ALL ROOTS LEAD TO ROCK

Legends of Early Rock 'n' Roll

Edited by Colin Escott

A BEAR FAMILY READER

Schirmer Books
New York

Photos courtesy of Bear Family Archives.

Schirmer Books
An imprint of Macmillan Library Reference USA
1633 Broadway
New York, NY 10019

Book design: Rob Carangelo

Library of Congress Catalog Card Number 98-33451

Printed in the United States of America

Printing number
1 2 3 4 5 6 7 8 9 10

All roots lead to rock : legends of early rock 'n' roll : a Bear Family reader / edited by Colin Escott.
        p. cm.
    Includes index.
    ISBN 0-02-864866-8 (alk. paper)
1. Rock music—United States—History and criticism. 2. Rhythm and blues music—History and criticism. I. Escott, Colin. II. Bear Family Records (Firm)
ML3534 .A45 1999
781.66'09—dc21   98-33451
                                                                        CIP
                                                                        MN

This paper meets the requirements of ANSI/NISO Z39.48-1992 (Permanence of paper).

Frankie Lymon and the Teenagers

Contents

Duane Eddy

Introduction

Colin Escott

The great bluesman Muddy Waters once cast himself in the role of musical theorist and declared "The Blues Had a Baby and They Called It Rock 'n' Roll." In the years since rock 'n' roll became a proper area of study, its birth has been reduced to a stupid little equation very much along the lines of Muddy's song: rhythm 'n' blues plus a little country plus a little pop equals rock 'n' roll. That's what the television documentaries tell us, that's what the history books tell us, and that's what the pop culture gurus tell us. As a generalization, it has a germ of truth, but the real story is numbingly complex. How can you say where rock 'n' roll came from when you can't really say what it was?

We all agree that Elvis Presley's "Hound Dog" is rock 'n' roll, but what about Freddie Bell and the Bellboys' big band version that Elvis heard in the Vegas showrooms and copied? Julia Lee would have been aghast at the thought that she played rock 'n' roll; the Kansas City nightclubs where she played were home to those who came to forget all about rock 'n' roll and its attendant problems. Yet, there was a licentiousness and anarchic spirit in Julia Lee's music that pointed nowhere if not toward rock 'n' roll, and even presaged shock rock. And then we have Ronnie Self and Bobby Lee Trammell, whose approach to making music was to start over the top and build from there. What did this owe to R&B, country, or early 1950s pop music?

This book draws together many different types of music that either contributed to rock 'n' roll or helped define it as a music apart from anything that had gone before. Our approach is an unusual one: these pieces were originally liner notes for Bear Family Records. Bear Family started in Germany in 1975, and over the years it has cultivated a reputation for unsurpassed quality in reissues. The Bear Family reputation rests largely on its boxed set catalog, but these boxes are neither for the faint of heart nor the faint of pocketbook. They are completist in the sense that they cover a musician's total recordings from one point in time to another; sometimes, they embrace an entire career. Bear Family's focus has been on country music, but almost from the start they have detoured into rock 'n' roll and rhythm 'n' blues. Boxed set booklets offer an opportunity to investigate an artist's career, and Bear Family has rarely passed up that opportunity. Some truly groundbreaking and original investigative journalism has gone into their booklets, and it hasn't always received the acclaim that it should. Bear Family boxes don't get nominated for Grammies, and the price tag often confines sales to the deeply committed. Hence this anthology.

I have worked for Bear Family on and off since the early '80s, and during that time I've annotated a hundred or so single or multi-CD packages and almost as many LPs. Inevitably, some of my own work is represented here, but I hope I haven't overrepresented it. If anything, I have tried to give exposure to work I wish I'd done. The selection here is not meant to imply that other essays in other boxes aren't as good; rather, I've tried to select pieces that work as stand-alone journalism. You don't need to hear the music to appreciate the writing, although the writing might lead you in search of the music.

If we try to draw a conclusion from all these pieces it's probably that rock 'n' roll did not come from Memphis, New Orleans, or New York . . . and certainly not from Cleveland. It came from everywhere. It was a spirit more than a music, an attitude more than white kids playing R&B. It came out of Niagara Falls, Canada, where a young Tuscarora Indian saw Little Richard in a local nightclub and declared himself for the shaking music; it came out of Arizona where a maverick deejay began experimenting with new sounds and scoured small desert towns for a grain silo with special echo; it came out of Las Vegas where the likes of Louis Prima and Freddie Bell reinvented the floor show; it came out of the fevered brain of Screamin' Jay Hawkins along with dark visions of mau-mau uprisings and constipation; and it came out of the Italian social clubs of New Jersey and the tenements of New York where the Four Lovers labored in obscurity and a 13-year-old kid called Frankie Lymon distilled the essence of something new, and died a has-been at the age of 25.

Preface

Richard Weize

When I started Bear Family in 1975, it was out of necessity. I needed to make a living for myself, my wife, and the kids, and I needed to pay back money I owed. I had started Folk Variety Records in 1972 with a partner, while we kept our regular jobs. In 1975, we parted ways. At the same time, I lost my job.

The first few years were a struggle. With lots of work, lots of luck, and a little help from our friends, Bear Family made it. There have always been two sides to Bear Family, our mail-order operation, which is now the largest mail-order supplier of specialty music in Europe, and the label. The label became a way of paying back a personal debt to those artists whose music moved me.

When I was ten years old, I bought Bill Haley's "Rock Around the Clock." As for so many others, that was the start of it all. I started to listen to any kind of music I could lay my hands on . . . which wasn't much in Germany during the '50s. Those were the days when one would buy a single, and, in case one didn't like the B-side, one would play it a few times every day, just to see if it really wasn't to one's liking. Radio didn't play much rock 'n' roll—and, if it did, it was mostly orchestrated versions. I managed to get hold of a number of singles, and the ones that made a deep, long-lasting impact were Johnny Cash's "Don't Take Your Guns to Town," Don Gibson's "Oh Lonesome Me," and Jim Reeves's "The Blizzard." These were unbelievable: the haunting feel of the Cash song, Gibson's extraordinary voice and phrasing, Reeves's way with a ballad. I also remember hearing Marvin Rainwater do "I Dig You Baby" (for some reason, only the German 45 and the British 78 had the count-off). The B-side was really fantastic this time; it was Marvin and his sister, Patty, singing "Two Fools in Love." It's no coincidence that Johnny Cash, Jim Reeves, Don Gibson, and Marvin Rainwater have been copiously documented on Bear Family.

I wanted to issue the complete works of artists I liked or artists I felt were important from a historical point of view. In the early '80s, I reached the point where I was able to do it, and that is what I've been doing for the last 15 years. Our boxed sets (first on LP and now on CD), range from 2 to 16 CDs with books that in some cases run to more than 200 LP-sized pages. It has been fun working with the writers, and the best sets are those that have been learning experiences for both of us. We have always tried to involve the artists, whenever possible, to get the inside story rather than the press-release version.

Some of our sets haven't reached breakeven point yet, and some never will. To issue something like a 16-CD box of Jim Reeves or a complete career retrospective of Hank Snow (39 CDs spread over six boxed sets), I have to keep the costs low. This means that our writers usually receive a fraction of what they would receive from a major label, and others help with photos, illustrations, disc dubs, and so on at no charge because they simply want to be associated with the projects. I'd like to take this opportunity to thank everyone for helping me realize a personal dream.

From the beginning, I have tried to make Bear Family a music-driven record label. I'm always willing to undertake a retrospective on artists who never amounted to anything in commercial terms, but who were important musically. That way, their work is preserved rather than forgotten. We also have some recordings by newer artists who couldn't get a major label deal if they tried—and most of them haven't. I believe that our reissues form the richest and deepest vintage country and rock 'n' roll catalog in the world. Legends like Conway Twitty or Jerry Lee Lewis sit next to quirky individualists like Ben Hewitt and Andy Starr. I can honestly say that we designed every set with the fan, rather than the bottom line, in mind. Our sets aren't the cheapest, but they are guaranteed the best.

Richard Weize
Vollersode, Germany

PS: Anyone wanting a complete catalog can get hold of us in the following ways. By mail at:

Box 1154,
D-27727 Hambergen, Germany

By phone at 011-49-4794-9300, by fax at 011-49-4794-930020, or by e-mail at bear@bear-family.de.

Our website (http://www.bear-family.de) contains a searchable database of all our recordings.

Screamin' Jay Hawkins

A Fan's Notes
Screamin' Jay Hawkins

Bill Millar

We begin with a piece that I regard as one of the best monographs ever written about a musician. It's part history, part memoir, and it's suffused throughout with a giddy enthusiasm for the subject's life and work. Screamin' Jay Hawkins doesn't tell us much about the roots of rock 'n' roll because he was a man apart, but it's hard to imagine his peculiar genius flourishing in any other era.

Screamin' Jay is the starting place if you want to chart gothic absurdity in rock 'n' roll. There are lines (or trails of blood) from his stage coffin to Alice Cooper, Ozzy Osbourne, and Marilyn Manson; fans of British esoterica will want to add Screaming Lord Sutch. It's not even stretching a point to say that much of the ghastly spectacle that surrounds heavy metal music began with Screamin' Jay's little excesses. (C. E.)

In a world that has never lacked characters, Screamin' Jay Hawkins is a performer apart. If one can imagine Jay McShann, Vincent Price, Billy Eckstine, Yasir Arafat, Little Richard, and a strong dash of '50s vaudeville in one glorious, treasurable stew, he is it. Hawkins's very extraordinariness defines his stardom. On one level, he works a seam between the weirdest comedy and the wildest rhythm 'n' blues. On another, he sings straight ballads in a tormented baritone which yearns for a role in *La Bohème*. Now and then, he descends into paroxysms of nonsense—a pure, incomprehensible language whose roots are as deep as any in Afro-American music. Most of all, he combines lurching, ear-cauterizing arrangements with murky private nightmares of voodoo violence. These are cryptic, self-degrading tales of mojo-bones, constipation, the Mau Mau, cunnilingus, and strange, bubble-eyed, flannel-lipped, bald-headed women. They virtually glow with their own parental guidance stickers.

Born Jalacy J. Hawkins on July 18, 1929, he grew up in Cleveland where he spent the first 18 months of his life in an orphanage and the rest of his infancy with a family of Blackfoot Indians. He studied piano and listened to Paul Robeson. He was besotted by opera, especially Caruso. On leaving high school in 1944, he joined the Army; World War II was still in progress and the forces accepted applicants as young as 15. Hawkins was only 14, but he was big for his age. After three years, he switched to the Air Force; he learned the tenor saxophone and joined the Special Services Division. By 1947 he was a competent boxer, winning the Cleveland Golden Gloves and eventually beating Billy McCan for the middleweight championship of Alaska. Following service in Japan, Germany, and Korea, he settled in Philadelphia where jump blues was casting a tall shadow over other forms of black music.

In 1951, Hawkins secured a steady $30-a-week position as singer, pianist, chauffeur, and valet to Tiny Grimes, the four-string guitarist already renowned for his contribution to the enduring brilliance of the Art Tatum Trio. By 1952 Grimes was fronting the Rocking Highlanders, whose Gaelic attire readily demonstrated the advantages of drawing attention to oneself. Grimes was quick to admit that donning tammies and tartan was a good career move ("the kilts really did it for us, they were the best threads on the scene") but he was soon upstaged by his young vocalist whose stage apparel often resembled something out of an ecclesiastical shop window.

Jay Hawkins's formidable discography began in Philadelphia over 45 years ago. As vocalist with Tiny Grimes's Rocking Highlanders he cut "Why Do You Waste My Time" for Gotham Records and "No Hug, No Kiss" (unissued until its appearance on a Tiny Grimes compilation in 1986). This, as far as can be determined, was Hawkins's first excursion into a recording studio and, like many a later rock 'n' roll auteur, his style sprang forth fully fledged. Right away, he asked serious questions of the listener's commitment. These intimidating, even bloodcurdling performances had no obvious precedent. He started way over the top and worked upward, establishing at once a persona that could only be described as "Screamin'" Jay Hawkins. In an interview with Stuart Colman on Radio London in June 1983, Hawkins described the genesis of the style which has made his reputation: "I couldn't sing that well until I went to a place called Nitro, (near Charleston) West Virginia. This is 1950. There was a big, big huge fat lady at the bar. Just allow your mind to roam free when I say 'fat' … Glutton! Beast! O-bese! She made the average elephant look like a pencil, that's how fat she was. And she was so happy. She was downing Black & White scotch and Jack Daniels at the same time, and whenever she looked up at me she shouted 'Scream, baby, scream!' I said to myself: 'You wanted a name? There it is!' and that's how the name was born, long before I got with any big name bands."

Atlantic Records came next. The venerable label grew into an institution noted for its taste and prescience, but in 1953 it couldn't handle "Screamin' Blues" by Jay Hawkins with Tiny Grimes. Our unrepentant boxing champ is said to have punched out Ahmet Ertegun when the company boss asked him to sing like Fats Domino. Atlantic has yet to liberate this mildewed tape from its vaults and connoisseurs may never hear this mysterious example of the screamer's art.

On leaving Grimes, Hawkins played or sang with a host of notable jazzers and pre-rock rockers including the Fat Man himself: in fact, he claims he was sacked for continually upstaging the comfy New Orleans megastar. There were equally short engagements with Johnny Sparrow (at Philly's Powelton Cafe in May 1953), James Moody, Arnett Cobb, Bill Doggett, and Lynn Hope, the tenor saxman who conjoined bar-walking hysterics with graceful, sweet-toned musicianship. Hawkins acquired an interest in the Moslem faith from Hope, as well as his preference for Islamic headdress. He was eventually encouraged to turn solo by Wynonie Harris whose gruff baritone voice remains one of Hawkins's more probable antecedents: others would surely include Slim Gaillard, Cab Calloway, King Pleasure, and Billy Eckstine. Two of Hawkins's records for Timely, "Baptize Me in Wine" and "I Found My Way to Wine," echoed the rumbustious drinking blues which Harris had already popularized. Another, "Not Anymore," with slide guitar wizardry from Mickey Baker, was perfectly illustrative of blues at its most exquisite.

In 1954, Hawkins signed with Mercury's Wing division. The eight titles might well have slipped between cup and lip at the time, but today they represent an ideal route to Hawkins's world. At first blush, they are less than revolutionary: little more than a clutch of antiquated R&B tunes by an above-average stylist with a lot of vocal power and a ripe sense of humor. To the fan, though, these recordings are akin to finding the Holy Grail in a record rack. These are dark, sere, seemingly inebriant performances with few equals in blues or rock (fans of Eugene Fox, Lloyd "Fatman" Smith, and Hurricane Harry can hang fire awhile here). "She Put the Whamee on Me" is demonic voodoo blues at its best; it demands to be played during a 3:00 A.M. thunderstorm with the lights out. (Parenthetically, the "Whammy," long meaning evil influence or hex, was popularized by Evil-eye Fleegle, a character in Al Capp's Lil' Abner comic strip.) "This Is All," "Well I Tried," and the latin-styled "Talk About Me" are essentially straightforward R&B wrought out of the ordinary by Hawkins's vocal inflections—that amazing whiskey-stained baritone swollen with blocked-sinus clearings, constricted screams, and low, dissolute moans.

In 1955, Hawkins recorded "I Put a Spell on You" for Grand Records. This original version remained unissued until the '80s, but the song has been revived again and again (not least by the great man himself). By 1986 there were 28 versions, including Creedence Clearwater Revival, Arthur Brown, Them, Audience, John Mayall, Alan Price, Manfred Mann, and Nick Cave; and, if you're thinking double figures is an exaggeration, how about Eddie Johns, the Atlantics, Johnny Angel? Of course, only one version still excites a glazed, ecstatic, knee-buckling reflex: OKeh 7072, which has also fetched up on Epic Memory Lane, Direction, Collectibles, Edsel, Crammed, Rhino, and the sound-track of Jim Jarmusch's cult movie *Stranger than Paradise*. It was conceived during a drunken session one dark September night after Columbia A&R man, Arnold Maxin, had posed the question "What do we have to do to make it real scary?" Hawkins and the musicians responded with a daring, virtuoso kind of mischief, transforming the original stark but pedestrian template into something as deep and primitive as the song tradition itself. Airplay was banned by many radio stations and Hawkins enjoyed the dubious distinction of having the only postwar million-seller that never charted. The record sold primarily on the strength of rumored cannibalistic sounds and a unique stage act encouraged by Alan Freed.

Hawkins had always been flamboyant. Now, he began to operate at the wildest, most unhinged limits of the music. He blended voodoo rhythms and horror film props with audacious panache. He rose from a rough board coffin into a blue spotlight. A skull on a pole was ever

. . . .

A FAN'S NOTES

present and he fed it cigarettes. He also carried fuse boxes which let out clouds of color coordinated smoke: "The cats dig my wardrobe," Jay told *Rock & Roll Stars* in 1957. "Sometimes I mix it up. Last night [part of a week's engagement at the Apollo with Dr. Jive's Rhythm & Blues Revue] I did a show wearing a green turban, red tux, purple tie and white shoes. Man, the chicks were gassed." Thus it was that Screamin' Jay Hawkins broke new ground by devising ghoul-rock, a subgenre which would invite many less musically credible comparisons including John Zacherle, Screaming Lord Sutch, Alice Cooper, Warren Zevon, Ozzy Osborne, and the rest of the rocky horror show. Even George "Funkadelic" Clinton admits the influence of Jay Hawkins's stage shows.

The OKeh recordings drew from every era of American pop music. Some were unutterably brilliant: "Yellow Coat," "Alligator Wine," "Little Demon." Others sounded like a man who had suddenly realized there was a limit to his versatility. His record sales never broke through to the wider awareness accorded, say, Fats Domino or Little Richard, and he was indubitably a difficult singer for listeners who preferred an easier time of it. He was aware of this: "My records have been selling pretty well," he told *Rock & Roll Stars*, "but I think you have to see me to appreciate me." That same year, his part in *Mister Rock 'n' Roll* was excised by Paramount Pictures in an act of self-censorship: "I walked on naked apart from a loincloth, white shoe polish marks on my face, my hair combed straight up, a spear in one hand and a shield in the other, like one of those wild Mau Maus, and I was singing a song called 'Frenzy.' The movie people claimed it would be an insult to the black people of the United States."

The period 1958–1962 was marked by intermittent recordings, a 22-month prison sentence, and a liaison with Pat Newborn, who suffered burns when one of Hawkins's fuse boxes exploded at a club in Miami while she was watching his act. They became close friends and formed a partnership: "Screamin' Jay and Shoutin' Pat." The duo recorded "Ashes," a Philadelphia breakout on the Chancellor label in 1962, and then moved to Hawaii where Hawkins played piano and emceed at the Forbidden City nightclub in Honolulu. Here he met and married Virginia Sabellona, a very pretty woman six years his junior. The nuptials did not please Pat, who plunged a nine-inch butcher's knife into Jay's chest, puncturing his lung and diaphragm.

Screamin' Jay Hawkins

In August 1964, Hawkins was rediscovered by John and Gloria Cann, jazz buffs who were holidaying in Hawaii. The Canns took the fully recovered Hawkins back to New York, secured a contract with Roulette and negotiated a tour of Britain with Don Arden's Galaxy Entertainments. Word of Hawkins's adventures had preceded him: "I Put a Spell on You" had been released in Britain on a Fontana 78 rpm and it was a regular favorite among the mods at Guy Stevens's Scene Club. There was a hero's welcome.

Cliff White and I were among those who rode from the airport to the hotel in the back of Don Arden's Jaguar. Jay played to the gallery: he broke into bloodcurdling screams for no apparent reason and shook Henry—a gleaming skull on a stick—at bewildered passersby. (I can well understand that readers have no great need to know all this but I need to tell them; I'm incapable of writing about Jay Hawkins without shoveling in almost every fact my megafan's brain has recorded.) We behaved like starstruck fans and asked the sort of questions starstruck fans ask. He told us that his favorite male singers were Roy Hamilton, Frank Sinatra, and Nappy Brown; his favorite female singers were Big Maybelle and Brenda Lee. Groups? He liked the Chantels, the Four Lads, and the Kingston Trio. He signed pictures with the phrase "I Love You Madly," a near-hit for Charlie and Ray with whom he'd shared an Apollo billing ("The All Gold Oldies Show") three weeks earlier. Wonderful stories emerged: of Esquerita's questionable gender; of Little Willie John, then standing trial for murder; of Huey "Piano" Smith, who allegedly stole "Don't You Just Know It" after seeing Jay perform this nonsensical rocker at a concert in Baltimore; of Larry Williams, who interred Jay in his coffin together with a diarrheic monkey. Back at the hotel, he unpacked two mammoth scrapbooks and more brain-bending goodies tumbled out: a mid-1950s poster of a Philadelphia concert with Jay and the Sensations, adverts for Apollo label-mate Solomon Burke (billed as "The 14-Year-Old Wonder Boy Preacher"), and a magnificent pictorial essay from *Ebony* which took me another 20 years to find.

A group of us flocked to all the London shows including the opening night at Wallington Town Hall. Hawkins was never in better form: He ran on- and offstage, did the splits, played piano, waved his cloak like a rabid bullfighter and screamed a slew of rock 'n' roll classics for well over an hour. Sadly, the louder his fans cheered, the more the locals booed. They came to the Town Hall every Tuesday to get pickled and practice their chat-up lines to the strains of Freddie and The Dreamers or Dave Berry and The Cruisers. They certainly didn't want anyone to complicate things by putting on a show. Eventually, fighting broke out and we escaped via the dressing room and car park, skulking along in the dark behind the former Golden Gloves middleweight. I don't think Jay was quite so wild again, but elsewhere audiences were ecstatic. Here's *Record Mirror*:

"Stars and showbiz personalities rubbed shoulders with mods and even some rockers in Soho's Flamingo last week (3 February [1965]) to witness a fantastic display by Screamin' Jay Hawkins. On his first British tour, Jay yelled his way through forty-five minutes of action-packed songs. 'The Whammy,' 'Alligator Wine,' 'Strange,' 'Party Doll,' and 'Little Bitty Pretty One' were delivered by a human tornado who whipped up the kind of storm not seen in these parts for some time. Jay clutched his friendly skull, 'Henry,' throughout his act and even made the thing smoke a cigarette. At Bromley Court Hotel on Sunday (7 February), Jay got so carried away that he ran around the ballroom and knocked over an amplifier. Then he returned to the stage and made flames shoot from his fingertips before playing his sax. 'Feast of the Mau Mau' and 'What'd I Say' got great cheers and it comes as no surprise to hear that Jay's stay here will probably be extended."

The spring of 1965 was memorable. Jay appeared on ITV's "Thank Your Lucky Stars" and disturbed the sepulchral quiet of the English teatime with "The Whammy." On April 6 we saw Larry Williams cutting his live album for Sue (hence the inclusion of impromptu verses like "Saw Screamin' Jay Hawkins with Long Tall Sally in the coffin / She don't love him but she do it very often"). "I Hear Voices" reached No. 14 on *Record Mirror*'s newly inaugurated R&B chart. We went to the zoo, and to the movies (*The Curse of the Coffin*, actually), and spent long evenings in Jay and Ginny's apartment at The White House overlooking Regent's Park. On June 4 there was a dramatic bust-up with Don Arden, and Jay decided to fly home immediately. We'd gone up to his flat with a view to catching Donnie Elbert at the Flamingo, but ended up deflecting threatening phone calls from the promoter and nervously watching Jay while he oiled a revolver. He couldn't take much luggage back in a hurry, and when we finally said our goodbyes we were loaded down with Henry, two capes, several gonks, a pair of zebra-striped shoes, a small but highly prized record collection (including his first LP, *At Home with Screamin' Jay Hawkins*), a foot-high jar crammed with threepenny bits, and a suitcase full of flash-powder and fuse boxes. It was 1:00 A.M. and we fully expected to be arrested.

On leaving Britain, Hawkins relocated to New York, hanging out with Little Joe Cook and Titus Turner (on a wave because RCA had released Elvis's version of Turner's song, "Tell Me Why"). Jay brought social conscience to R&B with "Poor Folks" and sent boxfuls of the Providence 45 to fans in Europe. The song was originally intended for Nina Simone, whose somber version of "I Put a Spell on You" had reached R&B Top 30 in 1965. Jay's letters, some on headed notepaper with David Waggett's line drawing of the screamer in manic pose, were rich in affection and anecdote: He and Ginny had guested at Lady Iris Mountbatten's wedding; he'd played at the Goldbug in Greenwich Village; did I know that "Hi-heel Sneakers" was really written by Welton Young, a.k.a. Dean of Dean and Jean? Then, after a brief sojourn in Hawaii and another Apollo appearance, some exceptionally welcome news: "I must let you know that, on 30 March 1966, I shall be putting in a very weird appearance at London Airport for a thirty-day tour. I hope that Henry, the fuseboxes and the capes are ready to be used again."

In any event, he arrived on April 1 and played the Ram Jam in Brixton that same night. Luminous-socked rockers had displaced West Indians for the evening and Hawkins came on as if it were still rock 'n' roll's finest hour. He eclipsed everything around at the time, agitating his way through "The Whammy" and concluding with "Shout," a feast of improvisation. The rest of the tour proceeded without difficulty. Only ten people (including New Orleans soulster Lee Dorsey) turned up at The Scene but Hawkins was no less vigorous or affecting. Before a crowd of black servicemen at Douglas House (a U.S. Air Force base) he completely transformed his act with an earthy recital of jokes and far fewer songs, though a version of Bobby Lewis's "Mumbles Blues" electrified this hippest of audiences. Another frenzied night at the Flamingo completed the London dates.

Back in the United States, Hawkins signed with Decca. Eight recordings resulted in just two singles. Rock 'n' roll greats were having to come to terms with the soul explosion, and Hawkins was no exception. His efforts were not, as it were, the scream of the crop, but the time warp factor has been reasonably kind to them. He was still screaming. Indeed, not content with screaming, he snorts, guffaws, and vomits.

9

The songs typify their era as surely as love beads and the scent of patchouli oil. Even the lyrics ("If you were a cloudy day you'd still be sunny") echo Smokey Robinson's self-contradictory statements. "Mountain Jive," a rewrite of "Little Demon," boasts the extraordinary couplet: "The lips on that chick were all out of place / She could kiss a man, and wash and dry his face." The souled-up version of "Spell" is quite listenable, though one inevitably misses the deeply unhinged character of the OKeh version. One last Decca factoid: producer Dick Jacobs included a pic of Jay and Ginny in his valuable reference work, *Who Wrote that Song?*

Mr. and Mrs. Hawkins spent the rest of the '60s in Hawaii. Though Jay spoke of being bored by the business and tired of the road, the best was yet to come. In April 1969, he signed with Philips and recorded a strange, ill-fated single, "There's Too Many Teardrops"/"Makaha Waves." The top deck, a straight country tune with a pedal steel player from the California Symphony Orchestra, was inspired by the C&W saloon next to the Forbidden City in Honolulu. The reverse, a tribute to the surfer's paradise on the west coast of Oahu, was written by Joseph Ryan, Hawkins's attorney in Hawaii. The record was only available in the Islands until reissued on Bear Family.

Philips followed up with a well-publicized and well-received album, *What That Is!* The cover showed Hawkins lying in an expensive coffin with his eyes wide open and one hand on the rim of the lid. This was going to be the finest comeback since Count Dracula's resurrection, and the music lived up to the promise of the sleeve. Here's *Billboard* columnist Ed Ochs on "Ask Him": "Can a gospel disk be a top 40 hit? More commercial than 'Oh Happy Day,' Hawkins' pop-gospel ballad makes rock 'n' roll out of a sax and guitar and a Baptist hymn. Blessed and sanctified by the glorious Billy Watkins Singers, 'Ask Him' could put religion in the jukeboxes—where it belongs. Black deejays and gospel fans who objected to the sacrilegious beat in 'Oh Happy Day' would have an unhappy day trying to sit still for this foot-tapper."

"Feast of the Mau Mau" inspired Ochs to alliteration ("Sardonic Jay Hawkins cackling like a cannibal at a cave-in") and its impact is hard to deny. This insane vision of the Kikuyu dinner table is almost as sickening as the Mau Mau's atrocities (the terrorist organization, formed in 1948, aimed to rid Kenya of European settlers and swore death to the white man). While "Feast of the Mau Mau" has some truly alarming lines ("pull the skin off a friend with a razor-blade"), it's not alone. What of "Do You Really Love Me—like a rat loves cheese?" Must remember to pop that one. Hawkins's female characters are generally alien, mephitic creatures with double chins, flabber-mouths and bald heads; "Thing Called Woman," with its compound eyes and solitary upper limb, doesn't disappoint. And what are we to make of "I'm Your Man?"—"If I can't be your man while you alive, I'll be your man when you're dead."

And then, of course, there's "Constipation Blues." This truly hair-raising meditation begins with a tugged and twisted play on sound as bizarre as any on record. The musicians surround these inventions with a skill that can only have been purchased by dedicated rehearsal, and Hawkins matches their concentration with an intensity derived from real experience. Dave Rosencran of KCMU in Seattle obtained the details: "I never before had been constipated in my life and it didn't dawn on me until I was five hours on the stool in the hospital that nothin' was gonna happen. I had doctors give me enemas and still nothin' happened. I had tears in my eyes, and I noticed this beautiful roll of toilet paper and I took out a pencil and, at the bottom of the toilet paper, I started writin' the song backwards, from the bottom up. The more I rolled out the toilet paper, the more I got into the song. I wrote exactly as I felt, each movement, each sound, each pain...." One critic was moved to ask whether the man who once opened his act by rising from a coffin now closed it by flushing himself down a lavatory.

Overall, I preferred the second Philips album. Three-quarters rich material, it was pretty much a history lesson under the aegis of Huey Meaux, a Texan producer with a swamp-pop pedigree, and a lately revealed taste for pubescent girls and cocaine—preferably in tandem. After Philips cut him loose, Jay recorded "You Put the Spell on Me" for RCA in 1974, then recorded albums for Versatile (1976), Koala (1979), Paris (1983), Midnight (1985 and 1988) and Spivey (1990). He blew himself up in 1976 and returned to the public eye in *American Hot Wax*, Floyd Mutrux's unashamedly soft-focus tribute to Alan Freed. He opened for the Rolling Stones at Madison Square Garden, returned to Britain in 1983, and toured Australia in 1986. Three years later, he amazed the Jarmusch glitterati by playing the manager-cum-night-clerk of a seedy Memphis hotel in the cult director's film, *Mystery Train*. His appearance at the Telluride, Colorado, film festival, where he screamed on the stage of the opera house before the world's most distinguished directors, actors and art-house distributors, will have

11

appealed to a constituency that ordinarily celebrates innovation and anarchy over the considerations of the marketplace. When he returned to Britain in 1989, his profile was very much higher. Instead of an audience in single figures at the Black Cat Club, Woolwich, he and his band, the Chicken Hawks (with veteran Beri Southern on screamin' saxophone), played to almost two thousand customers at London's Town & Country Club.

Suddenly, Hawkins was all over big and small screens, welcomed by media that had once shut him out. He appeared on numerous talk shows and in *A Rage in Harlem*. His marriage to Ginny ended after 20 years, and a brief union with a Japanese woman ended in 1991. His fifth marriage (and the last we know of) was in 1993 to a French woman. Today, Jay's profile is as high as ever. His version of Tom Waits's "Heart Attack and Vine" made the British Top 40 in 1993, and his recent CDs on Evidence, Aim, and Demon have been generally well received.

Now nearly 70, Screamin' Jay Hawkins remains one of the great R&B showmen and his luridly imaginative performances—live and on record—still contain rich, suggestive, and bizarre moments of twitchy genius.

These notes accompanied Spellbound, *a 2-CD anthology of Screamin' Jay Hawkins's work for Wing, Philips, Decca, and RCA between 1955 and 1974 (BCD 15530).*

2

Walk 'Em Rhythm
Buddy and Ella Johnson

Peter A. Grendysa

On one level, Buddy Johnson's music was the very antithesis of rock 'n' roll. It was almost as sophisticated and schooled as the music of Duke Ellington. His orchestra probably consisted entirely of sight-reading musicians, and his charts had chords and progressions that would have foxed most blues and rockabilly musicians. Buddy always stayed in touch with the black theater circuit in the South, though, and his records always returned at some point to roadhouse R&B. When rock 'n' roll erupted, Buddy Johnson must have thought it was a golden opportunity to reach a wider market. It turned out that he was too old and too sophisticated to stand much of a chance. The statistic books from the rock 'n' roll era show just two fleeting entries under his name. His story could be repeated any number of times for musicians like Wynonie Harris or Louis Jordan who thought that rock 'n' roll might be the biggest break they ever had, only to find themselves pushed further from contention than ever before. They contributed to rock 'n' roll but were swept away by it. (C. E.)

A line of golden saxophones held carefully aslant over the showy blue and white "BJ" bandstands catches the eye first. Arrayed behind are trombones flanked by piano, guitar, and bass, and watchful over them all are drums and a legion of trumpets. Unmistakable in pearl gray, while his troops are in black, the smiling general of this talented army stands facing the packed dance hall. As the emcee strides to the microphone, the roar of the crowd rushes against him like waves against a shore.

"Ladies and gentlemen, it is with the greatest of pleasure that I present for your dancing enjoyment the one-and-only Walk 'Em Rhythm man, the King of the Savoy Ballroom, star of radio and records, that young man with the Magic Touch on the piano, Buddy Johnson…with Ella Johnson, Arthur Prysock, and an all-sepia revue!"

Three or four hours later, weary musicians and band boys climb aboard their bus, senses still filled with whirling dancers, shouts, applause, screams of pleasure and, above all, the music—that indescribable, somehow intangible blend of rhythm and joy, love, and sorrow. While they sleep, the narrow highway will roll hundreds of miles beneath the wheels, with a destination no different from the dozens before, or the dozens to come.

This was the life of Buddy Johnson, leader and guiding light of the most successful big R&B band in American history. For two decades his band reigned supreme on the one-nighter circuit in southern states, an extraordinary feat that required an individual no less extraordinary to achieve it. In essence, the Buddy Johnson band was a very tight, hard-driving swing band easily the equal of anything the whites had to offer, and on a par with Count Basie, Duke Ellington, Jimmie Lunceford, and Lionel Hampton. Johnson wrote and played exclusively for blacks, and while this may have limited his commercial appeal, it certainly enabled him to keep his big band thriving for years after the big white touring aggregations had to disband.

Woodrow Wilson "Buddy" Johnson was born in Darlington, South Carolina, on January 10, 1915. His family was large, but only Buddy showed special musical talent at an early age. He began formal piano lessons at age four and by the time he was a teenager he had written songs and musical revues that were performed in his high school. He was also firmly hooked on classical music. In 1950, he surprised his interviewer by confessing, "The type of music that we're playing is not what I'd call music. Personally, I like classics, but I can't eat classics. We're very well aware of what we're playing. But we've set our style now and we can't change it to please New York because our bread and butter is in the South."

By 1950, when he made this statement, Johnson had been playing professionally and recording for over a decade, and was riding the crest of his popularity. This popularity had been built on a simple, fundamental premise: Find out what the people want, and give it to them. He was 23 years old when he moved to New York City and quickly learned that black men do not play classical music, nor do they sing it—a lesson learned by such widely disparate performers as Screamin' Jay Hawkins, Roy Hamilton, and Lee Gaines, late great bass of the Delta Rhythm Boys, all with operatic aspirations.

Work in the lounges and clubs was plentiful if you gave the audience what it wanted, and Johnson soon gained a reputation as a superb pianist, capable of adapting his style to his audience. When it came to pure and simple survival, he could and would play anything. In 1939, he was selected to play piano for the Tramp Washboard Band then embarking on a tour of Europe with the Cotton Club Revue. The high spots for the Revue were performances in London, Paris, Brussels, and Berlin.

While playing in Berlin, Johnson somehow offended the local bureaucracy, and received threats of physical harm. With the intervention of the United States Consulate, he made a hurried departure from Germany and returned to New York. Years later, the Allied Military Government uncovered a pile of his musical manuscripts, left behind in his quick exit, and returned them to him. The fate of his pre-war laundry is not known.

Back in New York, he landed a spot playing with a small combo at Barney Gallant's club in Greenwich Village and it was there that he was heard by a scout for Decca Records. Decca was especially attracted by his original material and, on November 16, 1939, he cut his first tracks. The keynote of the session was Johnson's clever "Stop Pretending (So Hep You See)," a jumpy number with a solid beat that told the story of a pseudo-hepster who may have been, after all, Johnson himself.

Although not a chart item by today's definition of the term, Johnson's original "Stop Pretending" sold very well, and a cover version by the Ink Spots made the pop charts in September 1940 (it was completely overshadowed the next month by the Ink Spots' blockbuster "We Three"). Significantly, Johnson's "Stop Pretending" was on Decca's Race series, while his label-mates, the Ink Spots, had their release on the Pop series. Johnson, however, had found that his musical training could be applied to writing hit songs.

Johnson didn't enter a recording studio for almost a year, and during that time he was joined by his younger sister, Ella. In later years Ella's singing became as much a trademark of the Buddy Johnson sound as his piano playing, but her coming to New York was merely by chance.

15

As she recalled, "My parents always told the older kids that if anything happened to them, the older ones had to take care of the younger. When our mom and dad died in 1940, I was sent to New York to be with Buddy."

Ella was born in Darlington on June 22, 1923, and the pudgy teenager had done some singing in church and in some of the original musical revues Buddy had written for the Darlington High School. Because of her youth, she had not developed a singing style of her own, but Buddy, faced with another mouth to feed, was quick to put her to work with him. It took a while to get her to stop imitating Ella Fitzgerald, but there is no trace of that "other" Ella in her first recording with Johnson, "Please, Mr. Johnson." If any outside influences have to be found, there is a certain resemblance to Rose Murphy, the popular black songstress whose trademark was a breathy, squeaky delivery.

"Please, Mr. Johnson," recorded on October 25, 1940, and released in the sepia series (which had replaced the Race designation) sold well enough to ensure that Ella's voice would be heard on Buddy's records for some time to come. By 1941 Johnson had a band of his own, with semipermanent membership of about nine pieces. Crooner Warren Evans joined Ella on vocals, but was soon replaced by James Lewis.

The band grew in popularity with every record release. "When My Man Comes Home" made all national charts in 1944, hitting No. 1 on the R&B lists, lasting 24 weeks. The wartime ditty had been recorded in July 1942, just before the musicians' recording ban put a stop to Decca's recording sessions for a couple of years. Since the Johnson band, good union members all, could not record, there was no reason to hang around New York City, so they hit the road.

The era of the great traveling bands was in full swing, and Buddy, Ella, and the boys headed south. This direction was not chosen by accident. "I'm a southern boy," Buddy explained, "and I remember going to dances when I was a kid and realizing that some bands made a good impression and some made a bad impression. People who go to dances on the watermelon route are closer to the musicians than in other parts of the country. Or, at least, they want to feel closer. The bands that don't make a good impression are the ones that don't get close to them. The music I play has a southern tinge to it. They understand it down there."

Playing for his chosen audience meant developing a special blend of music. A few years later he, or his promotion staff, developed the tag "Walk 'Em Rhythm" for the Buddy Johnson sound, the main ingredients being a strong beat, clear melodic line, and high volume. "They don't want the Ellington type of music in the halls where I play," said the maestro, "they want to hear a melody, which is why we play so many solos. They come to dance and they want to hear that beat. And we have to play loud because there are no p.a. systems. The acoustics are nil. They want to hear what we're playing so we have to play louder than the echo that's coming back to us." For the Decca publicity department, Johnson phrased this a bit more diplomatically, "The basic format of 'Walk 'Em Rhythm' is a tempo into which the dancers can easily swing. Furthermore, I believe it's the kind of tempo that makes dancing considerably easier for the beginner as well as for the dancer whose steps aren't too sharp." However it was described, the Johnson sound and style was extremely attractive to his audience, and traveling and playing one-nighters became his main source of income.

Southern orientation notwithstanding, the 14-man Buddy Johnson orchestra cut quite a chunk out of the Big Apple in the mid-1940s. Jazz journalist and producer Bob Porter has stated "The Buddy Johnson band was the most consistently popular attraction at the Savoy Ballroom for many years." And, the Savoy booked only the very cream of the black bands: Ellington, Basie, Gillespie, Eckstine.

When the recording ban ended for Decca Records in 1944, Johnson was ready with the perfect vocal counterpoint to Ella: the handsome and romantic crooner Arthur Prysock. Prysock was born in Greensboro, North Carolina, on January 2, 1925. The graduate of Dudley High School moved with his family to Hartford, Connecticut, in 1942. He soon found work in an aircraft factory and started singing evenings at local nightclubs. From this he moved to a featured spot as band vocalist with the Harold Holt orchestra, then holding down the house band spot at the Flamingo in Hartford. On the basis of these credentials, Johnson let him take the microphone during one of the band's appearances in Hartford, and the combination of the tight Johnson sound and the crooner's dark brown baritone voice pleased the audience to such an extent that Johnson offered him a permanent spot with the band. During his nine years with Johnson, Prysock came up with a number of hit records before leaving for a solo career in 1952. His departure left Johnson looking for a clone, and the remaining years of the Buddy Johnson organization spotlighted a number of Prysock soundalikes. Prysock himself had only one moderate hit on Decca in 1952 before suffering an eight-year absence from the limelight. He returned to the charts in 1960 and enjoyed a continuous run of popularity until his death in 1997, all without having changed his style or delivery one iota. When the times were right again for musical romance, Prysock was ready.

The big band momentum of the immediate postwar years swept the Buddy Johnson band along on the crest of the wave. Traveling incessantly, the band kept dancers lindy-hopping throughout the South and Midwest. In January 1946, they nearly broke house attendance records at the Kansas City Auditorium, their 4,285 paid admissions rivaling recent grosses of Count Basie, Lionel Hampton, and Jimmie Lunceford. The files of the late Jim McCarthy, press agent for the band, contain an incredible account of one-night stands and weekly engagements. From the appearance in Kansas City, for example, the band moved to Mississippi and Louisiana before hitting The Mosque in Fort Worth, Texas, on February 10. One week later, they helped reopen the Paradise Theater in Detroit.

Late in February, McCarthy filed this press release from Chicago, underscoring Johnson's philosophy of bringing his band close to his fans: "Buddy Johnson, who holds forth with his fast-rising 'Walk 'Em Rhythm' orchestra on the stage of the Regal Theater here the week beginning Friday, March 8, is one bandleader who believes in giving his musicians full credit for their individual efforts. No less than seven of the Johnson bandmen, in addition to vocalists Ella Johnson and Arthur Prysock, receive featured billing at each date Buddy plays. 'I believe the public likes to know the identities of the instrumentalists who are starred as soloists in their favorite bands,' Buddy explains, 'and for this reason I have always made it a point to introduce each soloist in my band to theater and ballroom audiences. I consider each musician an important part of our organization, and the more favor he can personally win with audiences, all the more interest is created in the band as a whole."

In March 1946, Johnson began work on a modern piano concerto. "I'm getting tired of playing piano concertos that were written hundreds of years ago by the old masters," he stated, "and I feel it's about time some of us present-day musicians and composers were getting a little more creative in our own right." Johnson had been exercising his classical proclivities by playing a swing version of Rachmaninoff's

Concerto in C Minor at some theater dates, and guessed that his audience wanted more of the same. It is a mystery why Johnson momentarily forgot his own credo of keeping his music danceable, but the project was a longtime dream of his.

The piano concerto was not set to wax until over a year later, when the first movement was recorded in New York City on October 30, 1947. Released as "Far Cry" in early 1948, the response to the record was not good. "It was a beautiful thing," he told *Downbeat* magazine in 1950, "but it didn't sell record one in the South. When Duke Ellington had his disc jockey show he used to play it and rave about it. Yet I remember walking into a restaurant in Jacksonville, Florida, and finding it in a jukebox there."

"Far Cry" continued to be a part of his stage shows, however, and he also added another complex serious piece, "Southland Suite," with vocal by Ella. Both were premiered in their entirety at a landmark Carnegie Hall concert in September 1948. There was no longer any doubt in Johnson's mind, however, that his fate lay in the hands of his southern fans and, as the big band business began to dry up, the longer runs in the big theaters and clubs were increasingly replaced by the dreaded one-night stands.

The session that produced "Far Cry" also marked the beginning of Johnson's own publishing venture, Sophisticate Music, BMI. He later added Jeanette Music, BMI (named for his wife) and Northern, ASCAP, to hold the copyrights of his numerous compositions. These valuable properties became the subject of an acrimonious court battle in 1979, two years after his death.

In the meantime, the Johnson band enjoyed some of its best years during the late '40s. "Fine Brown Frame" sparked a canny promotional gimmick used for years in every town the band was booked—The Miss Fine Brown Frame Contest. Another late '40s hit, "Did You See Jackie Robinson Hit that Ball?" was a direct result of Buddy Johnson's consuming passion for baseball, and was a sizeable pop hit. Jackie Robinson, the first black in major league baseball, was a universal black hero, but he did not take kindly to the use of his name in this novelty tune. Not until Johnson gave the ballplayer one-third of the writer's royalties in a move to smooth his ruffled feathers did talk of lawsuits subside.

In 1949, Johnson signed a three-year contract with Decca which guaranteed royalties of $50,000 a year. Despite this remarkable show

19

of confidence, the good times were nearing an end. The demise of the big bands became especially acute among black groups in 1950, prompting journalist John S. Wilson to take a close look at Johnson as a survivor in *Downbeat*, December 29, 1950: "The ebb in the big band business which followed the war has practically eliminated the big Negro band. Today only Duke Ellington and Lionel Hampton front big bands which are well known to the general public. Such still-surviving name leaders as Count Basie, Louis Armstrong, Dizzy Gillespie, and Cab Calloway have found it more practical to cut down to combo size."

Johnson's key to survival was the one-nighter tour, primarily through the South. Wilson tabulated a typical year in this life, calling it "no glory road." At the time, the Johnson band was doing two long tours a year, following each with a two-week vacation. "In 1949, for instance, outside of these two planned vacations, the band was off 18 days, some of these necessitated by the length of its jumps. Its itinerary for the year included 173 one-nighters, 14 weeks at the Savoy ballroom in New York, five weeks playing Negro theaters in New York, Washington, Baltimore, and Detroit, and two weeks at a Broadway jazz joint. This year it will wind up with pretty much the same schedule, except that it will spend less time at the Savoy and do more one-nighters."

The income from these dates was adequate in 1949 dollars. "On his one-nighters, Buddy's guarantees run from $600 to $1,250 against a percentage of the gross. On the lower guarantees his percentage runs up to 65 percent. Last year he grossed $300,000 on his bookings, which, of course, is added to by his income from records and his publishing house, which handles the originals he turns out for the band." One year later, a single tour covered 28,500 miles in 23 states, playing 133 one-night stands. On this one tour, Johnson grossed $286,257, or an average of $2,200 per appearance.

The human toll exacted by this grueling schedule can only be imagined, but in early June 1950, *Billboard* reported, "Orkster Buddy Johnson curtailed his southern one-nighter tour following a collapse on the bandstand during a date in Toledo last week. The orkster, following a couple of weeks rest, will take to action again with a date at the Howard Theater, Washington, June 9 for a one-week date...." By 1950, the band had actually grown to 17 members: four trumpets, four trombones, five saxophones, piano, string bass, guitar, with Buddy, Ella, and Arthur Prysock doing vocals. The veteran trombonist,

Buddy and Ella Johnson

Bernard Archer, was personal manager, and baby brother James Johnson worked as road manager. The entire aggregation traveled in a customized bus, with a huge "Buddy Johnson" sign painted on each side. The usual routine, upon coming into a one-night stand town, was to drive the bus up and down every street—a simple but effective means of advertising.

Beginning in 1951, the R&B scene began to change. More and more, the hit record became a key factor in getting personal appearance bookings. *Billboard* magazine noted in May, 1951: "Since the R&B disk trend has been inclined toward ballad stylists, blues stylists, vocal groups, and honk-and-romp combos for the past couple of years, the personal appearance quotas have been filled with these attractions in couples and threesomes to displace the former singular attraction of the band." From giving the public "two big stars for the price of one," the practice evolved into the huge star-studded road shows of the mid-1950s, with six or seven headliners, all of whom had had recent chart hits, and two full-sized bands.

As the disc jockey became the most important figure in R&B promotion, the pressure on acts to have a hit record increased. The last chart record produced by the Johnson band up to 1950 was "Because," a two-part dramatic opus sung by Arthur Prysock. At the end of Johnson's three-year paper with Decca, his contract was not renewed. Prysock left in early 1952, and Buddy made his final session for Decca in June 1952, with Nolan Lewis as Prysock's replacement.

Inexorably, the R&B and pop markets moved farther apart. Whether or not he had any choice in the matter, Johnson stayed with his black audience. A prime example of this is the tune "Hittin' on Me," with lyrics on a theme of abuse and far removed from the *I Love Lucy* nuclear family of the Eisenhower era. "Hittin' on Me" spent seven weeks on the R&B charts in the summer of 1953, and got even more action on the jukeboxes than it did on radio. It was Johnson's first hit since 1950, and his first for his new label, Mercury.

Johnson was on the road after his last Decca session, mulling over offers from several record companies, both major and minor. Mercury was pleased to add the Johnson band to its slim R&B catalog, then riding almost exclusively on the talent of Dinah Washington. Atlantic, King, and Savoy would have loved to get him, too, but couldn't afford the price.

"I'm Just Your Fool" followed "Hittin' on Me" on the charts and although Johnson continued to stuff his B-sides with baritone crooner Nolan Lewis and a few self-led novelties, it was apparent that vocals by Ella were going to be the hit-makers. Ella's delicate and deceptively sweet phrasing underwent a bit of a transformation on embarrassing rock 'n' roll songs in the later years, but she was perfectly suited for tough R&B anthems such as "I'm Just Your Fool," "Any Day Now," "What a Day," and the bona fide pop and R&B hit "I Don't Want Nobody (to Have My Love but You)."

An enigmatic and very shy person offstage, Ella was at ease in front of the band, with Buddy directing every aspect of her performance. She deferred to his every suggestion. "Buddy would pick my songs," she said in 1978, "and tell me how to sing them. If I told him I wanted to do a certain number, and he said 'No, it isn't right for you,' I wouldn't insist." Buddy also had the say on her stage dress and microphone technique.

With her fellow performers, she could be shy to the point of appearing aloof. Her peers ranged from ardent fans and friends such as

Screamin' Jay Hawkins and Ruth Brown, to detractors: "Ella wasn't nothing special," according to Jo Evans, a band vocalist with Maxwell Davis in the late 1940s, "although she acted like she was. Let's face it, anyone could have sounded great with that band behind them." Whether or not this falls into the category of sour grapes is a matter of opinion but for whatever reason, Ella was indeed "nothing" without Buddy, as later events proved. Even her "solo" efforts with studio musicians after the band broke up had Buddy directing and playing piano.

Johnson recorded for Mercury from 1953 to 1958 or, to put it in a different perspective, during a period when the No. 1 R&B songs ranged from "Money Honey" by Clyde McPhatter and the Drifters all the way to "Yakety Yak" by the Coasters. Aside from a few lame attempts at teen-oriented lyrics, the Buddy Johnson sound changed very little during that time, as it had changed very little from the first flush of success for Decca in the mid-1940s. Whether doing a searing instrumental with his own band, or directing Ella in front of a studio orchestra, Johnson always kept his original premise in mind: Let the people have something they can dance to. His was the only functioning and intact big band operating in the arena of R&B, and the accelerating changes in musical tastes soon left him behind.

It was no longer enough to put rock 'n' roll in a song title, and it didn't matter that this big band was tighter and tougher than most of the small combos and studio groups that had taken over the field. In late 1958, Johnson cut an album for Roulette Records that was to be his last. Two singles from Roulette and one from Old Town (not released until 1964) were the final attempts at getting airplay. By the time the band stopped traveling in 1959, it was the last black band on the one-nighter circuit. Johnson turned to administering his publishing companies, joined ASCAP in 1963, and helped out at brother Hiram's Johnson Record Company. Hiram produced classic New York vocal group records by the Dubs, Shells, and Cordovans until selling the property to Jim McCarthy, Buddy's former publicist, in 1960. Buddy supplied arrangements and played piano.

"Buddy was very active in church work from the early 1960s until his health started failing," recalled McCarthy in 1978. "The cause of his death was cancer and he endured considerable suffering for two years prior to his death. He divorced Jeanette in 1973 after being married 24 years, and they had one son, Woodrow, Jr., who was born

23

in 1951. Ella has not sung professionally since Buddy's band terminated in the early 1960s."

Ella, who had been living in Maryland, moved to New York to be near Buddy as his health began failing. She hasn't stepped in front of a microphone to sing since 1961, although the intervening years have not affected her wonderful voice. At the time of this writing, she is living in near poverty, reclusive and confused. For most of her career, she was merely the "girl singer" with the band, and she receives no royalties from the dozens of recordings she made with Buddy and has no song copyrights. In the early 1980s, the Route 66 Record Company in Sweden reissued some of her Decca and Mercury tracks for which she received $400. Even this paltry sum was almost stolen from her by an impostor in Los Angeles—someone who had fooled Johnny Otis into thinking she was the "real" Ella Johnson.

It is no mystery why Ella has not and will not sing again. No one puts it better than the singer herself: "In 1976 my friend Frank Driggs wanted me to record all my old songs, but Buddy was so sick. He said, 'I'll be there, but I won't be playing.' That was okay, because as long as Buddy was in the studio I would do better. Nothing came of that idea, though. You have to understand that Buddy was like my father. All my faith, my hope, everything was in my brother. When my brother left, the whole world closed in on me. If I had to make some records without Buddy around, I just couldn't do it."

The nature of Johnson's ailment made his last years very difficult for those around him. "Buddy had a brain tumor," Ella recalled, "and his personality changed as he got sicker. He was always the one who would drive around the neighborhood and pick up the old folks and take them to church on Sunday morning. He was very devoted to his wife and family and to the community. When he got worse, he left his wife and moved down to Georgia and started living with some dirty witchcrafty woman down there. He got mean and started drinking— things he never did in his life. He stopped going to church, too.

"One day he came up to visit me in New York and said, 'I've got a surprise for you, Ella. Come over and look out the window down at the street.' I went over and parted the curtains and he said, 'See that car down there? I bought that car for you. It's yours.' I saw a brand new Lincoln Continental parked on the street and I broke down and cried. I said, Buddy, 'Don't you remember? I can't drive.' His mind had gone so far he forgot that I didn't know how to drive a car. He was in my apartment when he died. He died in my arms."

Buddy Johnson died on February 9, 1977, and it took over two years to settle his estate. The hundreds of musical compositions he had copyrighted represented a considerable income for years to come. His former wife, Jeanette, had no claim on them because of their divorce, but their son did. He was opposed in the courts by the woman Johnson had been living with in Georgia. Ella also added her claim to the court battle, allying herself with Buddy's son.

"Before he died, he and me talked a lot of things over, and he told me that if he dies, 'Since I Fell for You' would be my song, and she would never get it. It's the son and myself against that woman claiming to be Buddy's common-law wife. If it goes right, everything will be mine, and Buddy's son understands that." But things didn't "go right" for Ella. In late 1979 the battle was over. "Georgia is a common-law state," a distraught Ella said, "and she proved she was his common-law wife, so the copyrights went to her and Buddy's son, so that leaves me out. I still have some things that Buddy never copyrighted, but the old ones are better. I especially wanted 'Since I Fell for You,' because I don't think anyone knows how to sing that song better than I can. I don't want to do those old songs anymore because I don't want to make any money for that woman."

Shortly thereafter, things went from bad to worse. Ella had to fly to Detroit to pick up the body of her only son, shot dead in a drug-related killing at the age of 25. Then, unscrupulous "fans" robbed her of most of her collection of photographs. Her life in the housing projects is not easy, but she has some dear friends. If nothing else, this fine and gentle woman deserves to live the rest of her life in peace.

In many ways, exploring the history of black artists and their careers bears more resemblance to strip mining than archaeology. Layer on top of layer of mystique and glamor is ruthlessly exposed and the landscape is never quite the same afterward. But if the truth about the lives and travels of these people reveals an all-too human side, perhaps that is the most important fact of all. You can't make music for the people without being one of the people.

These notes accompanied Buddy & Ella Johnson 1953-1964 *(BCD 15479), 4 CDs.*

Julia Lee

3

Kansas City Stars: Part 1
Julia Lee

Bill Millar

In case you missed it, there was a CD by the Dayglo Abortions a few years ago. It was the one with "Fuck, My Shit Stinks." If you can draw a line from Screamin' Jay Hawkins to heavy metal, you can easily draw a line from Julia Lee to the coarser end of today's music. There was no mistaking or overlooking the obscenity in Julia Lee's work, but, until the Bear Family boxed set appeared, many thought of it as her defining characteristic. Only when the full breadth of her work was revealed in the box did we see an eloquent jazz and blues stylist in the storied Kansas City tradition. Smutty songs were just a part of her repertoire. The Kansas City tradition gave much to jazz, R&B, and thence to rock 'n' roll. The profile of Julia Lee is followed by a profile of Jesse Stone who makes that contribution explicit.

It would take a far more serious volume than this to figure out what happened to gothic rock between Screamin' Jay and Marilyn Manson, or what happened to obscenity in R&B between Julia Lee and some of today's rappers. In theory, if you approve of one, you should approve of the other, but an encounter with the scrofulous end of today's music leaves one feeling sullied and dirtied in a way that an encounter with Screamin' Jay and Ms. Lee doesn't. There's a difference between ribaldry and obscenity, and Julia Lee was endearingly ribald. (C. E.)

A legend in Kansas City for more than 20 years, Julia Lee eventually arrived during the late '40s when she found her rightful place with a clutch of audacious hits that matched her ebullient personality and roly-poly figure. She called her music "Kansas City style with terrific rhythm" but the description says little for the elegance of her musical mind or the exuberance that bounds out of the grooves. Julia's contralto voice, rooted in the conventions of the so-called classic blues singers, possessed a rich intimacy and a warm knowingness. During an era in which popular music rarely strayed from the maudlin, her determinedly ribald style was conspicuous. Her piano-playing, full of melodic bounce with a strong left-hand boogie, echoed Fats Waller, Pete Johnson, and Count Basie. She followed regular blues sequences, but a sensitivity toward exact form and rhythmic balance attracted a sophisticated audience which often ignored or derided other kinds of black music. In her heyday, she was regarded as one of the most colorful, innovative, and refreshing stylists around.

Most biographical sketches state that Julia Lee was born on October 31, 1902, in Boonville, a small town in central Missouri some 100 miles east of Kansas City. Her death certificate, however, cites Kansas City as her birthplace. Her father, George E. Lee, Sr., was an accomplished violinist who led a string band. Her older brother, George, sang and played tenor saxophone. Under their guidance, Julia performed at house parties, acquiring an easy self-confidence which led to professional appearances at a tender age. Her parents bought a piano when she was ten and under the tutelage of ragtime players like Charlie Watts and Scrap Harris, both former pupils of Scott Joplin, Julia learned to play blues and a variety of popular tunes. She attended Attucks Elementary School and Lincoln High, and, after graduation in 1917, she embarked on further formal music studies which included training at Western University. Western, a black college, attracted many musicians including trumpet player Booker Washington, banjo and guitar player Charles Goodwin, and bassist Gene Ramey. During her early teens Julia was the featured vocalist with a local band that included a youthful Walter Page on string bass. They played at high school functions, churches, more house parties, and skating rinks.

In 1918, Julia formed a trio with her brother, George E. Lee, Jr., and a drummer. Apart from a brief period with Bennie Moten's band and some intermittent solo engagements, Julia remained with George for some 15 years. This was the era of the territory bands which crisscrossed the Midwest and Southwest playing in any town with a population big enough to hold a dance.

George Ewing Lee, born in Boonville on April 28, 1896, played piano and baritone saxophone in an Army band in 1917. On returning to Kansas City after the First World War, he and Julia hired a drummer and played their first professional engagement at the Lyric Hall. The only other local band of any substance was led by Bennie Moten whose five- or six-piece unit played an orchestrated version of ragtime at the nearby Panama Club. In 1919, Julia married Frank Duncan, manager of the celebrated Kansas City Monarchs, the city's all-black baseball team. The marriage, which lasted nine years and produced one son, raised her stature within the black community.

Bennie Moten and George Lee gradually augmented their bands during the '20s, and while Moten came to lead the first important Kansas City–style big band, George and Julia remained closer to the vaudeville blues tradition. George sang novelties and romantic ballads in a manner which prefigured Pha Terrell's work with Andy Kirk's Clouds of Joy. He also played slap tongue saxophone solos, but it was his voice, which could fill a ballroom without amplification, that made the women swoon. Julia played in most of the early piano styles and sang in a way that paralleled, perhaps even predated, the leading female blues artists of the day.

Julia Lee is often regarded as a close contemporary of Bessie Smith (who first entered a recording studio only months earlier) but the best of Lee's records are not necessarily blues or ballads but bouncy, ribald numbers. Ma Rainey and Bessie Smith sang as much blues erotica as anyone else in the sex-inundated race market of the '20s but Julia's frolicsome manner, her artful legerity, are characteristics perhaps most redolent of blues revisionists like Chippie Hill, Cleo Brown, or Georgia White. Dave Dexter, who signed Julia Lee to Capitol Records, recalled his record-collecting youth in *Billboard's World of Soul*: "Georgia White had the sexiest, most insinuating voice we ever heard, but you had to drive a few miles out of your way to hear her all-time hit, 'Don't You Feel My Leg.' It wasn't on any of the campus malt shop jukes we patronized." Inasmuch as Cleo Brown is known at all, it's for her variation of "Pinetop's Boogie Woogie," but her '30s best-seller, "It's a Heavenly Thing," also fueled the trend for female piano players who sang coy or risqué songs.

Sometime during the summer of 1923, probably late June, Julia traveled to Chicago. She might have worked there as a solo or OKeh Records may have invited her to an audition. Two recordings were made, but neither was issued. In this respect, she was in good company; Bessie Smith auditioned for OKeh in January 1923 and the company

29

rejected her test recording. By the time George and Julia made their first known recordings in 1927, they had been seen and heard by many thousands of people. During the mid to late '20s the columns of the *K.C. Call* featured advertisements and articles trumpeting George E. Lee's battles with other bands: George Lee vs. Walter Page and his Famous Blue Devils (billed as "The Battle of the Century") or George E. Lee's Singing Orchestra vs. Jesse Stone and his Blues Serenaders. Sometimes there was a black and white orchestra war, such as George Lee vs. Jack Owen and his Atcan Aces. Lee must have won that particular duel; one month later (April 2, 1929) the *K.C. Call* carried a provocative headline, "Can George Lee Do It Again? Another White Orchestra Challenges the Negro King of Syncopation to Contest."

George E. Lee's orchestra with Julia on piano first recorded for Winston Holmes's Meritt Records. Holmes, who may have dabbled in politics, began his career as a piano technician in 1898 and opened a piano repair shop in 1918. He subsequently stocked records, formed his own label and advertised his store, the Winston Holmes Music Co., as "the only Negro Music house in Kansas City." As far as the Lees are concerned, the Meritt record was not an auspicious debut. Lee was not a lucky man in the recording studios. Chuck Haddix, archeologist of the early Kansas City music scene, points out that George Lee's band was probably billed on record as the Novelty Singing Orchestra because they played an extended engagement at the Novelty Club (Julia doubled as intermission pianist), not because they played novelties. Either way, the Novelty Singers' next stop was Brunswick Records where the band cut six titles in November 1929. On this occasion, Jesse Stone directed a superior unit. Stone, the Kansas-born pianist and bandleader, went on to write "Shake, Rattle and Roll," and put the loping backbeat into so many of Atlantic's R&B records during the '50s that Ahmet Ertegun told Charlie Gillett that "Jesse Stone did more to develop the basic rock 'n' roll sound than anyone else."

Herman Walder also admired Stone's skills: "I was with George E. Lee's band, and I was so glad. See, we had Jesse Stone arranging for us. He taught us how to construct chords and all that kind of stuff. He took us down to 1823 Highland (the Musicians Protective Union Local 627) two or three times a week, teaching harmony and chord construction, how to write and all that kind of stuff." As this is written, Jesse Stone is alive and well and still driving his car at the age of 93.

The November 1929 sessions contrasted brother-sister vocals.

Julia conjured a spell over "He's Tall, Dark and Handsome" and "Won't You Come Over to My House"; both are marked by her sexy, coquettish singing and noticeably flamboyant piano solos. George crooned "St. James Infirmary" and the hugely popular "If I Could Be with You One Hour Tonight." The February 6, 1930, edition of the *Kansas City American* advertised the George E. Lee releases as "Hot, sweet, knockout records—both of them. Rhythm that makes you dance. Seething sentiment and golden vocal choruses by George E. Lee himself." The May 8, 1930, edition announced the release of Julia's Brunswick record—the first sides to be issued under her own name.

While George and Julia's pioneering records may have lacked originality, the band's live gigs were known to pack a greater punch as Andy Kirk recalled in his autobiography, *Twenty Years on Wheels*: "George and the band stopped in Tulsa to see us. I introduced them to the crowd and had them do some numbers in the intermission. Lee's was an entertaining band, they stressed dance music and had great variety. George himself played sax; his sister Julia played piano and sang with the band. They had a great brother-sister act. Both of them sang; they could sing pop tunes, ballads, blues—everything—together and separately, and always went over big." Count Basie later told Stanley Dance, "George and Julia Lee were one of the best teams you could ever hear," and Sammy Price, recalling the exciting musicians he had known in Kansas City, also put George and Julia at the front of a long list of stalwarts.

According to Julia's obituary in the *K.C. Call*, George Lee and Bennie Moten merged their bands in the autumn of 1932 and, for a brief period, Julia shared piano duties with Count Basie. George Lee reformed his own unit in 1933 but within months he and Julia, who never enjoyed touring, had parted company for good. In 1937 he worked in the summer resort of Eldon, Missouri, with a unit that included Carrie Powell on piano, Efferge Ware on guitar, and a teenaged Charlie Parker on alto saxophone. His band enjoyed residencies in Kansas City at the Brookside Club in 1938 and the Reno Club in 1939 but he retired from professional music-making in the early '40s.

By 1930, the Depression had enforced the decline of the TOBA circuit, with its notoriously poor facilities, and other small theater chains on which the territory bands depended. There was an alternative to playing before dwindling audiences in one-horse towns and Julia took it. In 1934, she appeared at Milton's Tap Room, a newly opened white nightclub unaffected by the financial crash. She worked very few out-of-town spots. In 1939, she and the one-armed trumpet player, Wingy Manone, played seven weeks at the Offbeat Club in Chicago, and in 1943 she appeared at the Silver Frolics and Downbeat Room in Chicago and at the Beachcombers in Omaha, but, by and large, Lee remained a fixture of Milton's Tap Room for some 16 years from 1934 to 1950.

Milton's was a flashy gin mill on Troost Avenue. Julia started there at the height of the Depression earning $12 a week. These were the rowdy years of the Pendergast era. Thomas J. Pendergast, boss of the local Democratic Party from 1927 to 1938, encouraged nightlife, protected gambling, and aided liquor interests. The laws relating to Prohibition and closing times were rarely enforced and jazz flourished during his reign. Pendergast lived in a $115,000 French Regency house in the best part of town and raked in huge amounts of cash from night-clubs and a corrupt police force controlled by a racketeer turned politician. As record producer and Kansas City music scene chronicler Ross Russell noted, gangsters and vicelords liked jazz and respected its value as a means of attracting customers and selling liquor, the real road to increasing profits.

For Andy Kirk, who rolled into town in 1929, Kansas City was a forehead-slapping revelation: "In other cities, lives were wiped out in an instant, rich men were committing suicide. In KC it (the crash) was like a pin dropping; the blast of jazz and blues drowned it out. People were crowding the clubs and ballrooms as usual. We had to get out of Kansas City to find out there was a Depression. It was the political set-up under Pendergast that kept everything moving." Some would say the decline of Kansas City jazz followed Pendergast's imprisonment on conviction of income tax evasion in 1938. A reform administration took power from the Pendergast machine in 1940; a number of nightclubs were shut and closing hours were enforced for the first time. Julia's career didn't suffer in the inclement political climate, though, and neither did Jay McShann's.

Given Lee's prolonged exile from theaters and records, news of her mesmeric hold on Milton's patrons was slow to emerge. *Downbeat* caught up with her on April 1, 1942; under the headline "Meet Julia Lee, Pace-Setter," the magazine reported: "An enviable record is being piled up here by Julia Lee, pianist and blues shouter, who is now completing her eighth year at Milton's Tap Room. Her individual

Julia Lee

pianistics and song style have made her Kansas City's favorite and stars of the stage and nite club world invariably dig her when they play engagements here." There's no byline to the piece, but it was probably submitted by Dave Dexter, a native of Kansas City who became a fan of Julia's when he was in high school. Born in 1915, Dexter served his apprenticeship as a jazz writer with the local *Journal-Post*. In 1938, he moved to Chicago to become associate editor of *Downbeat*, and subsequently opened an editorial office in New York. According to Haddix, Dexter often remained anonymous when promoting Kansas

City artists. In November of 1940, Dexter had helped write and produce Joe Turner's "Piney Brown Blues" for Decca which, as he recalled, "became a monster in the jukes, an unintentional smash hit that shoved a then youthful writer for *Billboard*, *Downbeat*, and *Metronome* into the ranks of professional, bedevilled, belligerent and ulcer-ridden A&R men."

By the mid-1940s, Julia's act, like Kansas City itself, was marginally cleaner. As well as such ribald songs as "The Fuller Brush Man" and "Two Old Maids in a Folding Bed," her repertoire also embraced "Stormy Weather" and "Night and Day." For two shots of bourbon she would sing almost any request. In a black lace gown with a clip of artificial flowers in her crimped and glistening hair, she resembled the already rare and consequently precious spectacle of a vaudeville blues artist. Benny Goodman, Bob Zurke, and Red Norvo and his wife, Mildred Bailey, were frequent visitors to Milton's Tap Room, and photos from the *Kansas City Star* show an all-white clientele crowding around Julia's piano, clapping and grinning ecstatically. Like Harlem's Cotton Club, Milton's Tap Room was off-limits to black customers.

Julia was now on a salary of $150 a week, and fans stuffed as much as sixty dollars a night into a white porcelain kitty which stood on the piano. The kitty, usually a cat-shaped jug or a bowl with a cat's face on it, was essential to the livelihood of club musicians who usually received only a guarantee against tips. Julia developed a routine to milk the kitty, breaking into the favorite song of a high roller as he came into the club in the hope that he'd respond with a large tip. Next to the kitty, there was a pitcher of water to wash down the whisky which customers supplied.

Dave Dexter, who had seen Julia at Milton's Tap Room, was devastated by her talent. He had joined Capitol Records as an A&R man shortly after the company's inception in 1942. Singer-songwriter Johnny Mercer, fellow songwriter Buddy DeSylva, and record retailer Glenn Wallichs did not expect to dominate a pop market controlled by Decca, RCA, and Columbia but they scored immediately with Mercer's own "Strip Polka" and Ella Mae Morse's "Cow Cow Boogie." Capitol survived the Petrillo ban as well as the wartime shortage of shellac. "Everything worked for us," Mercer remembered in 1962. "The war and even the musicians' strike only made our little company better known and more quickly recognized. Due to the shortage of other labels we got heard a lot. We could do nothing wrong." Capitol rapidly became a major force and much of its early success was due to Dave Dexter who has been credited with the signing of Peggy Lee and the discovery of Nellie Lutcher. The young jazz and blues collector was also instrumental in acquiring the Stan Kenton Orchestra, the Nat King Cole Trio, and Sammy Davis, Jr.

On November 1, 1944, Dexter took Julia Lee into Vic Damon's Kansas City studio and supervised her first Capitol session, which produced a remake of "Come On Over to My House" and the overly familiar blues, "Trouble in Mind." On both, she was accompanied by Jay McShann's Kansas City Stompers. The recordings were featured on a Capitol Records 78-rpm album in a series called *The History of Jazz*. Before they aroused any attention, Lee moved to H. S. Somson's Premier label and recorded a clutch of songs with a band led by Tommy Douglas, an alto player who reportedly influenced the young Charlie Parker. "Lotus Blossom," the headline side of the second Premier record, was a featurette all on its own. Julia rerecorded the song for Capitol in 1947. The first master, entitled "Marijuana," was withheld for obvious reasons and only the second attempt, a reversion to the less controversial title, graced the Capitol schedules.

By the summer of 1946, deejays had pulled Julia's 78 from *The History of Jazz* and played both sides more times than any other selection. Responding to the demand, Dexter signed Lee to Capitol and brought her to Hollywood where she cut eight titles in August. During the journey, she and her drummer Baby Lovett wrote "Gotta Gimme Whatcha Got." This suggestive boogie, coupled with the blues-ballad, "Lies," became the first of many Capitol releases by Julia Lee and Her Boyfriends. The first group of "boyfriends" included Henry Bridges from Oklahoma City who had played tenor sax with Charlie Christian and Harlan Leonard. Guitarist Nappy Lamare was a founder member of Bob Crosby's band; born in New Orleans, he would eventually tour Europe with the Night in New Orleans package. Baby Lovett, Pete Johnson's favorite drummer, was on all Julia's records between 1944 and 1949, but also played with Harlan Leonard and Charlie Parker, and deputized for Jo Jones in the Count Basie Band.

Surrounding Lee with a topflight backup squad illustrated Dexter's total belief in her abilities. "They knocked her out," Dexter recalled. "And she in turn genuinely excited them." Dexter has said that he christened the band "Her Boyfriends" after the succession of men on whom Julia lavished money and affection. (Following her divorce

35

from Frank Duncan, circa 1927, she married Johnny Thomas, another well-known Kansas Citian. That union lasted only two years and Julia had no more children.)

The immediate success of "Gotta Gimme Whatcha Got" (No. 3 R&B in 1946) led to bold comparisons with the late Bessie Smith. Bessie's rich and plangent voice plainly roused emotions that Julia's did not, but arguably Julia was the more versatile musician. The August 1946 sessions roamed through vaudeville, blues, boogie, and conventional popular song. There were concentrated studies in melodic sweetness ("When a Woman Loves a Man," "Have You Ever Been Lonely") and a pounding boogie version of Eduardo di Capua's "Oh! Marie" sung, as far as I know, in perfectly respectable Italian. The same date also spawned a second hit record in "I'll Get Along Somehow" (No. 5 R&B in May 1947). Dexter clearly sensed that Julia was someone who could sell to the black jukebox trade and those of paler skin. "Snatch and Grab It" was the song to fulfill these expectations.

Nothing quite suited Miss Lee as much as "Snatch and Grab It," a three-minute lesson in lechery bursting with thigh-slapping vulgarity. It was written by Sharon Pease, a Chicago pianist and *Downbeat* columnist, and fully illustrated his ability to etch material to match a performer's personality. The record spent 12 weeks atop the R&B chart and crossed over to a pop market ordinarily dominated by Bing Crosby and Perry Como. The title of Freddie Hart's 1956 rockabilly item, "Snatch It and Grab It," was clearly inspired by Lee's chart-topper. Merrill Moore's "Snatchin' and Grabbin'" wasn't (the song is a disappointing ode to consumerism), but Moore was a fan all the same; he cut a blinding version of "Gotta Gimme Whatcha Got" in 1955.

If some of Julia's material seems a tad eccentric ("Oh! Marie," "I'm Forever Blowing Bubbles"), it was at least tackled with intelligence and precision. When Capitol brought her back to the studio in November of 1947, she came to grips with material fully intended to charm a broad constituency. There were the usual hoary old standards like "Charmaine" (from 1913), "I'm Forever Blowing Bubbles" (1919), and "Pagan Love Song" (1929). There were standards of more recent vintage as well, but the core of the late '47 sessions resides in the playful, raffish raunch of "King Size Papa," "Take It or Leave It," "That's What I Like," "I Didn't Like It the First Time," and "Tell Me Daddy."

"King Size Papa," Lee's eighth single, exploited the frisky salaciousness of "Gotta Gimme Whatcha Got" and "Snatch and Grab

It." The slightly mocking vocal, enhanced by Benny Carter's sax solo, exudes genuine pleasure and wry irony. It wasn't a new idea (Claude Hopkins had recorded "It's Too Big Papa" in 1945) but it was guaranteed to amuse everyone, even the band. "King Size Papa" topped the R&B best-sellers for nine weeks and stayed in the chart for over six months. According to chart chronicler, Joel Whitburn, it also crossed over to the pop lists, peaking at No. 15.

As offers accumulated, Lee and her manager, Johnny Tumino (who also handled Jay McShann and the Five Scamps), accepted the best. Julia played New York's Apollo in May 1948 and Los Angeles' Million Dollar Theater in September. She and Baby Lovett also appeared in cabaret at a White House Press Association dinner before President Harry S. Truman. That event took place at the Hotel Statler on March 5, 1949. Julia sang "King Size Papa." A long-time fan and a pianist himself, Truman had helped Kansas City run smoothly during the Pendergast era when he was a county court judge.

For Christmas 1948, Capitol unfurled "Christmas Spirits." One part novelty ("Santa Santa Santa, I could go for your long [pause] whiskers") to nine parts holiday depression, it sold well past the season of goodwill, peaking at No. 16 in the R&B charts in January 1949. *Billboard* reviewed "I Didn't Like It the First Time" in February 1949: "A happy double-meaning romper in the spirit of 'Snatch and Grab It' and 'King Size Papa.'" In fact, "I Didn't Like It the First Time," a.k.a. "The Spinach Song" can be seen as a rare example of triple entendre, since spinach conveyed a reference to opium as well as sex. The record, a No. 4 R&B hit in March 1949, was coupled with "Sit Down and Drink It Over," an invitation which according to the *Kansas City Star*, was usually extended to any depressed spirits among the audience at Milton's Tap Room.

Most of Julia's best-selling records had been characterized by an audacious use of double entendre, and it was the dirty blues which provided the aesthetic motor for the 1949 sessions. Julia and her small band cut one after another: "Tonight's the Night," "My Man Stands Out," "Do You Want It?" and "Don't Come Too Soon." All were cherished by those who sought out anything risqué. In England, where Julia's records were issued in a rush during the early '50s (Capitol had no British outlet until 1948), she was much loved by reprobates who filed these selections between Oscar Brand's bawdy ballads and the faintly risible Paddy Roberts. The first ten-inch Capitol album even

37

came in a slate-gray sleeve without pictures, the equivalent of a plain brown wrapper.

The keynote in the performance of this often horribly contrived material is Lee's energetic good humor. It all hangs on her ardently carefree personality; she's so cheerfully offhand you can detect a gentle irony running through the whole spiel. Take "My Man Stands Out" ("especially on the beach") or the particularly sleazy "Do You Want It?" Here are two couplets: "The shortest thing 'bout a hog is his grunt /the best thing about my joint is my... hash" and "You can have anything you wish/I'd like for you to try some of my fish."

Sex was disguised as foodstuffs, drugs, weapons, methods of transportation, and money. On "Don't Save It Too Long" she urges: "Sister, open the doors of that little safe of yours." Promiscuity is encouraged on a heroic scale and the metaphors are multiplied with lines like "Guns that are idle soon lose their power / Remember that sweet cream quickly turns sour." By now, *Billboard* was actually warning deejays not to play the stuff. Reviewing "Don't Come Too Soon," released in July 1950, the trade paper declared: "Lyric is certainly too blue for airing and juke ops with finicky locations should listen carefully before installing this one." Capitol decided not to release "It Comes in Like a Lion (and It Goes Out Like a Lamb)" but this determinedly cheerful commentary on impotence and detumescence is redeemed by some ebullient protostride piano.

Julia Lee dented the R&B chart for the last time in November 1949. "You Ain't Got It No More," a common enough sex-automobile analogy, climbed to No. 9. These peppery tales of bedroom incompetence have helped to turn Julia Lee into a feminist icon. The women's movement has encouraged the view that many of the legendary black female artists were powerful heroic figures as opposed to passive victims. Biographies of Billie Holiday and Bessie Smith, unremitting accounts of disastrous bisexual relationships and great talents destroyed by enormous quantities of booze and drugs, do not support this revisionist approach but it may well hold true as far as Julia Lee is concerned. When she sang about mistreatment it was hard to believe; the readiness to impugn a man's poor performance is altogether more credible.

Despite her celebrity, Julia remained a hometown girl. Chuck Haddix notes that Milton Morris had strong underworld connections and that he frowned on out-of-town engagements even at the height of

Julia's career. Nevertheless, she also disliked flying (she once said she would travel if she could keep one foot on the ground) and rarely left Kansas City. "If you're not happy," she once remarked, "there's no percentage in the big money." The old showbiz cliché, "what you see is what you get," may be entirely true in this instance. Perhaps she was in real life the same lovable, bubbly, warm, naughty but nice character heard on record and seen on stage. Every shred of evidence points to a jovial, well-adjusted woman devoid of anomie or angst. Someone who, as Jon Newlin pointed out, could sing "All I Ever Do Is Worry" in so completely unneurotic a way as to sound like she was trifling with it. This lack of catastrophe summed up what Newlin liked most: "...no personal demons, this is not a woman gazing into the abyss at 5:00 A.M. Just the Mistress of the Revels fulfilling a request."

Maybe Julia Lee was a consistently good artist rather than a great one. Instead of recording when she had something fresh to say, she could only repeat herself, and the annual sessions which took place in the early '50s were not marked by any sense of real development. The final Capitol session produced one excellent single, "Goin' to Chicago Blues," a revival of the Basie-Rushing best-seller of 1941. Lee's version glowed with the music of her past without coasting on nostalgia.

For a while, Julia survived, maybe even thrived. She played the Cuban Room in Kansas City along with Bill Nolan's Trio, who accompanied her for the rest of her life. During the twilight of her career, Julia and Her Scat Cats recorded at least two singles for Vic Damon's Damon label. They probably sold well locally but received no national promotion. There might have been unissued Damon material but we'll never know for sure; when Vic Damon died, his sons trashed all his masters, recording logs, and equipment.

In the summer of 1955, Julia was filmed for an appearance in *The Delinquents*, the first movie produced, written, and directed by the then 33-year-old Robert Altman who was working for a Kansas City company that made industrial films. Later, of course, Altman would have an intermittently brilliant career, the latest episode of which was a rather beleaguered jazz-age movie called *Kansas City*. Alan Betrock described his debut as a gritty, realistic, and sometimes arty film often shot in cinema verité style using locals as extras and real cops, real drive-ins, and so on. The ads ran, "This is the hard-hitting motion picture that takes off the kid gloves and puts on the brass knuckles in a smashing expose of today's children of violence who just gotta have action!" Julia

39

and the Bill Nolan Quintet Minus Two perform "A Porter's Love Song" in a brief cameo at the beginning of the film which was made for $63,000 and subsequently sold to Warner Bros. for a whole lot more.

In 1957, there were two records for Foremost owned by Blevins Davis and John Sandusky. "Bop and Rock Lullaby" and a reworking of "King Size Papa" were creditable attempts to cope with the disturbance caused by rock 'n' roll's mass popularity. Her last-known recordings were "Trouble in Mind" and "Saturday Night" for the same small Kansas City label.

On December 8, 1958, Julia took an afternoon nap and died in her sleep. Until then she had appeared nightly at the Hi-Bar Lounge, another of the semilegendary clubs in downtown Kansas City. Her death, partially eclipsed by the deaths of Tommy Dorsey and Art Tatum, merited only brief paragraphs in *Billboard* and *Downbeat*, but her friend and personal maid, Mrs. Gady Gillum, gave full details to Bob Greene of the *K.C. Call:* "Julia called me Sunday morning around 9:00 A.M. and she told me she was cooking shrimp. I sent over for some later in the day. I called her back at 2:00 P.M....we made plans to go out somewhere later. I called her up at 4:00 P.M. but couldn't reach her. I called again at 6:00 P.M. and at 9:00 P.M. Monday I called twice but she still didn't answer. Then I went over to see if anything was wrong. I walked in and Julia was laying there as if she was asleep on the divan with a blanket over her. She always took a nap on the divan in the day while she watched TV. It wasn't until I touched her that I knew she was dead."

According to pathologist Dr. Lon Tillman, Julia died of complications from chronic hypertensive heart disease. The funeral service was held at Paseo Baptist Church and she was buried in Highland Cemetery. She left a son, Frank Duncan, Jr. (pitcher for the Chicago Giants), a grandson, an uncle, and a nephew. George E. Lee outlived his sister by a few weeks. He managed a Detroit bar during the '40s and died in 1959.

In his book *The Jazz Story*, Dave Dexter declared: "As Julia's producer for seven years, it was a labor of love for me to select songs, assemble musicians and try to catch her good-natured piano and vocal talents on records. At times she was Wallerish, at times Mortonish, but her delightful rhythm piano and husky vocals could always quickly be identified as Julia Lee's." Noting that she was in her 40s before she enjoyed a string of best-sellers, he added: "How much more effective might she have been had she recorded as a young woman."

In Britain, *Melody Maker* likened Julia's rhythmic phrasing and simple story-telling ability to a great many of the more publicized jazz singers and referred to the esteem in which she was held by English jazz collectors, including Jeff Aldam who gave her a place in *Melody Maker's* Critic's Poll of 1957. "So many musicians spoke highly of her," recalled Aldam, "it surprises me she was not more widely admired. Basie and Rushing, both friends of hers since the twenties, enthused when I mentioned her records. So did Mary Lou [Williams] and a lot more. On piano she swung more than most men, in a rock solid style that had echoes of Fats Waller and Pete Johnson. Solo or accompanying, her taste and tempos were perfect."

These notes accompanied Kansas City Star, *a 5-CD complete career retrospective (BCD 15770).*

41

Jesse Stone

Kansas City Stars: Part 2
Jesse Stone a.k.a Charles Calhoun

Peter A. Grendysa

They've got a Hall of Fame for rock 'n' roll now and a lot of the residents in that hallowed hall are craggy-faced and gray-haired, calling attention to the fact that this music of youth and rebellion has been around a very long time. As rockers look back in awe and satisfaction at over four decades of their music they are going to have to give some thought to the real artisans of the rock edifice. In particular, someday, someway, they are going to have to make room for the guy who made it all possible. It won't be easy. They have already used up all the honorifics: King, Father, Godfather, Grandfather, Prince, Boss, Duke, and so forth. Where, then, do we put Jesse Stone?

Now well into his 90s, but active and feisty as a 40-year-old, Stone is remembered by only a select few, a "fan club" with eclectic tastes and long memories: jazzmen, collectors, and record executives. Some were there when it all happened, and others simply know the music and the records. A few of them have given Stone a nod in their award acceptance speeches over the years, and others find their own self-aggrandizement too important to give credit where credit is due. But Stone, whose career in music spans six decades, knows his rightful place in the pantheon of American music.

Stone worked his show from black vaudeville to Kansas City jazz, Chicago jazz, hot swing, big band swing, bebop, R&B, rock 'n' roll, and soul. And he didn't waste any time getting started. Shortly after his birth in Atchison, Kansas, in the first year of the twentieth century, Stone was on the street grabbing coins with his dog-and-violin act. (Stone played the violin, the dogs just jumped around.) He told Nick Tosches, "All my people were in show business—cousins, grandmothers, grandfathers. I was taught at home by my parents. I had an uncle who was interested in the classics. I got the ability to write songs from my mother, because she wrote songs. My father was a producer. He arranged the numbers for the minstrel shows that we had. I started singing when I was four. I had a dog act. The dogs were so well-trained they could do the act without me. They just made me look good. The first instrument I played was the violin."

By the time he was 20 years old, Stone was working in Kansas City, then wide-open and full of jazz and gangsters, and he briefly put together a band that recorded for OKeh in St. Louis in 1927. He then parlayed his growing reputation as a pianist and arranger into a position with the George and Julia Lee bands in Kansas City, recording with them in 1928 and 1929. As the amoebalike bands split and re-formed, Stone worked with Terence Holder in Texas and Oklahoma and was codirector of Thamon Hayes's Kansas City Rockets from 1932 to 1934. The intense competition among the great bands of the Southwest ironically led to the demise of his attempt at a band of his own.

"Mamie Smith had the top black musicians in the United States at that time. Fletcher Henderson, in order to create a great, great reading band, raided her band and took these guys like Coleman Hawkins and all these great musicians from Mamie. By the way, Coleman Hawkins played with me before he worked with Mamie Smith. She tried to get me to go out as an arranger with her, but I didn't wanna go, because I wanted to have my own band. She wrecked my band, 'cause she could pay more than I could pay 'em, you know."

When the going gets tough at home, the tough form a traveling band. Stone and his Cyclones worked in Chicago, where he did arranging for Earl Hines and others and then traveled to Detroit. Duke Ellington caught his act and recommended him to Mills Music in New York City. Stone became a staff writer at Mills and began working the big-time theaters and venues such as the Cotton Club and the Apollo Theater. While house arranger at the Apollo, he took over the writing and arranging chores for the International Sweethearts of Rhythm, the supreme all-female big band.

"In the very beginning, they were very young. Most of the work was ensemble work. Then Helen Jones, she developed as a good solo trombone player and Pauline Braddy developed as a drummer, and these things happened gradually. When I came in, they started playing for dances, and that's when they started developing individually, because when you play for dances, you got to play solos and whatnot and it was different from the stage work that they did. I think Roxanna Lucas set a pattern for the rest of the girls to study. When they found that she was so serious about learning to read and all, then I finally got them to fall in, come in individually. I used to teach them one at a time. They made a bigger and more lasting name than any other female group in the country."

During this time Stone concentrated on writing. His first big song sale was "Idaho," written in 1942 and recorded with great success by Alvino Rey with singer Yvonne King, and Benny Goodman with Dick Haymes doing the vocal. Finally, it was used as the title song for a film by Roy Rogers. In 1945, Stone and the Sweethearts of Rhythm went on a year-long tour of Europe for the USO, but upon their return, "The best band broke up. Most of the girls got married. Their husbands took them out or they just quit or whatnot."

Stone was well positioned for the advent of R&B at the end of the Second World War. The loose-jointed, jumping jive that had been honed to a fine point by Louis Jordan and His Tympany Five in the early 1940s spearheaded the new music. Stone knew Jordan very well and he told Nick Tosches, "I also played with my band at the Club Renaissance in Harlem on weekends. That's where Louis Jordan picked up on my style of singing. I encouraged him, told him that if he wanted to sing, he should get away from Chick [Webb]. He took my band and they became the Elks' Rendez-Vous Band, the group on his first recordings."

In 1945, Stone began an association with Herb Abramson, the A&R Director for National Records. Abramson brought the label hits by Billy Eckstine, Joe Turner, and the Ravens and then tried a couple of labels of his own without success. In 1947, Stone began recording for RCA Victor as the major labels made a half-hearted attempt to gain some inroads in the new R&B market, already the province of the small, independent operations. For RCA, Stone provided original material of the novelty jive genre, lending his none-too-forceful vocals to stereo-typical images of black life (drinking, gambling, and wild women) in direct competition with Louis Jordan.

While Stone was with RCA, Abramson was putting together his Atlantic Recording Corporation with partner Ahmet Ertegun and

45

financial help from dentist Dr. Vadhi Sabit and record distributor Max Silverman. Stone was hired as a writer and arranger and subsequently guided the company into a swinging, urbane (as opposed to urban) blues sound, heavy on the rhythm section and glittering tenor saxophone solos. The combination of rough blues and meticulously crafted and rehearsed music soon led to Atlantic's first hit, "Drinkin' Wine Spo-Dee-O-Dee" by Stick McGhee in 1949.

Still on the artist roster at RCA, Stone found himself in competition with himself when he produced "Cole Slaw" by saxman Frank "Floorshow" Culley for Atlantic. Culley had brought in a tune he called "Sergeant" and Stone immediately recognized it as one of his own. "It turned out to be a song called 'Sorghum Switch' that I had written when I was a staff writer at Mills." This instrumental had been recorded by Doc Wheeler and His Sunset Orioles for Bluebird in 1942 and subsequently made into a minor hit by Jimmy Dorsey on Decca. "From wherever Culley had picked it up, he had gotten the title wrong."

The tune was retitled "Cole Slaw" when it was released in February 1949, as a tribute to influential disc jockey Max Cole at WOV in New York City. Stone then added some marvelous lyrics to the tune and it was recorded by Louis Jordan in April. One week later, Stone did his own version for RCA. Jordan's Decca disc was a runaway success on the national record charts. Of more significance to the development of rock 'n' roll, Culley's "Cole Slaw" was the first appearance of Stone's innovation—the pronounced bass line.

Stone, Ertegun, and Abramson had made a tour of their southern distributors in 1948 and found that their Atlantic records lacked a certain danceable quality. "The kids were looking for something to dance to. I listened to the stuff that was being done by those thrown-together bands in the joints down there, and I concluded that the only thing that was missing from the stuff we were recording was the rhythm. All we needed was a bass line. So I designed a bass pattern and it sort of became identified with rock 'n' roll—doo, da-doo, dum; doo, da-doo, dum—that thing. I'm the guilty person that started that. When we started putting that sound out on Atlantic, we started selling like hotcakes. The first big seller we had with the new sound was Ruth Brown, who we'd found in Philadelphia. After 1949, the hits just kept coming. I had to learn rock 'n' roll—we didn't call it rock 'n' roll then—and it wasn't something that I could do easily at first. I considered it backward, musically, and I didn't like it until I started to learn that the rhythm content was the important thing. Then I started to like it and finally I started writing tunes."

Quincy Jones, then a 20-year-old member of the Lionel Hampton band, recalled the revolutionary effect of the electric bass on this bass line in 1953. "It really changed the sound of music because it ate up so much space. Its sound was so imposing in comparison to the upright bass, so it couldn't have the same function. The rhythm section became the stars. The old style didn't work anymore and it created a new language."

In addition to directing the bands and, during the height of the vocal group explosion, rehearsing endless hours with rough-hewn singers from the street corners, Stone wrote original material for the Cardinals ("Please Don't Leave Me"), Clovers ("Good Lovin'," "Your Cash Ain't Nothin' but Trash"), Drifters ("Money Honey," "Bip Bam," "I Gotta Get Myself a Woman"), LaVern Baker ("Soul on Fire," "I Can't Hold Out Any Longer"), Odelle Turner ("Draggin' Hours"), Arnett Cobb ("No Child No More"), Ray Charles ("Losing Hand"), Ruth Brown ("As Long as I'm Moving"), Cookies ("My Lover"), Pearls ("Bells of Love"), Playboys ("Good Golly, Miss Molly"), Chuck Willis ("Juanita"), Titus Turner ("A-Knockin' at My Baby's Door"), Walter Spriggs ("I Pawned Everything"), Floyd Dixon ("Moonshine"), Willis Jackson ("Wine-Oh-Wine"), Roy Hamilton ("Don't Let Go"), and, of course, Joe Turner.

For a Joe Turner session in February 1954, Stone contributed a song that became the rallying cry of the rock 'n' roll revolution, "Shake, Rattle, and Roll." Two weeks before, Abramson had asked Stone to put together an uptempo blues for Big Joe. "I threw a bunch of phonetic phrases together—'shake, rattle, and roll,' 'flip, flop, and fly'—and I came up with thirty or forty verses. Then I picked over them. I got the line about a 'one-eyed cat peepin' in a seafood store' from my drummer, Baby Lovett. He was always coming out with lines like that."

The result, helped along immeasurably by saxmen Sam Taylor and Heywood Henry and the Atlantic "Piano Man" Van Walls, was, as Nick Tosches puts it, "a perfect record." After release in May, it sold heavily for nearly a year. Fledgling rock 'n' rollers of the white persuasion were moved along the path to enlightenment by the cover version by Bill Haley and the Comets, which reached places R&B records never went.

The aberration of an R&B song sung by a hillbilly shocked the racist establishment, and delighted white teenagers. As Haley recalled,

47

"I loved the song and I loved to hear Joe Turner sing. I'd sit for hours listening. So I thought, 'Well, I love that song so I'll do it.'" Haley and fellow Comet Joe Grande supplied sanitized replacement lyrics for some of Stone's more suggestive word portraits and the record became a national sensation. At the height of its popularity, another hillbilly cat was down in Memphis rocking the blues. King to be, Elvis Presley was just another courtier to Bill Haley in 1954. For Haley's pains in inventing a new teenage musical movement, he was branded a "nigger-loving communist" by certain elements of white society.

Jesse Stone

Stone gave Joe Turner more hits with "Flip, Flop, and Fly," "Well All Right," "Morning, Noon, and Night," and "Lipstick, Powder, and Paint." For all of his inestimable worth to Atlantic, Jesse Stone was never more than one of the hired hands at the label. His repeated requests to be made a partner were brushed aside as first Jerry Wexler and then Nesuhi Ertegun were brought into the company. "Ahmet was good to me. He'd say 'You're not charging enough,' and he'd write out a figure and say, 'This is what you should get. If you don't get it, the government will.' But I was after a piece of the company, and I could never pin them down to giving it to me. They kept offering me a lifetime job, but I didn't want that. I wanted a piece."

Stone wasn't the only one unable to cash in on the astounding financial success of Atlantic Records. Wexler himself is no longer with the company and founder Herb Abramson left in 1957. As Abramson explains it, "I sometimes look at it like a poker game, in that originally there are quite a few participants, but some of them are dealt out and some of them end up with all the chips. That's the way the cookie crumbles."

Stone also saw a need for a group of background singers, similar to the big Ray Charles Singers, but with the ability to sing in the new R&B style. Before this time, the concept of having a group solely for backup work did not exist. The immediate result was the Cues (Four Students), comprised of veteran group singers Ollie Jones, Robie Kirk, Abel de Costa, and Eddie Barnes. Although the Cues did record a few singles under their own name, they were much more prolific as Ruth Brown's Rhythmmakers, LaVern Baker's Gliders, Carmen Taylor's Boleros, Ivory Joe Hunter's Ivorytones, Charlie White's Playboys, and even Joe Turner's Blues Kings—and that was just for Atlantic.

As Ollie Jones recalled, "The Cues were the brainchild of Jesse Stone, a man who has never received the recognition he should have. The whole idea of having a back-up vocal group was his. Jesse wanted us to do demo records for his publishing company, and now there are a lot of groups who do just that and only that. But we were the first. They had the big studio reading type things, like the guy with the beard, Mitch Miller, had that big chorus, but that was not rock 'n' roll. So since we were able to do this we got a lot of work that way." Other Stone ventures included the Regals and the Cookies, who became the first Raelets for Ray Charles.

On advice from Ertegun, Stone used a pseudonym on his BMI

49

tunes to avoid conflict with his membership in the other performing rights society, ASCAP. He picked Charles E. Calhoun, the name of the man who had built his house in Hempstead, Long Island. "Chuck Calhoun" eventually made some records for MGM, Groove, and Atlantic. Stone even ran the New York office of Atlantic's archrival, Aladdin Records, for a time in 1954, and then started his own music publishing company, Roosevelt Music. His partners included song-writing giants Charlie Singleton, Rosemarie McCoy, Robie "Winfield Scott" Kirk, Lincoln Chase, and Otis "John Davenport" Blackwell. In 1958, he took over as music director for Lou Krefetz's Poplar Records, joining Atlantic expatriates the Clovers at the label.

Stone decided to take a less active role in recording in the late 1950s and retired to California. During the twist craze he was lured back into the studio and ended up doing work for Frank Sinatra's Reprise label. In the early 1960s he moved to Chicago to head a well-funded but shady independent label called Ran-Dee Records, notable only for being the debut label for soul chanteuse Joan Kennedy. After a few nervous years in the Windy City, Stone "escaped" to the East Coast again. Sitting in his office at Roosevelt Music listening to demo records, he heard a voice he remembered from the distant past.

Evelyn McGee, former vocalist with the Sweethearts of Rhythm, had been working in a duo with former Sweethearts' drummer Pauline Braddy after the failure of her first marriage. Stone told her, "You've still got the voice. It's a little rusty, but I'll work with you." They performed as the Jesse Stone Duo and were married in 1966. "I had fallen in love with him in the forties, anyway, long before I knew my husband. I had a crush on him. So it was meant to be. For ten years we worked together as a duo and he made me play the drums, which I became good at." After the team retired in 1978, they attended Kingsborough Community College, working for degrees in music.

In the interim, Stone recorded a few piano concertos of his own composition for RCA, but they were never released. Today he lives in Florida, still arranging and performing, a living national treasure with unequaled links to black vaudeville, jazz, swing, R&B, and rock 'n' roll.

Writers such as Nelson George and Nick Tosches have given Jesse Stone some long-deserved recognition, and in 1992 he was inducted into the Rhythm and Blues Hall of Fame in New York. Jerry Wexler said, "Jesse's musical mind had as much to do as anyone's with the transformation of traditional blues to pop blues—or rhythm and blues,

Jesse Stone

or cat music, or rock 'n' roll, or whatever the hell you want to call it. Jesse was a master, and an integral part of the sound we were developing." Ahmet Ertegun said, "Jesse Stone did more to develop the basic rock 'n' roll sound than anybody else." And someday everybody will know Jesse Stone—the Rock of Rock 'n' Roll.

These notes accompanied Alias Charles Calhoun, *an anthology of Stone's RCA, Decca, and Atlantic recordings, 1947–1958 (BCD 15695).*

5

Vegas Rocks and Reno Rolls: Part 1
Louis Prima

Billy Vera

Some would ridicule the notion that there was rock 'n' roll in the resort cities of Nevada during the 1950s. Everyone knows what happened to Elvis during his first stint in Vegas. The Nevada resorts were the playgrounds of the middle-aged, but they couldn't exist in a time warp. They had to adapt, and rock 'n' roll had to adapt, too, if it was to work there. The rock 'n' roll that became part of the Nevada entertainment mix was very different from what you'd hear on American Bandstand. *It was show-room rock 'n' roll.*

Like Julia Lee, Louis Prima's roots were in the big band jazz of the '30s, and he would have been aghast at the notion that he was a rock 'n' roller. Kids would have been aghast at the notion, too; this was their parents' music. What could be squarer than "Felicia No Capicia"? Plenty, as it happens. Looking back, we can see embryonic rock 'n' roll in the giddy energy and in the transformation of black hep into white hep. As Nick Tosches said in one of the first pieces to rehabilitate the man, "Prima presaged the Rock 'n' Roll of the Ridiculous. He perceived and embraced in all its tutti-frutti glory, the spirit of post-literate, made-for-television America."

Billy Vera's essay on Louis Prima is not only a wonderfully enter-taining monograph that seals the rehabilitation of a giant, but it's also a very personal journey. We all tend to jettison our parents' music, and it's not until later in life that we see some merit in it and discover its ability to evoke a lost time and place. (C. E.)

Is pasta fazool a.k.a. pasta e fagioli (macaroni and beans to the un-initiated) any less soulful than ham hocks and butter beans? Is a sausage, onions, green peppers, and scrambled egg sandwich any less tasty than fried chicken and collard greens? Does gnocchi with red gravy (marinara sauce) belong on a New Orleans kitchen table any less than shrimp and okra gumbo?

"If you don't know," to paraphrase Louis Armstrong, "ain't no way I can explain it to you." That does not mean, however, that you will never get it.

True Confession time: Yours truly did not always get Louis Prima. I have to admit that it is only in the past several years that his particular genius has become clear and apparent to me. But, now that I do understand, I am afraid I have become a bit of a proselytizer on the subject. In my late teens, I was a young turk starting out in the music business. It was the early '60s, and the music of choice for my crowd was New York soul: Ben E. King, Chuck Jackson, Baby Washington, and others. That, along with the requisite twist material for dancing, was the kind of stuff my band played when we first made our way from White Plains, in the Westchester County suburbs of New York, to the Times Square clubs where, for $15 per night per man, we played alternating sets of a half hour on and a half hour off with another band from 8:30 P.M. to 4:00 A.M. in joints like the Headliner, adjoining the Times Square Hotel next to the New York Times building on 43rd Street, or the world-famous Peppermint Lounge on 45th. You couldn't work next door at the Wagon Wheel if you worked the Peppermint because they were operated by opposing mob families. The alternating bands at that time fell into one of two categories: Joey Dee and the Star-liters-styled groups, playing impossibly fast tempos to keep the twisters twisting, or show bands, patterned after the combo of Louis Prima. These latter aggregations would inevitably feature the same instru-mentation as Louis's band, Sam Butera and the Witnesses: a rhythm section, with a trumpet and a wailing tenor sax and a chick singer along the lines of Keely Smith.

The goal, for these latter groups, was to become a lounge act, to get summer gigs down the shore, in Wildwood, New Jersey, preferably; to be signed by an agent, preferably Jolly Joyce; and to eventually make one's way to that Mecca-in-the-desert, Las Vegas, Nevada... to blow until dawn in the lounges—maybe even the one in the Sahara Hotel,

Prima's stomping ground, and wear sharp threads, sleep all day or get a nice tan by the pool, hang out with mob guys and bang lots of broads.

Except for the part about the broads, that scenario had no appeal for me in 1962. I was a pretentious young songwriter with eyes to becoming the next Bacharach and David or Leiber and Stoller, and as a performer, my dream was to play the Apollo on 125th Street, rather than some hitter bar in Atlantic City—even though the money was much less. I thought I was black.

Little did I know that countless hipsters before me yearned to live the life of a black musician. What did I know from Johnny Otis or Louie Bellson? What did some old Guinea with a bad rug singing some shit about "I eat antipasto twice, just because she's very nice" have to do with me? And all these wise guy club owners telling me "kid, you coo'be da nex' fuckin' Tony Bennett, Ah-sweah-t'God, if youse just get a chick singah and do 'Gigolo,' Whaddaya wanna be like sumfuckin' melanzane, woikin'fa peanuts, henh? Get wise, ya dumb giadrool!"

So, you see, I had to get rid of a lot of emotional baggage in order to get Louis Prima, to come to terms with a background that I had spurned 30 years ago in order to feel hip. He was of and for an older, cruder generation, as far as my crowd was concerned. That crap, and the Treniers for that matter, was bullshit for the carfones. A carfone, or gavone, in the Sicilian dialect so predominant in the area I grew up, is a slang expression for a loud, uncouth male—one who is given to wearing white-on-white shirts; silk neckties; flashy continental suits made of mohair or shark skin; large, shiny cuff links on cuffs extending two inches out from the edge of his jacket sleeve; gaudy, initials-in-diamonds pinky rings; and way too much cologne.

The carfone's taste in music may run from Sinatra to Jerry Vale; from Lou Monte's "Pepino the Italian Mouse" to Jimmy Roselli's "Mala Femina." His taste in automobiles runs from black Cadillacs to red Cadillacs. His taste in women runs from the Mother Cabrini he married to the putana or goomahd he has on the side. When he goes out to a nightclub or lounge, he wants his music loud, comical in a way that is familiar to him, a few off-color wisecracks thrown in here and there in Sicilian, so the squares won't know what he's talking about. (In this last, he is not so different from the black hipster, whose jive talk was a coded, cryptic method of keeping the outsiders on the outside peeping in—where they belong.)

In short, he wants to hear Louis Prima. All of this is not to cast

55

aspersions on the music herein—far from it—but to illustrate the distance one must often go to reach the state of mind where the heart will be open to enjoyment of the music and personality of a Louis Prima on their own merits. Or, perhaps this background might lend an air of exotica, the kind that first drew mavens of blues and jazz to the dives of Harlem or Chicago's South Side. You can dig it if you can set aside your cultural biases and relax and have a good time. It is thus possible to enjoy Louis Prima on a number of levels: as an insider who possesses the key to the code, or simply for the fun of the beat and the musicianship.

New Orleans, Sicilians, and La Cosa Nostra

Forget New York and Chicago. The place where the Mafia was born, bred, and nurtured after it made its way from Sicily to the good old U.S. of A., not long after the Civil War, was none other than that home of vice, sin, and other assorted fun stuff, New Orleans, Louisiana.

New Orleans, by the turn of the century, was home to more Sicilians and other Italians than any city in the United States. Maybe the southern Italians liked the climate; the temperature and sea breezes from the Gulf of Mexico were quite similar to those found in their homeland. Maybe the political corruption reminded them of the virtual anarchy and lack of government in their native Palermo. Whatever the reasons, they moved there in droves, bringing with them their own underground government, the Black Hand.

To this day, one of the most powerful families in La Cosa Nostra is that of Carlos Marcello (or, as he is often called, Marcellus). Marcello, for those uninitiated in JFK assassination lore, is often touted as the man behind the scenes who ordered the hit, sometimes in conjunction with Sam Giancana of Chicago. Both had allegedly been betrayed by the president's father, Joe Kennedy, after they had delivered the votes that gave America her first Irish Roman Catholic president.

New Orleans, with its population of French rather than English ancestry, suffered none of the puritanical Calvinist mores of the latter culture. Hence, prostitution, gambling, drugs, and other recreations were well established by the time the Sicilians arrived. The Crescent City was also the most musical of American cities, including, not only the well-documented brothel musicians, but also well-respected symphonies. It was the cradle of jazz, where masters, such as the tireless self-promoter Jelly Roll Morton, who claimed to have invented jazz,

Louis Prima

held forth in nightclubs, gambling joints, parades, funeral processions and on street corners, night and day.

It was into this atmosphere that Louis Prima was born on December 7, 1910, to Anthony and Angelina Caravella Prima in the Little Palermo section of the French Quarter. The French Quarter had, by that time, already become a bit of a misnomer, as the Primas' neighbors included Arabs, Jews, and blacks. Anthony, a passive, hard-working man, who distributed Jumbo Soda Pop well past the time when his son's fortunes would have precluded any need for him to work, and his wife had three additional children: Leon, the eldest; Elizabeth, who became a nun; and Marguerite, who died as a young child.

Angelina appears to have been one of those powerful personalities who forcefully ran her home. She was a legendary cook and the long Prima dining room table at their home on St. Peter Street was often filled with friends and neighbors. She was also a music lover and sang in shows at the local church, coaching young Louis to always smile when performing. Angelina gave Leon and Elizabeth piano lessons and Louis a violin, which he hated.

He hated it even more, once he began to hear Leon playing cornet. Leon, no mean musician himself, was playing in jazz clubs by the early 1920s. It is important to remember that, in New Orleans, jazz was the style of choice of not only black, but white musicians of that generation as well. While the races were not allowed to perform together professionally, they often listened to each other and even jammed in private sessions or after-hours clubs, many of which proliferated in Jefferson Parish, where the local mafia had control of the vice.

By this time, Louis had to have a trumpet. Besides his brother, local hero Louis Armstrong was then making a name for himself in the world of music. So, not unlike Elvis Presley (another favored son of a strong mother and a passive father), Prima, who could do no wrong in his mama's eyes, got his instrument and became very good at it in a very short time. At 13, he was photographed with his Louis Prima's Kid Band, which played at lawn parties and other private affairs. Members included Irving Fazola (a.k.a. Prestopnick) on clarinet, who later appeared with Ben Pollack, Glenn Miller, and Bob Crosby.

Louis quit Jesuit High School in the tenth grade and, with his friend and long-time guitarist, Frank Frederico, started playing for peanuts at New Orleans clubs like the Whip and the Studio Club on Bourbon Street. Both brothers gained local renown as respected players in a town where musical competition was tough. Leon formed the Prima-Sharkey Orchestra with Sharkey Bonano and played with Leon Roppolo, both important players in the history of New Orleans jazz. They performed at the Jefferson Parish gambling halls and over radio station WSMB, where, against the rules, they let black musicians sit in on occasion. In 1933, Leon opened the Avalon, later Prima's Beverly Beer Garden, on Metairie Road, his first in a string of nightclubs. Like so many New Orleans musicians, Leon preferred to stay in his hometown and did well there, relatively speaking.

Louis, meanwhile, had left town in 1929 for an aborted career with the band of Ellis Stratake. When that didn't pan out, he came home and married Louise Polizzi, his first of five wives. Continuing the life of a musician, his first break came when Lou Forbes hired him in 1931 to perform at the city's Saenger Theater, where Louis learned his craft as an entertainer, doing vaudeville sketches and musical comedy bits.

Before long, Louis was getting good reviews and had risen to second billing.

Later on, much was made about Prima's forsaking his musical abilities, which were considerable, and selling out to become a mere entertainer. The same was also said of Louis Armstrong who, despite his position as the major innovator of the century, never neglected his perceived obligation to connect with his audience. It must be remembered that, in a competitive atmosphere such as existed in New Orleans, the musicians who made that connection with their audiences were the ones who got—and kept—the work. It was this willingness to entertain that got Prima his next, and perhaps most important, break. He was playing at Leon's Club Shim Sham (a name suggested by Louis and Leon's friend Martha Raye) and was discovered there by fellow Sicilian Guy Lombardo, who was in town for the Mardi Gras, performing at the Club Forest, a gambling casino on Jefferson Highway near the Parish line. Lombardo later said he was walking down the street, passing by club after club, when he heard a trumpet that spoke to him with a sound more piercing than any of the many others on the street. Guy brought his brothers back to the club to see if they agreed with his assessment of Prima's talent.

Over the protests of Angelina (whose opinion was more important than Louise's), Guy took Louis to New York and introduced him around. To have the backing of a bandleader of Lombardo's stature was no small potatoes. Despite the fame of his mentor, Louis couldn't find work for six months. Guy had taken Louis to Leon & Eddie's on 52nd Street, only to be told by co-owner Eddie Davis that he wouldn't hire young Prima because he was a Negro. Louis's Sicilian coloring and features, combined with his New Orleans dialect, gave many people the idea that he was at least a mulatto. Ironically, this worked in his favor during some of his difficult periods, enabling him to work black theaters, whose audiences were also convinced he was mixed.

Through the efforts of Lombardo and publisher Irving Mills, Louis started his recording career almost immediately in September 1934 for Brunswick with a contingent of studio men, plus a couple of Crescent City homeboys, as Louis Prima and his New Orleans Gang. The hits came just as quickly: "Let's Have a Jubilee," "Chinatown," "The Lady in Red," and the No. 1 hit, "Chasing Shadows." In March of 1935, Louis opened at Jack Colt's Famous Door. He was an instant hit on opening night, causing columnist Robert Sylvester to later com-

59

ment that this was "the night 52nd Street plunged head first into the Swing Era."

Soon, trendy New Yorkers, teenagers, as well as women lured by rumors of Prima's generous endowment (which, ever the showman, he never failed to capitalize upon, dancing suggestively in pants custom-tailored to emphasize his gifts), packed the club for months. In September, Louis, reportedly in fear of mobsters trying to horn in on his success, returned home in triumph, appearing at his brother's Club Shim Sham. A month later, he headed for Los Angeles, where his growing fame preceded him. Not one to let any grass grow under his feet, Louis quickly began looking for opportunities—and found one. Singing star Gene Austin was looking to get out from under the lease of his Blue Heaven nightclub (named for his hit, "My Blue Heaven") and found a taker in Louis, who renamed it—what else?—the Famous Door.

Again, Prima was an instant hit, drawing the young Hollywood crowd and attracting young actresses, including Jean Harlow, with whom he allegedly had an affair. This led to appearances in the movies, the first of which was *Rhythm on the Range*, starring Bing Crosby, Frances Farmer, and his old singing pal, Martha Raye. Other films included *Swing It*, *The Star Reporter*, and *You Can't Have Everything*.

With friends like Crosby, Louis began hanging out at the race-track, which was to become a lifelong obsession. It was at the track with Crosby he came up with the idea for "Sing, Bing, Sing." Der Bingle responded, "Why don't cha just call it 'Sing Sing Sing,' and make it more universal?" Louis cut the first version of the tune in February 1936, in Hollywood, but it was elevated to legendary status when Benny Goodman recorded it for Columbia a year later at the famous 1938 Carnegie Hall concert.

It was in Hollywood that Louis met his second wife, actress Alma Ross, but he was soon back on the road taking the swing craze to the Midwest with a larger 12-piece band. His big gig, at Chicago's Blackhawk, was a flop; somehow the spontaneity of his combo was lost, perhaps through inadequate rehearsal. In late 1937, Prima returned to the New York Famous Door, where his intermission pianist was Art Tatum. There he played a successful 20-week run, after which he moved up to Billy Rose's Casa Manana.

There were more hit records on Brunswick and Decca: "Rosalie," "Pennies from Heaven," and "Exactly Like You." His band was now up to 14 pieces with the addition of vocalist Lily Ann Carol. Prima's big swing band was enormously popular with black audiences. Sam Butera says: "That was long before I was with him, but he told me he had this number, 'Nothin' Like a Long-legged, Brown-skin Woman to Make a Preacher Lay His Bible Down,' that used to knock 'em out in the black theaters, and had the women screaming from the balcony." Trombonist Milt Kabak, who joined Louis in 1942, says, "When I joined him, he was scuffling, playing black theaters almost exclusively. They loved him. He would imitate Satchmo. He'd sing 'I'm Confessin','' 'When It's Sleepytime Down South.'" Sammy Davis, Jr.'s first Apollo Theater appearance with the Will Mastin Trio was on a bill starring Louis Prima.

In 1942, during an engagement at Washington, D.C.'s Howard Theater, Eleanor Roosevelt, who was committed to racial integration, was in the audience. Seeing how blacks responded to Louis, she invited him to a party at the White House. When Louis was introduced to her husband, FDR, he said, "How you doin' Daddy?" The president replied, "Why did you call me 'Daddy'?" and Louis said "'Cause you da Father of our country."

Throughout World War II, the hits piled up on Majestic Records: "Robin Hood" (his theme song), "Brooklyn Boogie," and "Bell-Bottom Trousers." Prima's recording of "I'll Walk Alone" (with a vocal by Lily Ann Carol), put a lump in many a serviceman's throat. Louis also found a new, novel approach for himself: novelties with Italian subject matter like "Angelina, Please No Squeeza da Banana" and "Felicia No Capicia." As successful as these records were, wartime was hell on big bands. Milt Kabak remembers an unending run of "black theaters, one-nighters, late night trains." Kabak's first break with Prima came during "our first good gig at the Astor Roof, where Tommy Dorsey [had] played. Louis sat the band down and instructed us to clean up our act. We weren't to use the front elevator. He canned me one night when I came in through the front." The Astor represented an entré into big time show business via air checks and its prestigious location.

By war's end, Prima was breaking records at the Downtown Theater in Detroit, the Adams in Newark, the Panther Room in Chicago, and the Strand in New York, where the Prima Donnas, a fan club of 20,000 bobby-soxers did for Louis what they had done for Sinatra. At this time, his motto was "Play It Pretty for the People," and they responded by making his Majestic records of "My Dreams Are Getting Better All the Time" and "A Sunday Kind of Love" (which Louis cowrote with his manager, Barbara Belle) into best-sellers. A version of

61

the latter, by former Prima pianist Claude Thornhill with a vocal by Barbara Belle's management client Fran Warren was a big pop smash and, of course, became a doo-wop standard in versions by the Harptones, the Del Vikings, the Mystics, and others in the rock 'n' roll era.

Louis moved over to RCA Victor in 1947 and hit with his version of "Civilization (Bongo, Bongo, Bongo)." A year later, he married his third wife, 21-year-old Tracelene Barrett and bought a plot of land near Lake Pontchartrain, Louisiana, and named it Pretty Acres. That marriage was to be brief, however. In August 1947, Prima met a young half Irish–half Cherokee 17-year-old in a bathing suit at Virginia Beach, where the band was appearing at the Surf Club.

Lily Ann Carol had gone on to (very little) fame and fortune, leaving Louis to make his way with the likes of Florida Keyes and one Tangerine in the way of female vocalists. Lily Ann had become an important part of the act, playing, in essence, his straight woman-foil since at least 1943. She went on to record, as a solo act, unsuccessfully, for Victor and MGM. Back at the Surf, Louis held auditions for a new chick singer, when who should show up, but the babe in the swimsuit, Dorothy Jacqueline Keely (she says the Smith came from her stepfather, Jesse Smith). With his impeccable eye for female talent, he hired her on the spot. From the age of 11, when she appeared on the local Joe Broom Radio Gang show, young Keely wanted to be a singer. She had seen the Prima band a year earlier in Atlantic City at the Steel Pier and had gone out and bought his records.

By most accounts, Keely was, to say at least, a little green at 17. Her subsequent growth as a singer and performer owes as much to Prima's tutelage as to her own innate talent. Her very lack of stage training seemed to work in her favor. When she stood there and watched Louis go through his antics, she was somehow part of and yet, not of, the audience. In the words of Las Vegas publicity man Shelly Davis, "Louis and Keely invented Sonny and Cher," meaning, of course, that they were the duo's prototype.

Think about it. Louis/Sonny, the older, been-around-the-block showbiz pro, takes the unschooled younger girl (Keely/Cher) and molds her to his specifications. In the former case, Louis emphasized Keely's naturalness, telling her to "be yourself." He wanted her to appear unaffected, with an air of possibility. Her staring face, devoid of emotion, was a blank surface upon which the imagination could project any meaning desired, much like the face of today's high-fashion supermodels. This also freed Louis to evolve a new persona for himself, one more likely for a man of his age: the still-swinging, dirty old man. Keely's laid-back style suggested that she was disapproving and put off by his offcolor jokes and innuendos.

Of course, this process took years to develop. In the late '40s, there were other fish to fry. Though Louis kept his going longer than most, the decline of the big bands was imminent. Keely had made her recording debut with the band at the last RCA Victor session. With a new record deal at Mercury, Louis could be heard exploring the jump blues idiom he helped to pioneer on shuffles like "Over the Rainbow," while Keely crooned ditties like "Here, Little Kitty."

In 1950, Milt Kabak returned to the band after several years with Stan Kenton. "He still had the big band. Keely was already there. They weren't together yet; she had a thing for [drummer] Jimmy Vincent and Louis was married to Trace. Louie was after her, though. He was a big womanizer. He left notes on her door: 'If you want to really get somewhere…' The gigs ranged from the Steel Pier to the black theaters where Louis was still a big draw."

Bud Robinson, who with his wife had the dance team of Bud and Cee Cee, worked as an opening act for Prima and many other stars. He says, "We worked with him at all the theaters: the Paramount, the State in Hartford, the Fox in Detroit. That was his big town. Louis was real big in Detroit. I knew Keely. We were from the same hometown, Norfolk, Virginia." What were the differences between the black and white theaters? Kabak: "[At the white theaters], the band would open with an instrumental and one or two vocals, followed by a comic, maybe Henny Youngman, then a dance act or a dog act or a contortionist, then a singer, say Ray Eberle. We had to rehearse everybody's music." And the black theaters? "There would always be chorus girls first, then a dirty comic… Pigmeat or Moms Mabley-type, a hit record singer, then us."

What was Prima like in those days? Milt: "He was wild. He smoked pot, had tons of chicks, didn't drink, loved the horses, and paid lots of alimony, so he was always scuffling for bread, which was why we had to take any gig that came along." Bud Robinson concurs: "He forgot a lot. I remember once, he was supposed to introduce us and, although we'd worked together countless times, he couldn't remember our names … 'Ah… here's… ah… Buddy and ah… his chick!'"

Not long after Kabak rejoined, he and Louis wrote a huge hit. "We

63

were backstage at the Steel Pier one night and Louis wanted a tune based on a phrase which Satchmo used in between lyrics, 'oh babe.' You know, 'I'm confessin' that I love you ... oh babe.' I thought that was a good idea so we put our heads together."

The Mercury deal was short-lived and Louis, along with Leo Rogers and Ted Eddy as partners, started his own label, Robin Hood, based in the Brill Building in New York. The first release, "Oh Babe!" was a duet with Keely. It was a tremendous success, and, in the manner of the day, was the subject of numerous cover versions: Roy Milton, Wynonie Harris, Larry Darnell, Jimmy Preston, Lionel Hampton, and Jimmy Ricks with Benny Goodman's Sextet, all practitioners of the art of jump blues, as well as Kay Starr, who had a smash pop hit, and Lalo Guerrero, with a Mexican-slang version called "Chitas Patas Boogie." This latter version would, in the late 1970s, be used as a pachuco call-to-arms in the motion picture, *Zoot Suit*.

The success of "Oh Babe!" illustrates the great impact Louis had on R&B artists and, by extension, on the advent of rock 'n' roll. Milt, again: "We were on a one-nighter in Chicago. 'Oh Babe!' was on the radio. Number five. We played this big arena filled with lots of teenagers screaming, like Sinatra!"

Other records for Robin Hood didn't do as well. "Yeah Yeah Yeah," another Prima-Kabak composition, although covered by Paul Gayten, Joe Morris, and Peggy Lee, failed to ignite. Ditto a cover of Ruth Brown's groundbreaking "Teardrops from My Eyes" or Prima's original version of "Come On'a My House," subsequently a smash for Rosemary Clooney. In Louis's version, the invitation sounds positively lewd.

Hit records were becoming more and more important components in one's showbiz career. The lack of them was killing many of the old-line artists, including Sinatra. Keely: "Things got bad rather quickly." More often now, they dispensed with the band and, as Louis's price fell, had to make do with house bands. Early in 1952, Louis signed with Columbia Records, under the direction of the often-maligned Mitch Miller, whose commercial instincts usually overrode his musical talents. (Mitch was one of the finest classical oboe players in New York.) With Columbia, Louis did "The Bigger the Figure," a cover of Clovers' "One Mint Julep," a ballad version of "Oh! Marie," later a staple of his lounge act, and "Luigi," a tale of a numbers runner that went over the heads of most who heard it.

Louis Prima and Keely Smith

Keely became wife No. 4 in 1953. She was 21 and he was exactly twice her age. The marriage seemed destined to work for a number of reasons. He liked to control and, being a southern woman, she liked for the man to be the boss. She was also wise enough to let Angelina think things were her idea, that she was the boss. Acknowledging that his style of music had become dated, Louis toyed with the idea of retiring to Pretty Acres and running his hotel-golf course-country club among the alligators, while overseeing Keely's career. His own records, like his 1954 Decca cover of "The Happy Wanderer," did zilch.

Rock 'n' roll was waiting in the wings to pounce on a public starved for danceable music. Unlike his contemporaries, Louis understood it, and, in fact, had been successful all along with his own beautifully vulgar mixture of Dixieland, swing, jazz, and R&B. He wanted to put this kind of beat behind Keely's deadpan voice and face. To create an image for her, he cut her hair himself, giving her that famous look. But Louis's penchant for high living and the horses precluded his big dreams for his wife's stardom—at this point.

Vegas

Originally settled by Mormons, Las Vegas was founded as a city in 1905, but lay dormant until 1931, when the state of Nevada legalized gambling and eased the divorce laws to increase state revenues in an effort to lift the state out of the Great Depression. The construction of Hoover Dam in Black Canyon also aided in this cause. In 1941, the El Rancho Vegas hotel opened, and New York mobster Bugsy Siegel sent his henchman, Little Moe Sedway, to reconnoiter. Bugsy became

partners with Meyer Lansky and godfather Frank Costello in the Frontier Turf Club, the Golden Nugget, and the El Cortez. With backing from the above, Siegel's dream of a deluxe gambling casino-hotel, The Flamingo, opened on December 26, 1946, starring Jimmy Durante, and was an immediate flop. It reopened in March 1947 and continued to operate successfully. Three months later, Bugsy was blown away at the Beverly Hills home of his girlfriend, Virginia Hill.

In 1945, after the first regularly scheduled airline flights brought gamblers from the east coast, the various mob families divided up the town. First to stake their claim were the Jews: Moe Dalitz and the Cleveland boys (the Desert Inn), along with Longy Zwillman and his New Jersey wise guys (the Sands); then, the Italians: the Chicago Capone family (the Riviera, later the Stardust), Raymond Patriarca's Boston and Providence mob (the Dunes), plus Costello's various interests in the Sands and the Tropicana. Las Vegas was declared an open town with no one family in control. To keep order, Meyer Lansky, the one guy everybody trusted, acted as banker and referee in all disputes.

Costello, who held court at Manhattan's Waldorf barber shop, sent one of his lieutenants, Jack Entratter, to Vegas to protect his 10 percent interest in the Sands, which had been financed by the Cleveland mob. Entratter later went on to break the color line in Vegas by booking Lena Horne and Nat "King" Cole. Nowhere in my search have I been able to find anyone willing to say—even off the record—that there was mob involvement in the Sahara Hotel. In fact, when I asked, certain parties very closely involved made a point of saying that the Sahara was one of the few hotel-casinos not affiliated with organized crime. Hard to believe, but apparently true. I also asked various people connected with Louis—again off the record—if there were any mob connections as far as his business went. Again, the unanimous answer was "Never saw any of those types around" or "If he had any connections, he wouldn't have been scuffling so much."

The Sahara Hotel had its genesis in the Club Bingo, which opened in 1947 as a 300-seat bingo parlor. Milton Prell, described as "the top man in Montana" by Stan Irwin, longtime booker for the Sahara, founded the Sahara on the site of the Club Bingo. Irwin continues, "After World War II, steel was hard to get. To get priority [to buy steel with which to build], you had to expand on an existing property." Prell wanted his hotel and casino to have an African motif. To this end, the theme was carried out with camels erected in front of the hotel, life-size models of African warriors flanking the entrance to the main showroom, the Congo Room, the Caravan Room restaurant, and the lounge, which Stan Irwin named the Casbah Lounge. The Casbah opened in 1952 with *Wizard of Oz* scarecrow Ray Bolger and was a success from the start. "We booked purely by instinct, no marketing surveys," says Irwin. Other acts to play the Casbah included Don Rickles, who first gained notoriety there, in the lounge.

Things were looking bleak for Louis Prima in 1954. He and Keely had played in Las Vegas at El Rancho. Shortly after, Louis had a nervous breakdown. He had known Sahara impresario, Bill Miller, from Bill's Riviera Club in New Jersey and he called him, citing his financial problems, which were compounded by Keely's pregnancy. Louis was begging for work. He was a has-been. The best Miller could offer was a gig in the lounge, a big comedown for a star who had headlined theaters. Keely: "We had to take it." Bud Robinson, who, with his wife Cee Cee, had worked the main room as an opening act: "He asked us all kinds of questions, 'What's a lounge? What's it like?'"

Stan Irwin: "We gave him a three-year deal. He was so broke, we had to buy stage clothes for him and the band. He actually had holes

67

in his pants." It was a grueling schedule. Five shows a day. The first started at midnight and the last was from 5:00 to 5:45 A.M. The stage was tiny, no more than 30 feet across. How was Louis, who was used to strutting his stuff in the theaters, going to deal with that? The ceiling was so low, the performers could easily touch it. To top it off, at the edge of the stage, the bartender was ringing up change and operating the blender, which wreaked havoc on a ballad singer like Keely.

Like the Treniers, who had done well in the lounge over at the Frontier, Louis the pro knew how to overcome. His jump-styled mixture was just what the doctor ordered for a loud room full of hicks, losers, and carfones. He and Keely were an immediate success—just as he had been at both Famous Door clubs years before. Stan Irwin: "The idea of gaming is traffic. Move enough people around and they'll play." It was easy to move the people. "There was no admission—you didn't even have to buy a drink. You could just say 'No thanks.'" Asked if Prima's success at the Casbah led to his signing with Capitol Records, Irwin replies, "Betty Hutton worked at the Sahara in the Congo Room. Her husband at the time was [Capitol vice-president] Alan Livingston. You can draw your own conclusions."

After the first Sahara gig, Louis realized he needed a new band. To this end, he drew upon his New Orleans roots and chose as his bandleader hometown boy Sam Butera, recommended by Leon.

Seventeen years younger than fellow Sicilian Louis, Sam was born on August 17, 1927, in New Orleans' Seventh Ward—a largely black section, where his father, Joe, ran Poor Boy's Grocery & Meat Market. His mother's name was Rose and he had a brother, Joe, Jr. "Louis was from a different neighborhood, the French Market," says Sam. But, like the older Louis, Sam loved music, and was given a saxophone by his father. In 1946, *Look* magazine named him the "Best High School Saxophonist in America." Upon graduation, he went on the road with Ray McKinley, with whom he made his recording debut on McKinley's versions of "Civilization" and "Celery at Midnight." After stints with Tommy Dorsey and others, he returned home. Like so many New Orleans players, he found life out of town difficult. New Orleans musicians have traditionally been looked upon as strange by outsiders, as the entire culture is so different from other parts of the country.

Back home, Sam, with his five-piece combo, played at Leon Prima's 500 Club, backing strippers, bad comics, and acts like the Cat Girl. He also spent time jamming with the band of one of his father's

68

customers, Paul Gayten, who had one of the top bands in the city. A recording was made of Sam with Gayten for Regal Records in 1951, and, two years later, he cut a series of records for RCA Victor. Sam's sax style was strongly influenced by the honkers, Illinois Jacquet, Vido Musso, and others. He'll add Coleman Hawkins, Lester Young, Charlie Ventura, Bird, Zoot Sims to his list of influences. Butera also had something extra, the exuberance of youth, which gave him an edgy quality that might qualify him as an early protorock 'n' roller.

Asked if he remembers when he joined Prima, Sam says, "I remember exactly: December 26, 1954." When Louis was looking for his Vegas band, his brother reminded him of this kid Butera. Louis was gigging at Perez's Oasis with a 12-piece band and, after Sam got up to jam, it was, "Bring your piano and drummer to Las Vegas." Sam says today, "The bread was short at first, but it got better. A lot better."

Sam recorded for Cadence under his own name and—after the Capitol signing—for Capitol's Prep subsidiary as Sam Butera and the Witnesses, a name given to the group by Prima. The group was also given billing on all Prima recordings. Throughout the course of the three-year contract with the Sahara, Louis, in the words of Stan Irwin, "went from broke—not poor, broke—to affluent, due to the exceptional rapport between Louis and Keely, Louis's professionalism, and that shuffle beat. He moved to Vegas, into that house—the house the Sahara built."

69

Then, it came time to renew the contract. Remembering when he was a star, Louis saw himself and Keely as a main-room act; thus, to mollify him, Irwin had occasionally put them in there as an opener. But, at the end of the first three years, Stan had to do some fast talking and ego-manipulating when Louis said, in effect, "Give me the big room— or else." Knowing the secret of success lay in the magic synergy between performer and room, the smooth Stan moves in for the kill: "I said, 'Louis, we have a relationship. We want to give you a raise. You see how we put all the chairs on wheels so everyone can turn and look at you?' Then I got on the phone to my director of publicity and told him that, in the future, all ads, all promotions, all placards, all table tents, everything will read: 'Casbah Theater.' Louis Prima was the first artist to have a lounge turn into a theater."

Louis signed for another three years at a higher salary. Another thing, no more five shows. The group would now only do three a night. Other acts, like Freddie Bell and the Bellboys, would play in between.

From the time Louis and Keely signed with Capitol Records, the albums, mostly recorded live in the Casbah Lounge, kept coming out: *The Wildest*, *Call of the Wildest*, Keely's solo album with Nelson Riddle, 1958 Grammy nominee *I Wish You Love*. Live albums were the best way to capture the spontaneity of this volatile mixture. Louis was inspired by his audience as well as by Keely and Sam. Then, there were the singles "Old Black Magic" (best record Grammy, 1959) and "I've Got You Under My Skin"; those classic Sicilian-Vegas boogies, like "Just a Gigolo" (revived verbatim in 1985 by rocker David Lee Roth, who himself came on like a latter-day Prima); and a shuffled-up remake of his old stand-by, "Oh! Marie."

There were the R&B covers: Richard "Louie Louie" Berry's "Next Time," and Oscar McLollie's "Hey Boy! Hey Girl!" which became the title of a Louis-Keely movie, shot 30 miles outside of Vegas at Mt. Charleston. There were the medleys, of both jived-up standards and of Louis's '40s hits, "Robin Hood"/"Oh Babe!" and "Angelina"/"Zooma Zooma." And one I remember hearing on vacation with my parents in Miami as a kid, the wonderfully crass "5 Months, 2 Weeks, 2 Days."

Capitol engineer Jay Ranalucci, who still works for the company, was at some of the location recordings. He describes the proceedings: "We set up the equipment after the 2:30 A.M. show, next to the dumpster in the kitchen. The smell was awful. We had two vans, one for mono, one for stereo. Marlene Dietrich, who was playing the main room, came to see the show. I think she had a thing for Louis."

Stan Irwin describes Prima during this period as "the most disciplined, stimulating, professional act. He was like a general. If you see a photograph of them in action, the body language is such that it always gives attention to the soloist...you can always tell who is singing. Louis made them do that."

In 1958, Keely was voted best female vocalist in *Billboard* and *Variety*, and in a poll of the nation's disc jockeys. In 1959, she won the *Playboy* Jazz award. At the end of his second contract, Louis defected to the Sands for a reported record-breaking $3 million deal, 12 weeks a year for five years. Stan Irwin: "The Sands stole him from us because of their reputation as the hip place to be. They had Sinatra, Nat Cole, Lena Horne. We all stole each other's acts in those days." They also changed the record labels, to Dot, where they had a few more hits in

1959–1960—"Bei Mir Bist Du Schön," "Wonderland by Night," and Keely's "Here in My Heart"—before returning to Capitol.

But all was not well in paradise. Louis's philandering continued unabated and, by 1961, the golden couple were divorced. This resulted in canceled bookings, including the lucrative one in Las Vegas. Barbara Belle, after many years with Prima, went with Keely, who wound up marrying rockabilly artist and record producer Jimmy Bowen. For his part, Louis made the dreadful exploitation flick, *Twist All Night*, and married wife No. 5, 20-year-old Gia Maione, who he then proceeded to attempt to mold into another Keely Smith.

His career slid downhill, in the manner of many aging one-time stars. In 1965, his beloved mother died. By then, he and Gia were reduced to playing bowling alleys to make his alimony and child support payments. A 1966 voice-over speaking role in the Walt Disney cartoon feature *Jungle Book*—as King Louie, the ape, costarring with George Sanders and Phil Harris—was a high point of his later career.

He tried a move to New Orleans in the '70s, but the town couldn't support performers any better than it ever could, so he returned to Nevada, playing in Reno and Lake Tahoe and made a futile attempt to get Keely to return to the act. In 1973, he had his first small heart attack on stage. This came as a surprise, as Louis had always been quite athletic. Yet, he continued to suffer from chronic headaches and falling asleep and, in 1975, it was discovered that he had meningitis and a tumor of the membrane surrounding the brain stem. After an operation in Los Angeles, he was transferred to his hometown where he died on August 24, 1978.

Spurned by critics throughout most of his career, Louis Prima is only now getting some of the respect he deserves as both a fine trumpeter, a vocalist of brilliant phrasing, a songwriter of no small import, and an innovator who influenced the course of twentieth century music. He was an important player in the Dixieland era, the swing era, and the jump blues and R&B explosion of the 1940s. He was a precursor of rock 'n' roll and inventor of the Las Vegas lounge act. He and his band, Sam Butera and the Witnesses, were playing rock 'n' roll as early as anybody, but were not recognized as rockers due to Louis's age. Most of all, he was an entertainer par excellence. And when you're as good as Louis Prima was, entertainer is not a four-letter word.

Sam Butera, with his band, the Wildest, and Keely Smith are still performing. I recently saw them together in the lounge at the Desert Inn. Keely's singing was great, with none of that wide vibrato or other deficiencies common to female vocalists of a certain age; Sam's playing was as energetic and inventive as that of a man half his age. They were doing a lot of the old stuff, with Sam taking Louis's parts—and knockin' 'em dead.

These notes accompanied Louis Prima-The Capitol Recordings *(BCD 15776), 8 CDs.*

6

Vegas Rocks and Reno Rolls: Part 2

Freddie Bell and the Bellboys

Wayne Russell

Perhaps the first rock 'n' roll musician to figure out Vegas was Freddie Bell. He was doing well at the Sands in '56 while Elvis was stiffing at the New Frontier. Showroom rock 'n' roll is a neglected area of study because it was assumed not to exist. Within 15 years, though, many rock 'n' rollers would be playing Vegas because the teenagers who had been too young to get in to see Elvis in '56 were now in their 30s and Vegas was becoming their kind of town. That made Bell a prophet of sorts, albeit one without much honor. (C. E.)

One would assume that a group that toured Britain, France, Australia, and the Far East, and appeared in films like *Rock Around the Clock* and *Rumble on the Docks*, and had an album released on a major label would have had at least a few chart entries. Surprisingly, though, Freddie Bell and the Bellboys did not even make it as far as "Bubbling Under." In Britain, it was a different story. A Bill Haleyish novelty, "Giddy-Up-a-Ding Dong," spent six weeks in the *New Musical Express* Top 10, peaking at No. 4 in October 1956. That same year, Bell stood by as one of his arrangements became a standard of the rock 'n' roll era. So Freddie Bell isn't living off his hits, but he's still getting by as an entertainer. The reason is that he went to Vegas and quickly understood what it took to play there. He, along with Lillian Briggs, the Treniers, and Johnny Olenn virtually invented rock 'n' roll in the resort cities of Nevada. The older gamblers accepted a well-rehearsed professional performance that looked like an old-fashioned stage show even if it was rock 'n' roll. To an extent, Vegas is also the reason that there are more than one or two Freddie Bell records, and the reason that he can be savored in a couple of admittedly cheesy movies. Among the high rollers were the label execs and movie producers who signed him, thus reordering the usual process that would have taken Freddie Bell from a strong local teenage following to regional success on a small independent label to a major label.

Freddie Bell was born Freddie Bello on September 29, 1931, to Italian parents in South Philadelphia, the birthplace of singers like Charlie Gracie, Eddie Fisher, Frankie Avalon, Bobby Rydell, and Fabian. Freddie learned to play bass, trombone, and drums to go along with his singing skills. He played in the band of Charlie Ventura's less well-known brother, Ernie, who nevertheless recorded for King, Verve, Decca, and a host of other labels. Freddie left Ventura to form his own group, the Bellboys, when he was 20. His sound was rooted in the R&B hits of the day. Freddie insists that all the Philly groups were influenced by the Treniers, Steve Gibson and The Red Caps, as well as by Chris Powell and The Five Blue Flames. Those acts knew how to put on a show, and the virtue of *entertaining* stuck with Freddie Bell, much as it stuck with Bill Haley who was working in the same neighborhood and drawing inspiration from the same sources.

Freddie Bell formed the Bellboys from like-minded musicians. They honed their act in the Midwest before landing a plum booking with Jack Entratter, president of the Sands Hotel in Las Vegas. Around this time, they made their first recordings for Teen Records. Teen, a subsidiary of the equally obscure Sound Records, was owned by Bernie Lowe and Harry Chipetz. Lowe would go on to make a name for himself as the founder of Cameo and Parkway Records, and as the writer or cowriter of songs like "Butterfly" and "Wandering Eyes" for Charlie Gracie, "Teddy Bear" for Elvis Presley, and numerous hits for Bobby Rydell. Freddie's first record in 1955 was a belated, high-energy cover version of Big Mama Thornton's 1953 No. 1 R&B hit, "Hound Dog." As written by Jerry Leiber and Mike Stoller, the song was a bit raunchy for white radio, and was quite obviously a woman's blues. Lowe suggested a rewrite. Out went "snooping around my door," "wag your tail," and "weep and moan." The song was no longer a castigation of a black playboy; it was more a novelty in the Bill Haley mold with riffing saxes and group call-and-response. As things would turn out, Bell should have made a few more alterations and come up with his own

Freddie Bell and the Bellboys

song. As Elvis would later tell him, "If you had changed one more word, you would have made a lot of money."

"Hound Dog" got lots of radio play on the east coast, and Bell found himself with a regional hit, but no big payday. It became a staple of the Bellboys's act at the Sands, though, and it was there that Elvis heard it. Colonel Parker had booked Elvis into Vegas's New Frontier Hotel in April 1956, and while it proved to be one of the few mistakes the Colonel made that year, it afforded Elvis and his band the opportunity to catch Freddie Bell. Elvis had almost certainly heard the original version of "Hound Dog," but probably hadn't thought of it as a song a man could do. He suddenly realized that Freddie had transformed a mouthy woman's blues into a nonsense rock 'n' roll song. He fine-tuned Freddie's arrangement, and tested it on *The Milton Berle Show* on June 2, 1956, and again on *The Steve Allen Show* a month later. The day after the Allen show, he recorded it. Coupled with "Don't Be Cruel," it became one of the defining singles of the rock 'n' roll era. It stayed on the Hot 100 for 28 weeks, 11 of them at No. 1—longer than any other record in the rock 'n' roll era. It reached No. 1 on the R&B and Country charts as well. "Hound Dog" was also Elvis's introduction to Jerry Leiber and Mike Stoller. He would go on to record another 22 of their songs, including No. 1 hits like "Jailhouse Rock," and "Don't."

"Hound Dog" had been covered back in 1953 by artists like Little Esther and even Bob Wills' former vocalist, Tommy Duncan, but all the earlier versions were modeled after Big Mama Thornton's record. After Elvis, the song was only ever performed one way. Everyone who has done the song since 1956 owes an indirect debt to Freddie Bell, although few but Elvis ever knew it. Bell sensed the coming storm and rerecorded the song for Mercury Records in May 1956, some two months prior to Elvis, but Mercury sat on it. It finally appeared, squirreled away on Bell's album, *Rock & Roll...All Flavors*.

"When I gave 'Hound Dog' to Elvis, I thought I'd get tail sales," said Bell. Unfortunately, Mercury wasn't on the same page and Bell couldn't hitch a ride on the Presley hit. Elvis remained friendly. He returned to Vegas occasionally during the mid-1960s, and Bell remembers him giving karate exhibitions backstage.

76

Freddie had landed his Mercury deal soon after Mercury's New York A&R man, Bob Shad, was sent one of the Teen singles. He caught the Bellboys in Vegas and signed them. All told, the Mercury contract yielded five singles and an album. The Bellboys's Vegas shows were also caught by film producer Sam Katzman. In their book *Rock on Film*, David Ehrenstein and Bill Reed have the perfect description of Katzman. "In the scheme of corporate film making in the 1950s," they wrote, "Katzman was the cinematic equivalent of tabloid journalism." Katzman would latch onto a headline and have a movie scripted around it. He'd have the cast assembled, the film shot, and on the streets in a matter of weeks.

Rock Around the Clock was the first rock 'n' roll movie, and the 55-year-old Katzman was responsible. Bill Haley starred along with Alan Freed. Katzman also signed Freddie Bell and the Platters. He'd caught the Platters at the Flamingo the same night he'd seen Freddie at the Sands. Katzman simply asked Bell: "How would you like to do a rock 'n' roll movie?" Who could refuse such a graciously worded offer? The film did amazing business, and Katzman followed it with *Don't Knock the Rock* the same year. Five years later, he repeated the whole process with *Twist Around the Clock* and *Don't Knock the Twist*. He also produced two lesser entries in the Presley canon, *Kissin' Cousins* and *Harum Scarum*, which earned him the unenviable job of making Roy Orbison into a leading man in *The Fastest Guitar Alive*.

Katzman was good to Freddie Bell and the Bellboys. He featured them in another of his 1956 movies, *Rumble on the Docks*, which starred James Darren, best remembered for his appearances in the *Gidget* movies. Katzman used the Bellboys one last time in the 1964 movie, *Get Yourself a College Girl* a.k.a. *The Swingin' Set*. Bell and Katzman became good friends, and Bell jokingly called him "my personal producer." Katzman must have been a frequent visitor to Vegas because he used the Treniers in two of his films, *Don't Knock the Rock* and *Calypso Heat Wave*. The latter, in case you can't guess, was shot to capitalize on calypso's fleeting popularity in 1956. Not even Katzman could get that one on the streets fast enough.

The worldwide popularity of the *Rock Around the Clock* movie was good news for Freddie Bell. Almost everyone connected with the movie received lucrative offers from afar. The Bellboys's exciting performances of "Giddy-Up-a-Ding Dong" and "Teach You to Rock" were done live in Los Angeles over a three-day period, and, according to Bell, had to be rerecorded at a later date for Mercury. Freddie and his pal, Pep Lattanzi, had written "Giddy-Up-a-Ding Dong" after the Treniers gave Freddie the nickname "Ding Dong."

On the strength of the movie, the Bellboys played in Paris, Australia (with Bill Haley and the Comets, LaVern Baker, Joe Turner, and The Platters), Manila, Singapore, Hong Kong, and throughout South America. They were the first rock 'n' roll acts ever seen in places like Singapore and Hong Kong. Freddie found that the audiences liked the beat, but were a bit reserved compared with American and European audiences.

One of the most rewarding tours was through England, Wales, and Scotland in May 1957 when they were teamed with Cockney rocker Tommy Steele. British publicist Ken Pitt had seen the group in Las Vegas in January 1956, and described them in *New Musical Express* as "the most impressive white group playing in the R&B idiom." The tour did big business although the Bellboys had seen their first and last British chart action six months earlier when "Giddy-Up-a-Ding Dong" got to No. 4. Bell struck up a good rapport with Steele, who recorded "Giddy-Up-a-Ding Dong" on his 10-inch Decca album *Tommy Steele Stage Show*.

While in England, Freddie's bassist, Frankie Brent, quit the Bell-boys and cut four sides for Pye/Nixa, with Australian deejay Alan "Fluff" Freeman acting as A&R man. The guitarist was Bert Weedon who authored the most famous guitar instructional manual in British rock 'n' roll history, *Play in a Day*. Brent's four sides were issued on two singles, and set the stage for a long solo career on Vik, Palette, Calvert, Strand, Cameo (back with Bernie Lowe), Epic, Cutty, and Gold Standard. Eventually, he ended up with his own club in New Orleans.

The overseas tours were an eye-opener, but they did little to enlarge the popularity of the group at home. Bell sought to rectify that with a number of television appearances. He was on Dave Garroway's *Wide, Wide World*, and made an appearance on the Dean Martin/Jerry Lewis TV show. It all fell on deaf ears. "Giddy-Up-a-Ding Dong" flopped at home, as did Bell's subsequent Mercury Records. It all probably went to prove that Las Vegas patrons had no money left for records. Teenagers dictated which rock 'n' roll records became hits and the Bellboys were not reaching the teenage audience in Las Vegas. On top of that, Freddie was associated with the Bill Haley sound, and Haley's career was in an irreversible downward spiral by 1957. Mercury's termination notice was mailed that year.

During the 1960s, Freddie Bell and the Bellboys concentrated on their nightclub act. They could work steadily in Las Vegas and Reno, with plenty of time off during the day for golf. They also worked the New York lounges, and Johnny Carson and Ed McMahon were frequent guests after taping *The Tonight Show*. Bell married Lawrence Welk's original "Champagne Lady" Roberta Linn in 1961, and they merged their nightclub acts. They appeared in Sam Katzman's *Get Yourself a College Girl* alongside the Animals, the Dave Clark Five, the Standells, Jimmy Smith, Stan Getz, and Astrud Gilberto. The remainder of the 1960s was spent in much the same routine. Vegas, Reno, a little road work, and a few diddly record deals. Roberta Linn left. Jerry Lewis invited Freddie onto his telethon, and Freddie appeared for 22 straight years.

In the 1980s, Europe beckoned. Bell reinvented his show for Europe, taking it back to his roots in straightahead R&B. At home, though, the lounges were still his bread-and-butter. He now does comedy and impressions, but still manages to fit in "Giddy-Up-a-Ding Dong" during a nostalgia segment. He recently recorded three shows that have been edited down to a 90-minute souvenir video.

78

"I hope my career is more than giving 'Hound Dog' to Elvis," he says. Likely not. History dictates that achievements be narrowed to the smallest possible focus to register, and inasmuch as Freddie Bell will be remembered at all, it will probably be for reinventing "Hound Dog." He's still out there, though, playing and singing, and doing his high-energy act. He has been a music pro for 50 years, and he's justifiably proud of that. He has outlived Elvis and Bill Haley...in fact, most of his contemporaries. In the grand scheme of things, he's probably no more than a footnote in Elvis bios and a minor British chart statistic, but sheer dogged persistence in a legendarily cruel business makes Freddie Bell a winner... of sorts.

These notes accompanied Rockin' Is Our Business, *a single-CD anthology of Bell's Teen and Mercury recordings (BCD 15901).*

Smiley Lewis

New Orleans
···············
Smiley Lewis

Rick Coleman and Jeff Hannusch

Back in 1970, Liberty Records in England issued a Smiley Lewis LP. For those of us in Europe, this was an eye-opener. Years of listening to Fats Domino meant that the wonderful New Orleans backing tracks held no surprise, but nothing prepared us for that voice. It was deep and resonant …a huge voice, much bluer than that of Fats Domino. No roly-polyness here. This was blues so deep, you'd never find your way out. The original versions of "I Hear You Knockin'," "Blue Monday," and "One Night" were revelatory.

The reason there was a Smiley Lewis LP on the shelves in 1970 was that Dave Edmunds had just cut Smiley's biggest hit, "I Hear You Knockin'." Two fans of New Orleans R&B, Andrew Lauder and Alan Warner, were working for Liberty in England back then, and they took a chance on an LP tagged after Smiley's original record. A year or so later, I asked one of them if there would be a second volume, and was told it was out of the question; the first had sold 300 copies.

The 350-word liner notes on that old LP had just 50 words about Smiley himself. That comprised the sum total of what was known about him. His date and place of birth were unknown, as was the fact that he was dead. Bear Family's complete career retrospective 25 years later gave us the opportunity to commission a definitive biography of a vastly under-rated musician. We turned to Rick Coleman and Canadian researcher Jeff Hannusch, who lives in New Orleans. Smiley Lewis was never interviewed for posterity, but Rick and Jeff combed old newspapers and talked to everyone they could find who had ever known him or worked with him. What emerged was a compelling portrait of one of the hardest hard-luck singers of our time.

Rick Coleman has worked with Bear Family to document much of the New Orleans scene in the '50s. In addition to the definitive 8-CD box of Fats Domino's Imperial recordings, there's a double CD box of Bobby Mitchell, a 4-CD box of Shirley and Lee, two CDs of the Spiders, as well as single CDs on Allen Toussaint and Louis Prima's sidekick, Sam Butera. (C. E.)

"Blue Monday" framed a portrait of its singer. The hard-working, hard-playing life portrayed in the song was very much Smiley Lewis's life, and likewise the lives of a large segment of his audience. Smiley Lewis was never very famous and never received much money, but he loved his work, and he was very good at it. He and the superb New Orleans musicians accompanying him cut one great R&B record after another in the 1950s under the guidance of producer and writer Dave Bartholomew, yet Smiley Lewis came no closer to crossing over into the pop charts than pure bluesmen like B. B. King or Muddy Waters. The closest Lewis came to the pop hit that could have changed his workaday world was "I Hear You Knocking (but You Can't Come In)," a song that now resonates as an allegory for both the racial segregation of the time and Lewis's inability to make that elusive crossover.

These days, "Blue Monday" is thought of as a Fats Domino song; "One Night" is thought of as Elvis Presley's song; and "I Hear You Knockin'" is thought of as Gale Storm's song or Dave Edmunds' song. Yet, all three were originally recorded by Smiley Lewis. Anyone listening carefully will hear Edmunds shout Smiley Lewis's name during the instrumental break. Smiley couldn't hear; he was four years dead.

"He's got to be the most unfortunate man that's ever walked on the Earth," said Eddie Ray, former head of promotion for Imperial Records. "My goodness! I've often thought of this. I could never understand why I wasn't able to get him played on any crossover stations during that day—pop stations—because I was able to do it on 'Oo Poo Pah Doo,' 'Mother-in-Law,' all the Fats Domino things, of course, and even on the Spiders, but for some reason not Smiley. I said, 'What is it?' I tried to listen. It must have been something in his voice...."

Dave Bartholomew, who produced both Smiley and Fats Domino for Imperial, concurs. "I always call him a bad luck singer, because when

Smiley would get a hit it would do, say, 100,000. And after it'd get to 100,000 he would level off. Like he had a cover [by Gale Storm] when 'I Hear You Knocking' came out; I think this helped to kill him too. We always serviced 4,000 disc jockeys at the time. Imperial was one of the big independents. Everywhere Fats Domino's records went, Smiley's went, but we just couldn't break him nationwide. It's hard for me to believe that, and as for him—he never really accepted it. I call him just bad luck, because he had some hell of a [many] good records. On records like 'One Night,' he was so sincere. Smiley had one of the best voices we had around, but it didn't pay off."

It's no great mystery why Smiley Lewis didn't follow the tide of R&B performers who made the transition to rock 'n' roll. His records were simply too *black*. Dave Bartholomew, who had known Smiley since childhood, identified closely with Lewis's world and wrote dozens of songs for him, songs that compared sharply with the teen-slanted songs he was writing with or for Fats Domino. Smiley Lewis's world was not the world of the white baby boom rock 'n' rollers. His was rural shacks and harshly segregated cities. Though he often sang of romantic or even spiritual themes, he was at his best shouting about sex, cheating women, boozing, and jail time in his piercingly black and blue voice.

Lewis was never interviewed, but his records, delivered in his trademark bullhorn voice, stand as 180 proof New Orleans R&B masterpieces. They are his self-portrait.

83

Early life: "Oh, Lillie Mae, don't go away!..."

According to his first wife, Leona Robinson Kelly, Smiley Lewis was born Overton Amos Lemons, the son of Amos and Lilly Lemons in a small Louisiana town, DeQuincey, near the Texas line. The date was July 5, 1913. Smiley's sister-in-law, Thelma Lemons, who still lives in DeQuincey, says that Overton was the second of three sons, the first of whom, Jeffrey, was Thelma's husband. Smiley's mother died young and Thelma recalls the family living in West Lake, a town near Lake Charles, where the sons were raised by a stepmother and supported by their father. Lewis was affected deeply by his mother's passing. Years later, he named cars, guitars, and one of his most poignant songs, "Lillie Mae," after her. Decades before John Lennon's primal scream, "Mother," Lewis broke down and sobbed at the end of his song.

In his midteens, Overton made his way to New Orleans, as his second wife, Dorothy, relates: "You know how teenagers are, when they get a certain age they run off from home, they kinda wanna go somewhere. I remember one time he said he rode the freight train, him and some old boys. Wherever they wanted to get off, the boys jumped off, but he was scared to jump off, so he headed here where they stop at. So he stayed here."

Lost and alone in New Orleans, young Overton was lucky to find a family in the Irish Channel that took him in. His first wife remembered, "He was part raised by a white family that lived in Front o' Town. When Lewis was laying [on his deathbed] in Charity Hospital an older white lady who was in another ward came to visit him and called Lewis 'my baby.' Lewis said that was the lady who raised him when he came to New Orleans."

Dave Bartholomew remembers things differently: "Smiley was reared in the back of my father's barber shop about a couple of blocks away. He lived in the same neighborhood with my father, who [had] a barber shop in a place we called Silver City at that time. He used to sing on the front porch of his house. He always had this great big voice with a big, big sound. I said, 'One day when I get a chance I'm gonna record him.' And that's just what I did."

The Troubadour (1930s): "I love you for sentimental reasons..."

From his teens, Lewis was an all-around entertainer—a singer and guitarist with some comic skills. In the mid-1930s, he joined trumpeter Thomas Jefferson's band, which included Isidore "Tuts" Washington on piano and Edward "Noon" Johnson on "bazooka." New Orleans mythology has it that the bazooka was a trombonelike instrument made from a brass bedpost and a gramophone horn. Mississippi musician Bob Burns saw Noon playing the instrument, copied it, and coined the name *bazooka*, which gained renown on radio and later became the nickname for an armor-piercing weapon in World War II.

Bandleader Jefferson remembers, "Smiley Lewis was more like a hustler, you know. He went around from place to place, playin' and singin', pickin' up what people give him and what not. We'd play 'em a song and then go around the table with a hat. We wore frocktail coats and derbies with the high peak. That was our uniform. We were very popular. We played all the joints, colored and white."

Pianist Tuts Washington: "Lewis always was a good entertainer. He sang the blues and all of them sentimental numbers. He would walk off the bandstand and sing to the people in the audience. See, Lewis

84

had a voice so strong he could sing over the band, and that was before we had microphones."

During the day, Smiley hustled odd jobs and sometimes drove a truck for the Jahncke Barge Company. After the band dissolved, he worked spot jobs with Noon and guitarist Walter "Papoose" Nelson, Sr. Often the trio would play for tips on Bourbon Street. According to Leona, Smiley often returned "with a guitar full of change." One of Smiley's future saxophonists, Charles Burbank, saw the group as a child: "They used to play in these little joints all up and down Claiborne, St. Ann, and Orleans Street. I used to go past and—they wouldn't let me in the place—I'd stand on the outside and listen at 'em, because they had a funny sound, but the people'd be dancin' and havin' fun. Smiley was singin' blues and ballads. He was a good ballad singer. He'd make a medley of nothin' but the Inks Spots' numbers. His main thing was blues; he recorded blues. But I think his best singin' woulda been ballads. He'd imitate the Ink Spots just like the record."

Family life: "I'm the king of hearts and she's my queen..."

In the summer of 1938, Smiley met 20-year-old Leona Robinson, who recalls the meeting as "love at first sight." She never discovered how he adopted his name, but notes, "he sure did smile a lot." He probably got the name "Smiley" because he had no front teeth and did not obtain a bridge until later when he could afford it. He may have gotten the "Lewis" surname from the white family that took care of him. Smiley and Leona were wed in November 1938, and the couple stayed with the bride's mother in a small house on the corner of Thalia and South Tonti streets.

"Lewis didn't want me working," said Leona. "He didn't have a regular job, but he always supported us. Today you'd call it hustling. He drove freight, worked on the river, and did odd jobs. Some nights he'd play music and bring home some money, but he didn't have what you'd call a band. When Lewis and I met he was ever so slight. He didn't get stout until after we married. Lord, how he loved to eat my cooking. He liked red beans, gumbo, and greens. Lewis was a good cook, too. He loved to hunt and fish, and he'd cook rabbit or fish for supper. Sometimes Lewis would go to church with my mother and me. He loved to sing hymns and one time he entered a singing contest at church. Of course he won. He liked to go to the baseball games. I recall him taking me to Pelican Stadium to see Jackie Robinson play once."

The war and after: "Here comes Smiley, I hope you'll let me in..."

In the early 1940s, Tuts Washington was playing at a number of different clubs on Rampart Street. "Lewis was shoeing horses in those days. He was living Uptown then and he'd stop in to see me on his way home from the French Quarter. He was always telling me, 'Come on Tuts. Let's you and me get a little aggregation together and make some money.' Well, things were dead around here because the war was going on. So I took a job playing with Kid Ernest [clarinetist Ernest Mollier] and his brother Pat up in Bunkie, Louisiana, at the Boogie Woogie Club. The man at the club liked us but said he wanted a singer. I told them boys about Smiley, but they didn't want to hire him because he had a reputation for having a big head. I begged those boys to hire him and finally they did. We stayed up around Bunkie and Marksville for the best part of a year."

Leona even brought the couple's two children up to Bunkie in 1942 or 1943 for a couple of months. When Smiley returned to New Orleans, the house on Thalia had been razed by the city to make way for a federal housing project and his household had been moved into the Lafitte Projects on Orleans Avenue.

After the war, things began picking up in New Orleans. Many clubs reopened and there was work once again for musicians. The Kid Ernest band broke up, but Tuts and Smiley teamed up with drummer Herman Seals to form a blues trio. "We had the hottest trio in town," boasts Tuts. "Nobody could touch us. We played all through the French Quarter and down Bourbon Street—the El Morocco, the Cat in the Fiddle, the Dog House and the Moulin Rouge."

The August 23, 1947, edition of *Louisiana Weekly* reported 'SMIL-ING' LEWIS TO HEADLINE NEW DEW DROP FLOOR SHOW. The whole town knew that one of the best singers of the blues in this part of the country was poker face, 'Smiling' Lewis, who can get an audience in a dither over such blues renditions as 'Piney Brown Blues' and 'My Gal's a Jockey.' However, what the town didn't know was that 'Smil-ing' Lewis is equally versatile with the guitar.... On the bandstand will be Dave Bartholomew's orchestra." Judging by the songs Lewis was singing at the time, he was already closely associated with the blues shouter who most influenced him, Joe Turner.

The trio's popularity was such that in late 1947 they were recorded by David Braun, who, along with his brother Jules, owned DeLuxe Records in New Jersey. The label had already found success with New

Orleans stars Paul Gayten (featuring Annie Laurie), and Roy Brown of "Good Rockin' Tonight" fame. On November 1, 1947, the *Louisiana Weekly* reported on the release of the first records by two legends: "That sensational 'Stardust' arrangement of Dave Bartholomew's can now be found on platters. A batch of the combo's numbers were released last week by DeLuxe. DeLuxe also released some groovy blues waxings of Smiling Lewis...." Smiley's first sides were "Here Comes Smiley," and "Turn on Your Volume, Baby." The latter was rife with radio repairman double entendre ("your tubes is gettin' hot"). Both songs were written by Leo Franks, who, according to Tuts, was a white bartender in the French Quarter. They were classic New Orleans piano blues. Smiley sang softly and took short guitar breaks. Radio play was negligible and sales were poor, although the record got the group some gigs in Texas. A second release was scheduled and numbered, but apparently canceled as no copy has ever surfaced. Smiley went almost unpublicized for the next two years, playing mostly French Quarter clubs like the El Morocco with a repertoire slanted toward sentimental ballads for the all-white customers.

1950: "Tee nah nah nah nah nah..."

On January 14, 1950, Vernon Winslow, who had become the city's first black disc jockey in May 1949, wrote a *Louisiana Weekly* column under his moniker, "Dr. Daddy-O," that must have encouraged Smiley: "The next time ya see Smiley Lewis please compliment him on having a much mad band!!!...Those boys are real crazy...Drummer man Seals...Piano man Washington...Both sound like they oughta be recorded RIGHT NOW on Apollo wax!!!...(Talent Scouts, please note!!!)."

Winslow took matters into his own hands when he began to play an audition disc on his radio show. On February 4, he wrote "That new audition disc of Smiley Lewis is a honey, and if the talent scouts don't pick it up someone else will...." Exactly a month later he wrote: "'Teeny-na' [sic] is my nomination for the year's surprise hit." The next week he wrote of a show at Sal's Place in the Irish Channel: "When Smiley Lewis began to tap his foot and play 'Tee Ny Na'...man, the cats almost tore up the place!!!" Nearly four decades later, when Winslow returned to announcing an R&B program on WYLD, he produced the mysterious all-black acetate and played it on the air again. It seems to be a slightly different recording, predating the released version.

"He cut it for me on a lacquer disc," said Winslow, "and I played it on the air like that. I heard him at this little spot. It might have been the Club Desire. I said, 'Man, I want you to have my engineer tape what you got.' He made the first cut for me. Then Imperial got it and recut it." Dave Bartholomew realized that "Tee-Nah-Nah" was a ready-made hit because it was already receiving heavy airplay on Daddy-O's show, so, in his capacity as Imperial Records A&R man, he took the trio into the studio to recut the song.

"We started bummin' around the J&M Studio," said Tuts Washington. "They had an old German-made upright piano that I liked to play. I wrote a lot of those numbers for Smiley that I never got credit for. I wrote 'Dirty, Dirty People Done the Poor Boy Wrong,' and I gave Smiley the words to 'Tee Nah Nah.' That was one of those prison songs they used to sing up in Angola, but Lewis and me was the first ones to put it out."

"In that time," said Dave Bartholomew, "we used to have what is called a New Orleans-type music that was actually sang in prison by some of the guys in Angola. And all the musicians, every old piano player could play what was called 'The Junker Blues.' Tuts had it. Every piano player. So I can't say who really originated that, because my father had a band and the old man who played piano with him played that type of piano. I was a little kid then. My father died when I must have been about ten. All of them played that type of music. What we call funk, no one actually originated that in the last 25 or 30 years. When I was born I found that here."

The phrase "tee nah nah" had been used in New Orleans song titles since at least 1910 and may have been slang for marijuana. "The Junker's Blues," best known in a 1941 recording for OKeh by Champion Jack Dupree, was, of course, a song about junkies, explaining the reference to a bad habit in "Tee-Nah-Nah." "The Junker's Blues" was the standard eight-bar New Orleans blues, closely related to "Stack O'Lee," and very much the basis for Fats Domino's "The Fat Man," Lloyd Price's "Lawdy Miss Clawdy," and more than a half dozen Smiley Lewis songs, most notably "Blue Monday."

A couple of show reports illustrate the red-hot New Orleans R&B scene circa 1950. Dr. Daddy-O wrote on May 20 about a show the previous weekend at the San Jacinto that featured Dave Bartholomew performing ten choruses of "Ain't Gonna Do It," Roy Byrd (Professor Longhair) stomping out "She Ain't Got No Hair," Smiley Lewis with "Tee-Nah-Nah," and Fats Domino knocking out "Junker's Blues" in a

88

blue suit. Daddy-O rightly exclaimed, "'Twas the grandest Mothers' Day ever was!!!" On June 24, Smiley met New Orleans habitué Joe Turner in a Battle of the Blues promoted by Frank Painia, owner of the Dew Drop Inn. Dr. Daddy-O commented in the July 1 *Weekly*: "It was 'Tee Nah Nah' against 'Adam Bit the Apple' last Saturday at the Jacinto as Smiley Lewis and Joe Turner tangled up in a blues battle...But here's the joke: didja ever hear Joe Turner sing 'Tee Nah Nah'???...it's kicks!!! ...The next night Block-bustin' Bartholomew took over and presented Tommy Ridgley, Prof. Roy Byrd and Archibald in a frantic session that had everybody in solid perspiration!!!"

Early recordings (1950–1951): "Lowdown"

Smiley Lewis's first session closely paralleled Fats Domino's early blues sessions. On the second session in April 1950, he adopted the more strident vocals that would become his trademark, along with a tighter, more energetic R&B approach that showed Bartholomew's influence. "His repertoire didn't go too far," said Dr. Daddy-O Winslow. "He relied on his few melodies and his tunes that he had. Nothing extensive. He was very friendly, always anxious to perform, always anxious to tell you things that would happen to him, some of his unfortunate love affairs. He liked to peel off certain layers of his life and express them, not at any level of sophistication, but as someone from the country, and he had learned two or three melodies that the people liked. He was more like a deacon in a church with a sense of syncopation than a star."

During this period Smiley met the lady who would play an increasingly important part in his life, Dorothy Ester, a divorced nurse from the rural town of Convent, then living on Toledano Street. "The first time I remember seeing him," she said, "he was at a barroom, a little nightclub, playing music in the Irish Channel. Tuts was with him and Herman. When I met him, him and his wife wasn't together....I don't know where he was livin'. He had a lot of other women that he was runnin' with. He was a very honest, very nice, sweet man that any woman would love to be with, a lovely man. He kept himself up very well, though he was on the heavy side. He had a beautiful smile."

"Tee-Nah-Nah" had made Smiley an overnight sensation in the Deep South. It would probably have made the national R&B charts if—in a trend that would plague Smiley Lewis—he hadn't been covered. Atlantic Records rushed out a version by Van Walls (the pianist on Joe

89

Turner's "Chains of Love" and "Shake, Rattle and Roll"), featuring a vocal by Brownie McGhee as "Spider Sam." Atlantic advertised its version as "the most unusual blues record ever made." Ahmet Ertegun and Jerry Wexler of Atlantic were so impressed with "Tee-Nah-Nah" that, according to Wexler's autobiography, they later had Professor Longhair create "Tipitina" in its image in 1953.

"'Tee-Nah-Nah' went everywhere," said Tuts Washington. "Every time I turned around I heard it on the box. We traveled all over on that record. Florida, Mississippi, Oklahoma. We went so many places I had to write my aunt just to let her know where I was. Lewis was the best singer we had around here, and he could sing them sentimental tunes like 'Someday You'll Want Me' just as good as the blues. Some people called him the black Bing Crosby. Lewis could imitate Amos and Andy on the bandstand, and you'd have to look twice to really believe it was him and not the radio playing. He could do something with a guitar that I never saw before in my life. When it came time for him to take a solo he would put a pick-up under the strings, lay the guitar next to his amplifier and it would keep on playing. Then he'd get down off the bandstand and grab some old gal and start dancing. Some nights he'd do that for ten, maybe fifteen minutes before he came back and started playing again."

Changes (1952–1953): "Don't you hear those bells a-ringing?..."
An evocative sentimental blues, "The Bells Are Ringing," snuck into the national R&B charts for two weeks at No. 10 in September 1952. It was his first official chart entry. Smiley was once again a hot property. Still working the road, he augmented his lineup with Joe Harris on alto sax and James Prevost on bass. "He did a lot of traveling between Louisiana, Georgia, and Tennessee," said Prevost. "Every time I'd turn around we were goin' to Nashville. He'd tell you what he liked and he disliked and if you were down on the things he didn't like, he would tell you about it. Like some drummers they wanna tap on everything, especially if they're ridin' in the car. He got rid of [Edward] Blackwell [who'd] have his sticks and start rapping. Smiley wanted it to be quiet, and I heard that he put him out one night, told him to get out! [Blackwell's practicing paid off, though, as he later gained renown as a jazz drummer with Ornette Coleman.]

"We played Grady's in Nashville and the Bijou Theatre. He had a big name in the place and every time he went it was just about packed.

When he started his solo he would put the guitar behind his head. He had a long cord where he could go out in the audience and play like that. Everybody liked that kind of thing, because it was new at that time."

The strain of one-nighters caused personality conflicts. "Lewis got ornery and big-headed," said Tuts Washington. "Everywhere we went he was behind a gang of women running around and drinking. He threw me out of his car in Nashville over a woman one night and made me walk back to the hotel. Another night we was crossing the [Mississippi] River on a ferry and he said he was gonna kick my ass. I told him, 'If you try, I'll take this knife and juke you in your big fat belly and throw you in the river.' Well, if someone wouldn't have joined in between us, we probably would have killed each other. But, hell, I didn't need that; if it hadn't of been for me, Lewis would still have been shoeing horses. I told him, 'Lewis, I was playing long before I knew you. I don't need you.' So that's when Dave Bartholomew grabbed him. He tried to get me back in the band later on when his records stopped selling, but I had had enough of Smiley Lewis."

1954: "Blue Monday, how I hate Blue Monday…"

On December 14, 1953, Smiley was recording at Cosimo's studio right after Fats Domino had recorded one of his lesser entries, "You Done Me Wrong." It was Smiley's record that would become the standard, although, ironically, it would be Domino's version everyone would remember. Smiley should have known his star was cursed when he received a sign of sorts in the studio.

"We was in the studio recording 'Blue Monday'," said sax player Herbert Hardesty, "and Smiley was playing his guitar. He accidentally touched the microphone stand and the whole guitar blew up!" Engineer Cosimo Matassa also remembers that Smiley nearly killed himself recording that number: "His amplifier was hot, it wasn't grounded properly. And he touched his guitar strings up to the mike stand. There was a blue flash of light and the strings all burst! It was serious, he could have really hurt himself."

The song was Dave Bartholomew's portrait of the man who suffered from working and partying in an unending cycle. "I was workin' in Kansas City," he says. "This was during the rhythm & blues age and on Mondays nobody worked. And I went in from one joint to the other and [the bands] started around five or six o'clock in the evening. So that's where I got the idea for 'Blue Monday.' I said, 'Hell, nobody in this town works!' Actually the story was right there. That was Smiley's big, big one. He did about 150,000 on that one. Lew Chudd, who owned Imperial Records, said that was the best song I ever wrote, because it was actually life itself."

Touring with Joe Turner: "Too many drivers"

After signing with the Shaw Booking Agency out of New York in March 1954, one of Smiley's first tours pitted him against the red-hot Joe Turner, whose current hits included the New Orleans-recorded No. 1 R&B hit, "Honey Hush," and his new release, "Shake, Rattle and Roll." New Orleans' Lastie brothers provided backing on the tour.

"We wanted to make him mad," said David Lastie. "We all was young then. We called him 'Overton.' See, his name was 'Overton Lemons.' Boy, he couldn't stand that! Smiley rode all over the country, man, by himself. I don't want to badmouth the man, but that's the kind of person he was. He was a loner. We left here going to Denver. The second job was from Denver to Vallejo, California. Then the next stop was Oakland. We had a nine-passenger Suburban, a DeSoto with the rack on the top. And I turned it over down in Tijuana, Mexico, and we all had to ride with Smiley and Joe, 'cause Joe had a Cadillac then. So some of us rode in the Cadillac—the ones that wanted to smoke and drink, 'cause you couldn't do none of that in Smiley's 'Lillie Mae.' It had his name all over it, phone number and all that. He'd keep two shotguns and a pistol. We'd be driving across the desert shooting at jackrabbits and stuff. It was a great trip!"

The fall of 1954 found Smiley touring with Shirley and Lee and blues singer–harmonica player Alexander "Papa" Lightfoot, then impersonating Little Walter. The New Orleans band on the tour included several young musicians who would make their mark later— Milton Batiste on trumpet, Nat Perrilliat on tenor, Wilbert Smith on tenor and piano, Charles Connor on drums, and Edwin "Guitar Red" Mayer. "Smiley was kinda strict," says Milton Batiste. "He was an alright guy, but he didn't go for no bullshittin'. He mostly liked to stay off by himself. He was a real flashy dresser. Always clean. Shiny shoes at all times. Even if he was wearing a pair of dungarees around the house, they'd be pressed to a point. He must have had dozens of suits. He could drink, too, man. Drank straight gin by the fifth. One time him and Papa Lightfoot got in a hell of a fight. We were up in

Tennessee. Before the show those two were drinking that gin and throwing dice. Papa Lightfoot was winning and Smiley wasn't too happy about that. Smiley started calling Papa Lightfoot 'Tangle Eye' [Lightfoot was cross-eyed]. So Papa Lightfoot took Smiley's money and sat in the front seat of his car and started eating a ham sandwich! Well, that was worse than taking Smiley's money! Next thing you know they were rolling in the snow beating the hell out of each other. It took the whole band to pull them apart. But we did the show and everybody was friends at the end of the night."

Bill Boskent, the road manager with Lloyd Price at the time, remembers encountering an altogether different Smiley Lewis in Atlanta. "I seen him after he made 'Blue Monday,' 'cause I know how hard and for years he was tryin'. That station wagon had all kinda names of records that he had recorded, and he couldn't get a good one. He told me, 'Bill, all my life I've been tryin' to get a hit record so I could make a livin' on the road. Now I got one, and I'm too old and too tired!' And he...cut [the tour] off right there in Atlanta."

The hit: "I hear you knockin'..."

In July 1955, just as Fats Domino's "Ain't It a Shame" was following Pat Boone's cover version into the pop charts, Smiley Lewis released the biggest hit of his career. "I Hear You Knockin'" was covered by several pop artists, including Josephine Cottle, a 33-year-old actress from Texas, who had been dubbed "Gale Storm" by an impish agent. Storm had just finished a three-year run as the mischievous daughter on the *My Little Margie* television sitcom. Her No. 2 hit of the song on Dot (Pat Boone's record label) led to a successful recording career and her next television show, *The Gale Storm Show*. Smiley Lewis's No. 2 R&B hit of the song led to his being a footnote in rock 'n' roll history. He was knockin' on the door, but he couldn't come in.

"To be frank," said Dave Bartholomew, "during that time, when white people were covering the black peoples' songs it stopped a lot of the blacks from progressing. The proof is 'I Hear You Knockin'.' Gale Storm killed Smiley's record completely. Because I wrote the song, I wasn't too disappointed because I did fine moneywise, but I also could see that Smiley wasn't going to make it because a white girl had cut him out completely, and I felt bad for him. 'I Hear You Knockin' came from a skit. We used to have a lot of black nightclubs in the New Orleans area. This comedian, who was considered one of the best in the country,

93

was Lollypop Jones. He had a skit with a girl where she would come on stage and say, 'Yes, I'm leavin' you, I done met me a young man, I'm goin' to New York.' In our time all the musicians wanted to do was to get to New York. Down here in the South there was so much that we could do and after that, being black, we couldn't get any further. We had to go where we could make it big. Sure enough, she packed her clothes and left. While she was gone, he got him a good job, he was doin' good, havin' a brand new car. She heard about it in New York City; she was doin' pretty bad, 'cause the guy she left with had left her. So when she came back she knocked on the door. He said, 'I hear you knockin', but you can't come in!'"

Smiley received the largest royalty check of his career, which he used (along with the trade-in of his beloved station wagon) to purchase a 1955 Cadillac, also dubbed "Lillie Mae." By this time Lewis had set up housekeeping with Dorothy Ester in an upstairs apartment on 4628 Freret Street. "I had just come home from work," said Dorothy, "and I was still in my nurse's uniform. He told me to put something on. So I did, and there was a Cadillac down there. So we took a ride in the country. We used to have fun, ridin' around, laughin' and talkin', meetin' the people, stuff like that."

1955–1956: "The tune they call the rhythm and blues..."

Starting with a session on October 26, 1955, Dave Bartholomew began recording Smiley Lewis with more rhythm and less blues, and, over the next year, Smiley recorded one classic after another. On the last day of March 1956, his original version of "One Night" entered *Billboard*'s R&B Disc Jockey charts for three weeks, reaching No. 11. "There was a young lady in Mobile, Alabama," said Bartholomew. "I used to play most of the black society dances in Mobile. A very respectable lady. She said, 'One night, I'm gonna have one night of sin.' I never did know what she meant from that. I put the title down. I always considered her a beautiful person who could do no wrong. She had a husband and kids. I said, 'Maybe, you know, in the back of her mind, one night she just wants to go out and see the other side of the world, how the other side is livin'.' That's how I wrote that tune."

Smiley's original version of "One Night (of Sin)" expressed guilt for a sin (presumably adultery) for which he lost his "sweet helping hand." It's the guilt-wracked lament of a middle-aged black man. He was 42 when the record was released. Elvis Presley clearly loved it, but knew he couldn't get it played if the lyrics weren't rewritten. A gut-wrenching blues, in which too much fulfillment has taken place, was transformed into a dream date in which fulfillment waits tantalizingly in the distance. Presley's record was no lame Pat Boone record, though. It was a lascivious performance that no black singer could have got away with. Strictly speaking, it wasn't a cover version, either. Presley recorded his rewritten version two years after Smiley's record had been and gone.

1957: "Shame, shame, shame..."

In January 1957, the *Louisiana Weekly* advertised the New Orleans premieres of two movies that featured Fats Domino, *Shake, Rattle and Rock* and *The Girl Can't Help It*. Also showing that month was Smiley Lewis's movie debut, although no one knew it.

Baby Doll, a Tennessee Williams story filmed by Elia Kazan (the Oscar-winning director of *On the Waterfront*), was about the moral, financial, and sexual bankruptcy of a white southern racist in the person of Karl Malden. His childlike teenage bride, sultrily played by Carroll Baker, slept only in a cradle (thus her nickname) in a decaying, empty southern mansion (filmed on location in Benoit, Mississippi). For all Kazan's liberalism, the blacks around the house and in the town were shuffling stereotypes. In an act of revenge, Malden was symbolically cuckolded by an Italian-American "wop" played by Eli Wallach. In the midst of his chase and seduction of Baby Doll, Wallach discovers a record player in her "nursery." He puts on a 78-rpm record and rocks in the saddle of her rocking horse as horns blast and Smiley Lewis shouts, "Shame, shame, shame on you, Miss Roxy!!"

No doubt Lew Chudd's Hollywood connections led to Smiley's bizarre and unprecedented presence in such a prestigious dramatic work. The song was written by a radio, TV, and movie scorer, Reuben "Ruby" Fisher, and the film's musical director, Kenyon Hopkins. It was originally recorded by Bartholomew and crew in August 1956, but apparently Hopkins—or possibly the musically minded Elia Kazan—was not satisfied with that recording and had the studio band rerecord the song in October 1956 in New Orleans, likely with precise instructions on alterations to be made. Incidentally, that same month Specialty Records president Art Rupe closely supervised Little Richard's recording of the title song to *The Girl Can't Help It* in New Orleans under strict instructions from Twentieth Century Fox. Smiley's session

95

produced the extraordinary soundtrack recording. It was the most rocking recording of Smiley's career, but, unfortunately, it was only available on the *Baby Doll* album on Columbia Records. The earlier version, released on Imperial, got little play.

The "Adults Only" tag on *Baby Doll* served as a reminder of the gulf between Smiley and the white and black teens flocking to see Fats Domino in his movies. It could be argued that Domino's softer vocals on just about any of Smiley's 1955–1956 songs would have made them smash hits. In fact, Fats went on to record several Bartholomew songs that Smiley had cut earlier. He says he never sensed any resentment from the blues shouter. "He didn't have nothing to do with the songs," says Fats, "That wasn't his songs. I never did talk to him about that."

1958-1960: "I shall not be moved"

On the weekend of July 26, 1958, Smiley was appearing at the High Hat Club. An old photo, circa 1953, spoke only of old news: "On Monday night Lewis will again headline a special 'Blue Monday Party' and will play the recording hit which made him headlines—'Blue Monday.'" Around that time, Smiley was one of several New Orleans artists dropped by Imperial. The unsentimental Lew Chudd was doing very well with Ricky Nelson and didn't need R&B singers who appeared to be somewhat past their sell-by date. "We just couldn't get Smiley started," said Dave Bartholomew. "He always had the best material. His records would sell great all around New Orleans but we just couldn't break him nationally like everyone else. It was a frustrating situation." In 1960, Bartholomew persuaded Chudd to take another chance on Smiley, this time with more sophisticated big band arrangements. The results were no better.

"He had to be frustrated," said Smiley's daughter, Hazel. "I couldn't understand how Fats could make a hit out of 'Blue Monday' and my father couldn't. He had some bad things to say about Dave, but him and Fats were friends. I remember going to Fats's house where Fats had a bar that was covered with hundreds of silver dollars, and we were living in the Lafitte Projects." It was late 1960 when Smiley visited Domino's new $200,000 mansion in the Ninth Ward. "We just paid a visit to his home," said Dorothy. "He'd came up where we was. And he said, 'Y'all follow me and see my home.' He just was getting straight with it then, but it was very nice."

Smiley was down on his luck throughout the '60s. He no longer carried a band, and most of his work consisted of spot jobs around New Orleans. He often opened for up-and-comers like Irma Thomas or Ernie K-Doe, and occasionally played the Sands on Jefferson Highway. His Cadillac had been wrecked in an accident, so he had to load his equipment on the Jefferson Parish bus at the end of the night. He often played the French Quarter, sometimes as a ballad-singing troubadour once again. He filled in at the Court of Two Sisters when Clarence "Frogman" Henry was on the road.

There were some recordings for OKeh in December 1961, which were reminiscent of the glory days on Imperial, but the many years of hard living, heavy drinking, and smoking were catching up with him. He entered the studio just once more in December 1965. Allen Toussaint produced lackluster remakes of "The Bells Are Ringing" and "One Night of Sin" for Warner Bros.' Loma label. Smiley's once booming voice was weak and strained, leaving Toussaint to finish the session with a bouncy instrumental. Smiley's last show was at the I.L.A. Hall on Claiborne Avenue with Sugar Boy Crawford and the Sugarlumps. Soon afterwards he entered Charity Hospital a very sick man.

"It got to the place he didn't want to eat," said Dorothy. "Then he started losing weight. Then he stayed hoarse all the time. So then I had him under the doctor. And they treated him. He started getting worse all the time, so then I put him in the hospital. They said he had an ulcer. So when they operated on him they found he had cancer."

Pianist Tuts Washington played at a benefit concert. "They had a benefit up in the hospital for him so they could get blood for him," he remembered. "Smiley called me and asked me to come up and play a party for people to donate blood the day before his operation. I hadn't seen him in a long time, but I could see that the cancer was eating him up. He tried to play with us but could barely hold his guitar. I walked Lewis up and down the hall and he had his arm around me and his eyes got full of water. He said, 'Tuts, you taught me all I know. If I'd have listened to you I'd still be doing all right today.'"

After the operation, Smiley was sent home where Dorothy used her training as a nurse to tend him. The March 19, 1966, issue of the *Louisiana Weekly* revealed his plight and asked his friends to visit him and "drop by some of the green stuff." On June 18, Dorothy and Smiley finally got married in a small service. Earl King remembers passing Smiley on Freret Street not long after he got out of Charity Hospital. Although only just over 5 feet tall, Smiley had once weighed as much

97

as 225 pounds. Earl would have kept on walking had Smiley not stopped him: "He couldn't have weighed 100 pounds. I couldn't even recognize his voice."

Others paid their last respects. "When I saw Smiley he was sick," says Fats Domino. "I went to see him before I left town. When I came back he was gone." "Fats came to see him about three days before he died," says Dorothy. "And Fats told him when he got where he was going he would call him that night and he did. I think he was in Chicago."

A benefit show was organized by Benny Spellman and Dave Bartholomew for October 10, 1966, but Smiley didn't live long enough to see it. He died on October 7, 1966. "He died in my arms," said Dorothy. "He told me that he wanted some water. And I gave him some water. Then he said, 'How about some juice?' I gave him some. Then he didn't say anything else. He just looked at me. I felt it when he gived away. So I just shook my head to my sister, told her he was gone. He just passed right on, just that quick. At the wake it was covered with people. A lot of them went to the country with us, even though the weather was very bad. They all was there, what was in town." A large funeral was held at the Dennis Rhodes Mortuary on Louisiana Avenue, and Smiley was buried out in the country where he and Dorothy used to take rides, behind a little Methodist church at the St. James A.M.E. Cemetery in Dorothy's hometown of Convent, Louisiana.

These notes accompanied a 4-CD complete career retrospective, Shame, Shame, Shame *(BCD 15745).*

The Joint Is on Fire
Clyde McPhatter

Colin Escott

Another long piece, this is, as far as I know, the only extensive biographical sketch of Clyde McPhatter. As said earlier, achievements tend to be narrowed to the smallest possible focus, so McPhatter gets in the history books for a few rather trite hits like "A Lover's Question," "Ta-Ta," and "Lover Please." When those same books talk about gospel passion and phrasing revolutionizing secular R&B it's usually Ray Charles and Sam Cooke who are mentioned. The truth is that Clyde McPhatter was doing it first. His leads on some Billy Ward and Drifters records pointed unerringly toward soul music. His solo records were intermittently brilliant, undermined by his lifelong ambition to be a legit entertainer like Johnny Mathis. By the time he realized he was a soul pioneer and was willing to capitalize on it, he was all but finished.

This essay accompanied an LP boxed set of McPhatter's MGM and Mercury recordings that has now been discontinued. I hope that we will be able to reissue it on CD one day, ideally with the earlier and later titles to show the broad sweep of McPhatter's career. In search of McPhatter, I contacted many industry people, and I had hoped to contact family members to provide a full portrait of a man who was clearly not without personal troubles. As it was, I was only able to locate McPhatter's widow, Lena, who was both charming and guarded. As a result, this essay concentrates on Clyde McPhatter's career and only hints at the complex mix of problems that dogged him. A pioneer deserves better, and perhaps if we get a chance to do the CD box I can revisit this piece. (C. E.)

Traditionally, black music has been dominated by voices that are full, deep, and rich. Clyde McPhatter sang in a high, almost strangulated tenor, and in that beseeching voice you could sense some of the self-doubt and querulousness that riddled him. As the founder and leader of the Drifters and subsequently as a solo artist, he was in the charts from the early 1950s until the mid-1960s; yet, by the time he died in 1972, he was in such wretched shape that he was barely able to capitalize on his status as a faded hit maker. His influence is everywhere, often second or third hand. Virtually all latter-day R&B stars who sing high, from Smokey Robinson to Michael Jackson, owe something to him. Elvis Presley was a fan, dipping into his Clyde McPhatter collection throughout his career ("Money Honey," "Such a Night," "Without Love," and an arrangement of "White Christmas" that followed McPhatter's arrangement almost note for note). Tom Jones poured more sweat into "Without Love," but only managed a shadow of the passion.

No career as long as Clyde McPhatter's is without ironies and contradictions. McPhatter was a soul music pioneer whose career sputtered and died in the soul music era. He was also a soul pioneer whose biggest hits were trite pop novelties, and whose aspirations lay with supper club music.

Born Durham, North Carolina

Little is known about Clyde McPhatter's early years. His curiously Scottish name apparently reflected the fact that he had Scots ancestry. He was born in the tobacco town of Durham, N.C., probably on November 15, 1931. Most biographies quote 1933 or 1934, although government documents cite the earlier year. His parents, George and Beulah, were religious people; George was a preacher, and Beulah was the organist and choir mistress. "We all sang," Clyde told Marcia Vance. "We all got started in my mother's choir. She'd get us all together for rehearsals every Wednesday night. I've been singing as far back as I can remember." In 1945, the McPhatters moved to New York. The following year, Clyde joined the Mount Lebanon Singers at the Mount Lebanon Church on 132nd Street. Others in the group included David Baldwin, the brother of novelist James Baldwin.

"I hate to say it," Clyde told Lee Hildebrand shortly before his death, "but religion in my family is very closely related to suspicion, or, as my father would say, 'The Fear of God.' Religion…was nothing but another word for discipline. 'God don't like this' and 'God don't like that.' One day I said, 'God damn it,' and my father beat the hell out of me. What the hell has God got to do with all this? That's how my early life was. Everything was built around God."

It seems unremarkable now to talk about introducing gospel passion to secular music, but McPhatter was bridging the two solitudes before Ray Charles, Sam Cooke, or the generations of soul men who followed. Bill Millar put it best: "He took exceptional liberties with the melody, creating daring and climactic vocal lines which stemmed from his previous experience in spiritual groups. He jumped octaves, juggled keys, and stretched single syllables over numerous notes. All these mannerisms helped convince the listener that pop singing was unable to express the enormity of real emotions. 'You weren't supposed to sing with sincerity unless it was to God,' he once remarked."

In 1948, he sang Lonnie Johnson's hit version of the old pop song "Tomorrow Night" at Amateur Night at the Apollo. He insisted that he won, although other reports have him placing second. In 1949 or 1950, he came to the attention of Billy Ward. Stories conflict on how McPhatter and Ward came together, and we still don't know who took the initiative to contact whom. Ward was a shrewd judge of talent, and, at the time, was nurturing the idea of managing and fronting a vocal group to be called the Ques. His ideas on vocal harmony came from the Ink Spots, and he saw McPhatter taking Bill Kenny's role as high tenor. McPhatter thought otherwise. "I had been so oriented to gospel music," he said, "that I couldn't sing along those lines."

The Dominoes

Billy Ward was damned memorably by McPhatter as a "wrong man." Ward was born and, at last sighting, still living in Los Angeles. He began piano lessons in infancy. In 1935, at age 14, he won a competition with a self-composed classical piece he called "Dejection." The Ward family then relocated to Philadelphia, and, during the war, Billy Ward directed the Coast Artillery Choir and staged USO shows. After his discharge, he worked as a sports editor for Transradio Press in New York and continued his music studies at Juilliard.

At some point in the late 1940s, Ward became acquainted with an agent and manager, Mrs. Rose Marks. Together they hatched the idea of forming a vocal group; Ward would look after the music while Mrs.

101

Marks would handle the business. At some point in 1949 or 1950, the Ques became the Dominoes, and, in October 1950, Mrs. Marks got them on Arthur Godfrey's show to sing "Goodnight Irene." This shows the sort of legitimacy Marks and Ward had in mind. Next came the record deal. Syd Nathan's King Records started several subsidiary label partnerships with independent producers. In October 1950, Nathan launched Federal Records in partnership with producer Ralph Bass. Ward and Marks appeared just as Bass was scouting out his roster.

"Ward came into my New York office," Bass told Michael Lydon. "The cat had a dub of an aircheck on 'Goodnight Irene.' I said, 'Man, I can't use this. It hasn't got it,' but he was so insistent that I told him to bring the group down. They came in and I said, 'This ain't fish nor fowl. It ain't R&B enough to be R&B and it ain't pop enough to be pop. It ain't got a thing.' He asked me what kind of music I wanted to hear and I played some records to him, including some by the Orioles— the only group that was selling. Ward said, 'I can write songs like that all the time.' I said, 'Baby write ME one.' He came up with 'Do Something for Me.'"

"Do Something for Me" was released in the first batch of Federal records in December 1950. Clyde McPhatter took an astonishingly confident lead. All the McPhatter hallmarks were already in place, and the record was enough of a success to encourage Ward and Bass to persevere. The breakthrough came with "Sixty Minute Man." It was released in May 1951 and ruled the R&B charts for the rest of the year. Bill Brown took the deep, measured lead like a man intent on taking his time while McPhatter contributed the excitable, priapic shrieks in the background. Several commentators have noted that the song conjoined the words *rock* and *roll* in the line "I'll rock 'em, roll 'em all night long, I'm a 60-minute man," and although the words had been conjoined before (the Boswell Sisters had recorded "Rock and Roll" as far back as 1934), the Dominoes' record almost certainly helped popularize the phrase and made its original meaning abundantly clear.

The Dominoes' next No. 1 hit, "Have Mercy Baby," caught McPhatter in full flight. All the church-based mannerisms for which he became famous are here. It has as good a claim as any to be the first soul record. Now clearly the star of the Dominoes, McPhatter became increasingly disenchanted. He was on a salary with no participation in record sales. On top of that, Ward and Marks ran the group with militaristic discipline, levying fines for petty infractions. Ward also did nothing to discourage the notion that *he* was singing lead, even going so far as to introduce Clyde as his younger brother. The parting of the ways came in 1953. "I was only making a hundred dollars a week," McPhatter told Marcia Vance, "and after taxes of twelve dollars and food [I was making nothing]. My father told me to pack up and come home. He said, 'You can make more in the garment center.' That's why I say Billy Ward is a wrong man. When I got ready to leave he took back the uniforms I was wearing and left me with one damn suit."

Jerry Wexler, then a vice-president at Atlantic Records, takes up the story:

"One night in the early spring of 1953, my partner, Ahmet Ertegun, went to Birdland to catch Billy Ward, mostly to hear Clyde McPhatter sing 'Have Mercy Baby.' For Ahmet this was an all-time R&B classic and he loved it for its pure gospel feel and the incredible funk of Clyde's high lead tenor. The Dominoes came on and Clyde was missing. Ahmet went backstage after the show and asked Billy about Clyde. Billy said, 'The reason he's not here is I fired his ass today.' Ahmet exited Birdland like a shot and headed directly uptown where he found Clyde in a furnished room. Ahmet reached an agreement that Clyde would assemble a vocal group behind himself."

In the interest of accuracy, it's worth noting that in an interview with Alfred Duckett of the *Chicago Defender* (May 15, 1954), McPhatter stated that Ertegun discovered him at Birdland, although it's possible that McPhatter did not want to admit that he had been fired. Either way, he was now an Atlantic Records artist.

Let the Boogie Woogie Roll

Clyde McPhatter signed with Atlantic in May 1953. It was the right place at the right time. The owners were in sympathy with his music, allowed him ample time to rehearse, and placed him with Jesse Stone. "We were making records in tune," said Jerry Wexler. "We would rehearse anywhere from four weeks on. It was super professional because Clyde would work on his harmonies and his voicings. At the same time, other legendary indie record labels were lining up street corner groups in the wings and pushing them out to sing two songs— one take each. That was the record….The bands didn't even have a chance to learn the chords. God help us, there's a cult for that shit!"

McPhatter brought in two members of the Mount Lebanon Singers, William "Chick" Anderson and David Baldwin. Fourteen-year-old David Baughan sang tenor and James "Wrinkle" Johnson held down the bass. They decided on the name Drifters, although there has never been any consensus on how they arrived at it. After rehearsing for six weeks, they went to Atlantic on June 29, 1953. Ertegun and Wexler were less than impressed with what they heard. McPhatter's supper club leanings shone through, and Ertegun lost no time telling him that "Clyde McPhatter and the Drifters" sounded like a hillbilly band. McPhatter refused to change his name, but rethought his music. He recruited a hard gospel group, the Thrasher Wonders, and returned to Atlantic with an arrangement of Jesse Stone's "Money Honey." Ertegun and Wexler were floored. It hit No. 1 on the R&B charts in November 1953 and stayed there the rest of the year.

"Money Honey" was followed by "Such a Night" and the only slightly less suggestive "Honey Love." For many, though, the highlight of McPhatter's tenure with the Drifters came with Ahmet Ertegun's composition "What'cha Gonna Do." Ertegun had borrowed the song's structure from gospel records (some have suggested the Radio Four's "What're You Going to Do" as a direct source of inspiration). For a Turkish immigrant, Ertegun got off some good lines ("What'cha gonna do when the joint is on fire," etc.), but it wasn't the lyrics that mattered. The gospel structure was the best possible showcase for the group's harmony; McPhatter's piping, insistent lead crossthreaded through the relentless ebb and flow of the backing vocals. It was wondrous and imperishable.

By the time "Honey Love" got to No. 1 on the R&B charts, Clyde McPhatter was in the Army. "We had so much success that Billy Ward called the Army on me," McPhatter told Marcia Vance. "He told me not to register when I was with the Dominoes." McPhatter spent his Army hitch at Grand Island on the border between Canada and the United States, near Buffalo, New York. "The Army was real good to me," he insisted. "I was able to fly home on weekends. They were very lenient." While he was away, McPhatter agreed with Ertegun, Wexler, and the group's manager, George Treadwell, that he would go solo. Treadwell assumed control of the group, and, taking his cue from Ward and Marks, made the singers into salaried employees. He collected all royalties and personal appearance fees, and treated the members as indentured servants. "Thank God, I'm out of that," McPhatter remarked later in life.

Clyde McPhatter

Solo

Atlantic tried to keep McPhatter in the spotlight while he was away. He cut a lightweight single with Ruth Brown, important only in that its pop leanings were a clear indication of where he would be heading after his discharge. "Seven Days," released just as McPhatter was exiting the Army, confirmed the new direction. There was a very white arrangement from a very white arranger, Ray Ellis. For his part, Ellis insists that he went out and bought some R&B records to get a feel for working with McPhatter, but his work still owed more to what he'd been doing for Mitch Miller. Another of Ellis's arrangements, "The Treasure of Love," was released to coincide with McPhatter's first solo tour, and went on to become a Top 20 hit. It was a very different view of love than the one expressed in "Honey Love" a couple of years earlier. Gone forever were lines like "I want it in the middle of the night"; in their places were lines like "The treasure of love is found in no chart / To find where it is, just look in your heart."

"Without Love (There Is Nothing)" hit the pop charts in February 1957, and peaked at No. 19. One of the great performances of McPhatter's career, this song started with a simple piano accompaniment and built to an emotional crescendo that has challenged generations of singers. Elvis and Tom Jones are among those who have never quite recaptured the specialness of Clyde McPhatter's performance. Jones is just one who replaced McPhatter's vulnerability with a grim, sweaty determination to hit those final notes.

Jerry Wexler maintained that McPhatter's pop aspirations were not matched by sales: "He wanted to be Perry Como, but we weren't selling in pop quantities. The litmus test is this: Was it being played on pop radio? The answer is that it wasn't. There's a lot of romanticizing about crossover and Clyde was more or less strictly on black radio. We certainly didn't get Bobby Darin sales off his singles. We treated the songs with respect. We didn't get into vomitacious productions. My only regret is that we used a white vocal group, as we did on some of Chuck Willis' sessions. And we rehearsed. Very few companies rehearsed like us in those days."

Ahmet Ertegun was less charitable about the productions. Talking to the *New Yorker*, he said: "I don't think they hold up that well. The singing holds up pretty well, but the background sounds dated to me. The inventions of arrangers give it leaden feet. It's like an automobile. A simple body design of 1938 on a Delage or some of those simple French cars looks beautiful today, but a Buick Roadmaster, with a lot of chrome, looks funny. It's of its time, but not something one would want to copy in any way. There's too much chrome on those records."

Atlantic had scheduled a session for August 7, 1959. That morning, Jerry Wexler was handed a demo by Clyde Otis, a young songplugger and songwriter at Eden Music. On it, a failed recording artist named

Brook Benton sang an irresistibly catchy song that he had cowritten called "A Lover's Question." Wexler borrowed the arrangement to the point of bringing in Benton and Otis to snap their fingers in the background. It was released on September 5, 1958, cracked the charts in January 1959, and spent almost half the year on the Hot 100. During that time, McPhatter's contract with Atlantic Records was up.

The Year of the Lion

Clyde McPhatter's decision to move from Atlantic to MGM Records was portrayed at the time as a simple dollars-and-cents decision. Reporting the switch in March 1959, *Billboard* reported that MGM had offered $60,000 up front. Atlantic was at pains to point out that they could have afforded the up-front guarantee, but chose not to. Clyde Otis later hinted at hidden agendas.

"Clyde was militant but not political. It was his militancy that made him have problems with Ahmet Ertegun and Jerry Wexler. Their perception of him was different from the way he wanted to be perceived, especially in a business way. I remember when we talked about signing him to Mercury, Irvin Feld was his manager and Irvin confided in me certain aspects of his relationship with Atlantic which made it impossible for Clyde to continue."

McPhatter was signed by MGM president, Arnold Maxin—the former head of Columbia's Epic division and the man who had notionally produced Screamin' Jay Hawkins's "I Put a Spell on You." A month after signing McPhatter, Maxin brought in Ray Ellis as A&R manager. The first album, *Let's Start Over Again*, showed them striving for the legitimacy McPhatter craved. The LP's title song provided evidence of his new direction; it was about the dissolution of a marriage. The only kids in it were the ones about to be hurt by the divorce. The arrangements were sterile, and the rhythm tracks had none of the crispness that the moonlighting jazzmen brought to the Atlantic and, later, the Mercury sides.

The first MGM single, "I Told Myself a Lie," rose to No. 70, sputtered, and died. The best showing McPhatter ever got on MGM was when "Let's Try Again" peaked at No. 66. Several songs came within a hairbreadth of greatness, but McPhatter and the arrangements were at cross-purposes. Ray Ellis's sight-reading musicians tried to play blues fills, but the results were stilted. If McPhatter loved the sound of himself cushioned by a full orchestra, he must have been bitterly

107

. . . .

ALL ROOTS LEAD TO ROCK

disappointed at how few embraced his new direction. Clyde Otis, watching intently from the sidelines, thought he could succeed where MGM had conspicuously failed.

Clyde McPhatter

Mercury 1: Clyde Otis

When Clyde Otis left Prentiss, Mississippi in his early teens, he probably had everything he owned in his valise; when he returned to show his children something of their heritage, it was in a Lincoln Continental half the length of Main Street. Otis has nothing if not steely persistence. He fought his way up the New York music publishing industry to become one of the most successful black music business executives. He was, in many respects, the polar opposite of the querulous, self-doubting Clyde McPhatter.

After a brief, unsuccessful stint as a drummer, Otis became a song-writer for Meridian Music, then entered into a partnership with Irving Berlin's one-time professional manager, Dave Dreyer. Together, they wrote and/or published hits like "Looking Back" for Nat "King" Cole. Otis also produced his own demos, and his demo of "The Stroll" land-ed him a job with Mercury Records. "I had sent the demo to Nat Goodman, the Diamonds' manager," said Otis, "and they asked me to produce the session. I did, and it became a million-seller. Then Art Talmadge from Mercury came and asked if I'd be interested in assuming a position at Mercury because Bobby Shad had just left. I knew that up to that point no black had ever held the administrative responsibility in addition to the creative responsibility. One of my conditions was that I wanted both."

The personal chemistry between Clyde Otis and Mercury president Irving Green was never good. Otis was never shy about placing songs he owned with the acts he produced, which was against Green's policy, and Green tended to like effusive, happy-go-lucky characters like his other black A&R man, Quincy Jones. Otis was many things, but effusive and happy-go-lucky he was not.

Green couldn't argue with Otis's success, though. Otis brought his demo singer, Brook Benton, to Mercury, and their first record together, "It's Just a Matter of Time," was not only a million-seller but one of the most elegant records of the '50s. That same year, 1959, he revived Dinah Washington's career with "What a Diff'rence a Day Makes." On June 13, 1960, Clyde Otis signed Clyde McPhatter to Mercury. Otis knew exactly how successful "A Lover's Question" had been because he was still cashing the royalty checks. He wanted to recapture that groove, but found an artist with aspirations that still ran in an altogether different direction.

"He wanted a more progressive or contemporary backing," said

109

Otis. "He had seen the things we had done with Brook Benton where we had a preponderance of strings, and he said he'd love to be cut that way. I told him it would not be the best set-up for him, but he insisted and I went along with it. Black artists wanted to sing with strings because it was something that had been more or less denied them. Some black artists just shouldn't mess around with strings and lush arrangements but you can understand the urgency they felt to explore it."

On Clyde McPhatter's first Mercury album, *May I Sing for You?* he and Otis tried for the sweet-and-sour formula that had worked to unbearably poignant effect on Billie Holiday's last recordings and would soon work so well for Ray Charles. Unfortunately, they chose some of the clunkiest entries in the great American songbook, songs like "Put Your Arms Around Me, Honey" and "Three Coins in a Fountain." McPhatter sang them as straight as he could. This was so clearly what he really wanted to do, but his high, somewhat thin voice, simply didn't work effectively against string instruments because the two had much the same timbre and worked the same range.

In a sense, McPhatter was onto something. The LP market was a thing apart from the singles market in 1960. Careers came and went in an instant in the singles market; the LP market was the key to long-term growth and prosperity because adults bought LPs while kids bought singles. That's why so many of Sam Cooke's albums were chocked full of standards similar to, if not clunkier than the ones McPhatter was recording. Much as he wanted it otherwise, though, this was simply not Clyde McPhatter's forte. Otis saw it as something McPhatter needed to get past.

With the singles market very much on his mind, Otis presented McPhatter with "I Ain't Giving Up Nothing," a song that he and Brook Benton had written and first tried with Canadian rockabilly singer Ben Hewitt. McPhatter had also taken the rare step of writing some original material in conjunction with session guitarist Jimmy Oliver. They had even taken a page out of Otis's book and formed a joint music publishing company, Olimac Music. "Clyde brought in 'Ta-Ta,'" said Otis, "I said, 'That's a cute song. Who wrote it?' Clyde said, 'I did.' I said, 'I don't believe you.' Then Jimmy Oliver spoke up and said, 'Yeah, we wrote it.' I said, 'Oh, WE wrote it.'" The giddy string arrangement and Otis's crisply miked rhythm track made it perfect Top 40 radio fare circa 1960, and it gave McPhatter his best chart showing since "A Lover's Question" two years earlier.

Clyde Otis had given a clear indication of the direction he wanted to pursue with McPhatter, but he left in 1961 before he really had a chance to bring that vision to fruition. Otis was a pioneer, albeit one who barely rates a mention these days: "In 1958, black musicians were only used in the rhythm sections at recording sessions," said Otis. "When I decided to do the Brook Benton sessions with strings I asked my contractor if there were any black string players. He said, 'Yes.' I said, 'Where are they working?' He said, 'In the pits of the Broadway shows.' I said, 'Why don't they play recording dates?' He said, 'Nobody calls them.' I said, 'If they're good, I want to see them on these dates.' Out of twenty or so string players we used, four or five might be black. Now they're predominantly black, which is the reverse of what I was trying to get away from."

Otis also made a point of using the brilliant black photographer, Chuck Stewart, for photo shoots instead of Popsie, Kriegsmann, and the established showbiz photographers. He had only been with Mercury a shade over two years, but he had made an impact.

Mercury 2: Shelby Singleton

On the face of it, Mercury's choice of Shelby Singleton to replace Clyde Otis as the New York head of A&R was an odd one. Singleton was from Shreveport, Louisiana, and, in the space of a few months, had revitalized Mercury's Nashville operation. With artists like Faron Young and Leroy Van Dyke, Singleton was accomplishing for country music what Otis had accomplished for R&B; he was staking out the middle ground where minority-interest music attracts pop sales. Singleton took over the New York office on the condition that he didn't have to live there. He took a bachelor apartment on 57th Street and commuted back and forth from Nashville.

Singleton preferred to record in Nashville, and could never get the New York musicians to work up "head" (i.e., on-the-spot) arrangements like their counterparts in Nashville. He even tried bringing a planeload of Nashville sessionmen to New York to lead by example, but it didn't work. One of Singleton's favorite musicians was Ray Stevens, and Singleton brought McPhatter to Nashville to record while Stevens was working on his "Ahab the Arab" single. In deference to the visiting star, Stevens named Ahab's camel "Clyde."

Singleton found a hit for McPhatter just weeks after taking over. After leaving Elvis, Bill Black had started his very successful combo. He used the proceeds to launch a record company, Louis Records, and a publishing company and studio, Lyn-Lou, in Memphis. In 1961, Billy Swan came to Memphis with a song he'd written, "Lover Please." Bill Black recorded it with an artist he had under contract called Dennis Turner. Singleton takes up the story:

"I tried to buy the master from Bill Black, but he wasn't selling. The record was breaking wide open in St. Louis, and I told Bill that if he didn't sell me the master I was going to cover him. He said, 'Go ahead, you can't take it away from me.' So I covered him—and did. We had a session set up for Clyde, but we didn't have a song I thought was strong enough. I decided to put 'Lover Please' on the session. Clyde didn't want to record it. He thought it was a terrible piece of material. I said, 'Okay, Clyde, you can cut three songs you want if you cut "Lover Please" for me.' I got Stan Applebaum to do the arrangements because he was very hot with the Drifters at that time. When it got to the middle break, he had an elaborate arrangement with violins and oboes. I didn't like it, so I got King Curtis to play the sax solo and got all the string and woodwind players to clap hands. Some of them were afraid they were going to hurt their hands. After the session, I cut thirty acetates, sent them out to Mercury's promo people, and told them to take the acetates to the pop stations. Every station put it on the air immediately."

It peaked at No. 7 and became Clyde McPhatter's biggest hit on Mercury. Even so, that didn't mean McPhatter could retire off the royalties: "'Lover Please' probably sold 700,000 or 900,000 copies," said Singleton. "Artists were mostly signed to contracts calling for five percent of retail. Singles retailed at 99 cents, so the artist was getting five cents a record. So Clyde would have made $35,000 on a hit, but recording costs were deducted, and the album sessions that followed might have eaten up as much as $20,000 of the $35,000. Most acts back then made their money off personal appearances. Records were their advertisements."

The hits grew ever smaller after "Lover Please." Shelby Singleton tried all kinds of experiments; none worked. His last bold move on McPhatter's behalf was to commission a concept album, *Songs of the Big City*, inspired by the success of *West Side Story*-styled ghetto records like "Spanish Harlem," "Up on the Roof," and "Uptown." Singleton brought in Alan Lorber to direct the project. Lorber had made his mark producing and arranging at Scepter-Wand Records, and went on to arrange several early '60s urban classics that have weathered well.

Lorber played to McPhatter's strengths. "Clyde had such a beau-tiful velvet voice," he said. "His voice had a sound that had to be very carefully cast. He was a very fragile man, and you had to watch for sparks. Sometimes, something in the arrangement would ignite him and he would dig much deeper into himself. He was drinking and singing off-pitch, so we laid down a scratch vocal and Clyde went in and redid it later. He had that vulnerability in his voice. He was half-way to the grave, I guess, but that enhanced the fragility of his performances."

If the sessions held a bitter irony it was that several of the songs McPhatter and Lorber decided on, such as "On Broadway," "Up on the Roof," and "Spanish Harlem," had been hits for the Drifters or ex-Drifters. Ten years after leaving the group he founded, McPhatter was following desultorily in their footsteps. "Deep in the Heart of Harlem," a single pulled from the *Songs of the Big City* LP, spent two weeks on the charts peaking at No. 91. It would be Clyde McPhatter's last hit.

Lena

Anecdotal evidence suggests that the ups and downs of Clyde McPhatter's career were played out against a troubled personal life. With proceeds from his early success, he bought a house in Englewood, New Jersey, near a house he'd bought for his parents in Teaneck. He sent his younger brothers to private school in New York. His first wife, Nora, is a shadowy figure. An early press release said that she had sat behind him in junior high school. "During our nine years of marriage," Clyde said in 1962, "her companionship has been a wonderful part of my life." That year, they divorced. McPhatter started dating Lena Rackley. Originally from South Carolina, Lena was working at the time for *Ebony* magazine in New York. Clyde closed up his house in Englewood, but couldn't find a buyer. In the meantime, he lived in an apartment on 57th Street in New York. Lena lived on 90th Street, and she and her three poodles would take taxi rides to Clyde's place.

"He was really a home person," said Lena. "He liked to eat and I liked to cook. He played a lot of records at home, including a lot of his own records. He'd play them back and try to perfect his technique." Clyde and Lena married in 1965. Wedding notices mentioned that she was a vice-president of Atlantic Fiscal Corporation at the time. They reopened the house in Englewood. "We built a swimming pool," said Lena, "and Clyde would invite underprivileged children to come and swim. He never had any children himself, and in the end we adopted

113

Patrick, who was his uncle's grandson. We brought him up from Raeford, North Carolina. The adoption wasn't complete when Clyde died, so I adopted him."

The photos in Lena's scrapbook show a happy suburban couple, small dogs around their feet. Clyde's parents came over for cookouts, and his brother Joe lived in Englewood, as did Clyde Otis. The black middle-class society in New Jersey left Clyde deeply ill-at-ease, though. "He associated with doctors and lawyers," said Lena, "and to them he was a star, but he had a real inferiority complex because he had never graduated from school. I told him that he had a talent that these doctors and lawyers would love to have. I had a college education, but I never threw it in his face. I tried to use my education to help him. I even thought about becoming his manager, but I had no background in it."

As success faded, McPhatter's drinking grew worse. He would hole up in his apartment on 57th Street. Shelby Singleton was in the same building. "Clyde used to come in at four or five in the morning," said Singleton. "He'd beat on my door, wake me up and want to talk about why he was black and I was white. Clyde and I were fairly good friends but I was getting sick of this. I said, 'Clyde, if you wake me up one more time, I'm gonna shoot you. You know I ain't got nothin' to do but wake up at four or five in the morning and talk to you.' He left me alone for a month or two, then one night he was half-drunk and he rang the door-bell over and over. I got up, looked through the peephole, saw it was him, went back to the other room, took a .22 pistol, loaded it with blanks and went back to the door. I said, 'Who is it?' He said, 'Clyde.' I opened the door, shot six blanks at him, slammed the door and locked it. Didn't say a word. Looked out the peephole and saw him go back into his apartment. The next day he called about three in the afternoon. He said, 'Hi Shelby.' I said, 'Hi Clyde, I ain't seen you in a while. Where you been?' He said, 'Oh, I been on the road. I got in late last night. I went to bed and had the damnedest dream. I dreamed I went to your door and you jerked the door open and shot me. It was so real even my chest is sore.' I said, 'Really?' He said, 'Yeah, it was the realest dream I ever had in my life.' The blanks had paper wads in them that had hit him in the chest and stung him. I never did tell him any different."

The problem was that McPhatter was a loner who hated being alone. "All the years I knew Clyde," said Singleton, "I never knew him to have any personal friends. You'd never see him with the same person twice."

The last Mercury album was cut live at the Apollo. It wasn't the landmark album that James Brown's Apollo album had been, but it showed that Clyde McPhatter could have had a place in the coming soul music explosion if he'd found the right songs and the right producers.

"We still had the home in New Jersey," said Lena, "but Clyde couldn't spend like he used to. People were calling for money and he couldn't afford full-time musicians any more. One time I even had to play piano on stage with him." McPhatter also saw his physical appearance change. He had been a strikingly handsome young man, but had been wearing increasingly obvious toupees since 1960, each one more luxuriant than the last. His features were becoming coarser. "Clyde was very vain," said Clyde Otis. "He cared an awful lot about his appearance. It was paradoxical. We all cared an awful lot about him, but we couldn't reach him. Couldn't reason with him. I felt it imperative to talk about the things that were destroying him, but there were tremendous problems just being with him." One of those problems was the issue of McPhatter's sexuality. He had been told he was effeminate for singing in a high voice, and he saw his inability to father a child as further proof of his effeminacy. He had tried to live in a normal family setting but it wasn't working out. He had been attracted to men all his life, and came to believe that he was gay when in fact he was probably bisexual.

It galled McPhatter when singers like Smokey Robinson and Dee Clark began doing well with what he regarded as his style. He was 35, but the industry had collectively decided that it was unreturned-phone-call time. Clyde Otis, who was ultrasensitive to racial issues, detected something else in McPhatter. "He had no problem with the racists down South. They were what they were," said Otis. "His problem was dealing with the white power structure in New York in the music business. He thought he had earned a certain level of respect, which was not forthcoming." It all preyed upon Clyde McPhatter, a man much given to worry and self-doubt at the best of times. After he and Lena adopted the baby, their relationship fell apart. "I tried to get him in for treatment for alcoholism, but there were no programs in those days," she said. "For me it was a matter of survival and retaining the sanity for the baby, so I decided to go."

115

England

It's hard to know what motivated Clyde McPhatter to take up residence in England. Perhaps he believed the focus of the music business was shifting there. Perhaps it represented a fresh start. Perhaps he hoped that he would be different in a different country. He had toured there in March 1960 with Duane Eddy and Bobby Darin, but he was hardly a household name. He had seen just one hit, "The Treasure of Love." McPhatter left Boston on the overnight flight on January 30, 1968. He arrived at Heathrow Airport the following morning with $2 in his pocket and a copy of a record he hoped to lease. He had an offer of work at $1,000 a week from Universal Dancing, but he didn't have a work permit. At noon, McPhatter was on a flight back to New York. A few days later, he arrived back. "I have not felt so content in my life for years," he told the British music press. "I felt I was becoming stagnant in America. What started fifteen years ago as an extremely enjoyable way of life where I was performing my art turned into just a job. I was playing the same venues and just making money. So many artists have come to see me and said they patterned themselves on me—Jackie Wilson, Smokey Robinson, Dee Clark, Bobby Hendricks—just about every lead singer of vocal groups in America. I felt it my duty to expand." He said he was selling his house in the United States and planning to buy a place in England.

There were two singles for the Deram imprint of British Decca, then McPhatter signed with Tony Stratton-Smith's B&C/Action/Charisma Records, the label that later launched Genesis. One single flopped, and a planned LP never materialized. McPhatter was arrested in 1968 for importuning young men (or "loitering with intent," as the British legal system quaintly termed it). Depositions from the case provided a rather desolate picture of his finances, and showed that the new beginning wasn't amounting to much. McPhatter had made just $368 from the sale of his house in Englewood. His royalties from Atlantic totaled just under three thousand dollars that year, and Atlantic's Progressive Music paid him a shade under five hundred. BMI paid him $11, and he was still unrecouped at MGM and Mercury. The British gigs were paying around £150 to £275 a week. He often worked for as little as £15 a night.

On August 1, 1970, Clyde McPhatter returned home.

The End

McPhatter had nowhere to go but his parents' house, the house he had bought them in less troubled times. He began picking up gigs on the oldies circuit.

"I had heard he was back," said Clyde Otis, "and I'd never got him out of my mind. I rang him and asked him what his plans were. He said he didn't have any. He just needed to come back. I spoke to the people at [U.S.] Decca. I said, 'Clyde McPhatter's back. I don't know what his condition is, but why don't we do an album called *Welcome Home?*' We did, but it didn't sell very well. It was a travesty really. I just couldn't keep him sober. We recorded in Philadelphia. Gamble and Huff were very popular and we were using their sidemen. I'd look out from the control room and Clyde would be sneaking a bottle out from somewhere in his garments. I confronted him about it, and he said, 'I just can't sing unless I'm drinking now.' When I heard that, I just gave up."

We can only guess at McPhatter's frustration singing "Lover Please" and "Ta-Ta" twice a night when he wanted to grow as an artist. He called Jerry Wexler and Shelby Singleton, but they turned him away. He tried for a reconciliation with Lena, but she could see that his problems were worse than ever. He was interviewed by Marcia Vance at Brooklyn's Camelot Inn on April 29, 1972. When she was introduced to him as one of his fans, McPhatter looked up bleakly and said, "I have no fans." On May 24, he appeared at OD's club in Houston. The *Houston Post* reported that he kissed the pianist's neck, stumbled around the stage, and unzipped his fly. OD canceled the remainder of the shows.

By now the chest pains from an enlarged heart were causing McPhatter considerable distress. He had found a woman named Bertha who liked to keep him company on his binges. On the night of June 12–13, 1972, they went to bed after an evening of heavy drinking. Bertha woke up; McPhatter did not. There were short, "famous long ago" obituaries; one or two bracketed him with Basie's blues shouter Jimmy Rushing who died the same week. Rushing was 68; Clyde McPhatter was 39.

117

Tommy Sands

Nancy Sinatra Between the Sheets

●●●●●●●●●●●●●●●●

Tommy Sands

Bill Millar

Shreveport is one of those cities (Cincinnati, Dallas, and Springfield are others) that just missed being Nashville. The focus of the music business in Shreveport was KWKH, a 50,000-watt clear channel station that hosted a Saturday night jamboree, much like the "Grand Ole Opry" on WSM, Nashville. The Opry attracted its fair share of talent, but when KWKH's "Louisiana Hayride" dubbed itself "The Cradle of the Stars" it wasn't kidding. The artists who got their start there included Hank Williams, Kitty Wells, Faron Young, Webb Pierce, Slim Whitman, Johnny Cash, Jim Reeves, Johnny Horton, Claude King, Elvis, and Tommy Sands among others.

Sands was one of the great might-have-been, should-have-been stories in rock 'n' roll. He had the looks, the talent, the drive, and the major label deal. All the right factors went into the equation to deliver the wrong answer. His story runs curiously parallel to Elvis's. Not only did they both start on the Hayride, but their ambitions did not begin and end with country music. More than anything, the Tommy Sands story is a study in frustration. Success seemed tantalizingly close a few times, only to disappear from view. (C. E.)

T ommy Sands had been the one to watch. His was thought to be the next golden larynx after Elvis's, and he was the boy considered most likely to survive when the hip-swiveling stopped. Unlike Elvis, a phenomenon of mystified repulsion to many adults, Sands was seen as a neater, PG-13 model; a conservatively groomed, threat-extracted innocent who grinned when he could have sneered. His biggest hits, which wallowed in teenage ritual and adolescent mooning, reinforced the air of inoffensive soppiness. Alone among early rockers, Sands started out with uninteresting material that got better. By 1959 he was into crude, hard-driving music with a fine rockabilly band. But it couldn't last. Torn between the urge to make decent records and the crushing embrace of show business, Tommy Sands became the lost boy of rock 'n' roll, denied glowing references in the history books and long regarded with skepticism even by those who ordinarily liked the music.

Thomas Adrian Sands was born of Scots and Irish ancestry in Chicago's Grant Hospital on August 27, 1937. Benny, his father, was a professional pianist who traveled away from home a good deal. His mother, formerly Grace Lou Dixon, spent some time as a band vocalist including several years with Art Kassell's orchestra. She'd been raised in Louisiana and frequently took the children, including Sands' half-brother, Edward, to stay with relatives who owned a farm near Greenwood, a few miles from Shreveport. For part of the year, Sands went to school in Chicago where his father played the hotel lounges. In the winter, when Benny went out on the road, his wife returned to Louisiana with the children. That was how early publicity put it; according to Sands, his parents were always fighting, splitting up, and getting back together again.

Tommy was not a blissfully contented child. At Greenwood Grade School he was teased for being a "Yankee." Brother Ed, 11 years older, couldn't provide the companionship he needed. By the age of 7, he was infatuated with country music. "Tommy," his mother recalled, "haunted the radio the way other kids haunt the icebox. He'd rather listen to the radio than eat, sleep, or romp around. No sooner would I settle down in another room when he'd be after me to come back. 'Mama,' he'd yell, 'it's Jimmie Davis! Mama, it's Harmie Smith! Listen to those guitars.'" Mrs. Sands put a down payment on a guitar in time for the boy's seventh Christmas: "It became a part of him, flesh and soul. He taught himself at first because we couldn't afford the instrument and lessons. He played all the time, before school and after, evenings and weekends. We all felt he was getting real clever at it but none of us realized how clever until we went shopping in Shreveport and he walked into the radio station and got himself an honest-to-goodness job."

At eight years of age, Sands had toddled into KWKH lugging a guitar as big as himself. Station manager Henry Clay was probably as much amused as impressed, but the child became a twice-weekly afternoon attraction at $2.50 per performance. "At first," producer Pop Echols remembered, "I told the audience not to expect too much but we were surprised. Tommy cut out with the prettiest rendition of 'Oklahoma Hills' you ever heard."

Sands took to the South. He spent hours in H. C. (Hard Cash) Wilkerson's J&S Music Store listening to hillbilly records; he joined the Greenwood Methodist Church and stood on an apple crate to preach; he even told classmates that he was born in "South" Chicago and that made him a rebel. Back in Chicago he appeared on WBKB-TV's "Barn Dance," and *TV Forecast* lived up to its name by predicting that Sands was a star in the process of rising.

Down South, Sands began singing with Harmie Smith, one of his earliest inspirations. Others included Hank Williams and his namesake, Tex; Tommy was obsessed with Tex Williams's 1947 hit, "Smoke, Smoke, Smoke that Cigarette." He and Harmie were heard on KWKH where Sands, now 10 or 11, dressed in a cowboy outfit and sang "My Mommy Bought Me an Ice-cream Cone." Tillman Franks, who'd played bass with Pop Echols, gave the kid a few tips. Franks also worked on Webb Pierce and would later make a star out of Johnny Horton. It was probably Franks who persuaded Horace Logan, producer of KWKH's "Louisiana Hayride," to give Sands a shot. Logan wasn't too keen: "I was inclined to class Tommy as one of the 'maybes.' He was attractive and winning but many lads of twelve will please a crowd. I definitely felt his talent was in the projection of a song rather than in any unusual quality of voice. I hesitated at taking on Tommy but, luckily for my reputation as a talent scout, I did put him on the Hayride." Sands made his Hayride debut on September 3, 1949; he sang "Candy Kisses," a hit for George Morgan. Nine months later, on his final appearance (May 27, 1950) he sang "Who Shot a Hole in My Sombrero."

That same year, Mr. and Mrs. Sands divorced. For a while, Tommy stayed with his father in Chicago before rejoining his mother in Greenwood. Ever ambitious for her youngest son, Mrs. Sands thought Houston might provide a wider audience for his talents and Tillman Franks agreed to take him. They sought out prominent deejay Biff Collie, who also hosted KPRC-TV's "Hoedown Corner." Sands appeared in a spot sponsored by Sun-Up Ice Cream.

Houston's Sidney Lanier Junior High School welcomed Sands as a ninth-grade student. He pursued an interest in acting as well as singing. "Crowds liked him," recalled Horace Logan with the benefit of hindsight, "but I felt it was more for his personality than his singing talent. As an actor, I knew he'd make it." Sands played a sensitive adolescent in *The Magic Fallacy* at the Alley Theater ("The kid has something on the acting ball," noted the Houston press). He also appeared in a radio series on KXYZ and alongside Reginald Owen in *Open House*, a play that narrowly missed a Broadway opening.

In 1951, Sands cut his first record for Saul Kahl's Freedom label. When he sang with Biff Collie and the Hoedown Corner Gang he'd usually concentrate on Little Jimmy Dickens's uptempo novelty songs, and "Love Pains" and "Syrup Soppin' Blues" had their Dickensish aspects. Credited to Little Tommy Sands (the West's Wonder Boy), he sang with an assurance and maturity that his teachers attributed to his association with older people in radio drama. But the Houston-based Freedom label was known for its R&B roster and nothing on its hillbilly series sold very well.

By 1952, Sands had been taken under the wing of Colonel Tom Parker's Jamboree Attractions, then representing Pee Wee King, Jimmie Davis, Mac Wiseman, and Eddy Arnold whose RCA Victor records had already sold 25 million copies. Parker, who had heard Sands singing at a Houston club, placed him with RCA, a move that raised his profile without shifting too many records. His RCA discs (seven during 1953–1955) were pure cornball. He rerecorded "Love Pains" and covered "A Dime and a Dollar" from the movie *Red Garters*. Guy Mitchell, the knee-slapping star of the film, sold more copies.

1954 was a busy year, and the trade papers reported Sands' affairs in increasingly attentive detail. By June, he was voted Thirteenth Most Promising Male Vocalist in *Cashbox*'s Folk and Western Poll. Before the year was out, he'd covered Terry Fell's minor hit "Don't Drop It," staged appearances with Biff Collie at Houston high schools (Sands was still a full-time student at Lamar Senior High), and obtained a three-hour show as a deejay on Houston's KNUZ, where he received a visit from Capitol's A&R man, Ken Nelson. "Biff asked me if I would go and talk to Tommy because he was feeling down in the dumps," Nelson told Rob Finnis. "I said 'Sure.' So I went to the station and I spent two hours while he was doing his deejay show and after that we went to dinner. He took me to a hamburger stand in a beat-up old Ford he had. I listened to his record on Victor and I said to him, 'If I were you, I would write to Mr. Sholes [RCA's country A&R man Steve Sholes—then toying with the idea of signing Elvis] and ask him not to record you for at least another two years.' He was recording the wrong kind of stuff. It just wasn't Tommy Sands, it wasn't the right kind of song for him. What I didn't know was that Tommy had that day gotten a letter from Steve saying he was off of Victor. Anyway, what happened was, I said to Tommy then 'Tommy, if you get off Victor and you're still around and you haven't got a record contract in a couple of years you come to see me and I'll sign you. You can't sell immaturity in a voice.'" Nelson concluded, "The only thing an artist has to sell is their emotions and a kid that young is not emotionally developed. Brenda Lee was the only one able to get through."

Early in 1955 Sands appeared with Elvis Presley on shows Biff Collie promoted in Houston. Sands' girlfriend, Betty Moers, recalled leaving Eagles Hall with Sands and Presley whose first pink Cadillac had been stripped of its hubcaps: "Elvis was getting popular by then but he wasn't being mobbed by souvenir-hunters. So it's anybody's guess whether they were taken by fans, vandals, or plain old thieves."

A year or so later, Presley put a call through to Sands while the teenaged deejay was hosting "Tommy's Corral" on KCIJ, a Shreveport station which he'd flunked graduation to join. Mindful of Sands' prowess as an actor, Presley promised to try and get him a part in his first picture. Fellow KCIJ deejay, Vern Stierman, was impressed by Sands' ambition: "The Sands's made no bones about their plan to get to Hollywood as soon as possible. They lived simple, worked hard and saved, saved, saved. Mrs. Sands tried to get Tommy to rest more but he had the bit between his teeth and he had to keep going. The nights he wasn't making personal appearances he'd pick up extra money doing TV commercials. All the while the dream got bigger and bigger. You could just see him reaching…."

Sands left Texas in May 1956. He and his mother moved to an apartment in the Hollywood hills, close to Pasadena where his half-brother and family were living. He auditioned for Cliffie Stone's "Hometown Jamboree," which went out live on Saturday night over KTLA-TV. Stone, who also managed Tennessee Ernie Ford and effectively A&R'd many of Capitol's country sessions, became Sands' manager (Colonel Parker, who didn't get along with Mrs. Sands, had dropped out of the picture, although he and Tommy remained friends). Despite Stone's ties with Capitol Records, Sands was not signed to the

123

label immediately. Nonetheless, he was about to define the phrase "overnight sensation."

In December 1956, Sands was invited to New York to audition for the leading role in the "Kraft Theater Hour" production of *The Singin' Idol*, a play by Paul Monash. Teens ordinarily watched "Kraft Theater Hour" because this NBC-TV series often featured singers in dramatic roles (e.g., Ferlin Husky and Julius La Rosa). Indeed, the part of an up-and-coming rock 'n' roller had been offered to Elvis Presley upon whom the story was loosely based. Presley, however, was now fully committed and Colonel Parker pitched for Sands, who got the job.

When Ken Nelson heard that Sands had landed an hour's prime-time TV he kept his promise and drew up a five-year contract with Capitol. "Teenage Crush," the song chosen for Sands' Capitol debut, was written by Joe and Audrey Allison, then in their mid-30s. Joe was a country deejay at WMAK in Nashville where he acted as a representative for Cliffie Stone's Central Songs, a company which Ken Nelson surreptitiously owned. Three years on, Joe and Audrey would give Jim Reeves's career a lift with "He'll Have to Go."

On January 30, 1957, Sands sang "Teenage Crush" in *The Singin' Idol* and NBC was swamped with 8,000 requests for information and pictures (7,000 more than they'd ever received before). Released the day after the broadcast, "Teenage Crush" reached the Top 3 in both *Billboard* and *Cashbox* (and Kraft probably sold an awful lot of cheese). The song was not an instantly memorable pop masterpiece nor was Sands' mush-mouthed singing especially attractive; he'd been advised to lose his southern accent if he wanted to work in films. Nonetheless, Sands wore the magic halo that provoked calf-love in abundance, and thousands of teenaged girls gave a sensational boost to a career that had struggled for a dozen years. Within 24 hours, he was offered contracts by four major film companies, including Twentieth Century Fox, which bought the rights to *The Singin' Idol*.

The question has to be asked: How could someone who "played" at being a rock 'n' roll singer do so much better than the dozens of truly authentic artists whose telephones rarely rang? Sands himself has no illusions: "It wasn't because of the song. It was the impact of the TV show. Every girl in America was watching that show just to see what an Elvis Presley was like, and the story happened to be a real tear-jerker. It was an excellent drama, the kind of role that was destined to make whoever played it a star."

Sessions in March 1957 produced "Ring-A-Ding-A-Ding," which climbed to No. 50 in *Billboard*, and a revival of Faron Young's breakthrough hit, "Goin' Steady," which became Sands' second and last Top-20 hit. On March 27, he sang "Friendly Persuasion" at the Oscars ceremony, and on April 10 he was on *This Is Your Life*. The host, Ralph Edwards, had told his director: "Look, with a kid like Tommy we could reassure millions of parents that rock 'n' roll is not nearly as dangerous as they think."

There was nothing remotely subversive about the first album, *Steady Date with Tommy Sands*, which contained ten shriveled old standards from writers who were born in the previous century. It reached No. 4 on the LP charts where it stayed for 18 weeks. Elvis, Ricky Nelson, Pat Boone, and Fabian sold more albums than Sands but no other roughly contemporaneous teen idol came close.

Sands never quite lived up to that first public burst of fame. The "Next Elvis" tag became an instant burden and his new manager, movie executive Ted Wick, lacked Colonel Parker's entreprenurial acumen. Sands' material was also badly judged. Ken Nelson, who preferred show tunes to rock 'n' roll, generally chose the songs. Much of the time, Nelson had the good sense to supervise rock 'n' roll sessions without imposing his own artistic values, but for Sands' fourth single he picked "Let Me Be Loved," the theme song from *The James Dean Story*. It was written by Ray Evans and Jay Livingston, the Tin Pan Alley tunesmiths responsible for "Mona Lisa," as well as "Buttons and Bows," Nelson's very first hit back in 1948. That Sands could sing this stuff was without question; his voice was smooth, accurate, versatile and technically accomplished, but those around Sands profoundly misunderstood or misinterpreted what was happening. It would not be long before Tommy Sands could walk unmolested in public places.

Sands himself wrote his fifth single, "Man Like Wow!" It oozed rock 'n' roll toughness but sold like Bibles in Baghdad. He had to be seen as well as heard. In late 1957, Sands reprised *The Singin' Idol* role in *Sing Boy Sing*, filmed by Twentieth Century Fox who'd already made movies with Elvis and Pat Boone. He played Virgil Walker, an orphan raised in the South by his gospel-preaching grandfather and aunt. Grandad wants Virgil to thump the Bible too, but he's lured into the corrupt world of rock 'n' roll by a duplicitous manager (none other than veteran Hollywood heavy Edmond O'Brien, who'd been a singing gangster in *The Girl Can't Help It*). The kid's a hit but when grandpa

125

Tommy Sands

suffers a heart attack Virgil promises to give up rocking for religion. He's saved from this dreadful dilemma by his aunt who convinces him that God wants him to sing. Roles were built in for three disc jockeys (including Biff Collie), and the film was well received by *Variety*: "Tommy is not only a slim and vital juvenile but, what is more unexpected, he is a surprisingly sensitive and sincere young actor."

The sound track, which reached No. 17 on the LP chart in 1958, lived up to its title with a dozen unexpectedly eclectic songs. Neo-blues (Sands' own "Your Daddy Wants to Do Right") crackled alongside gospel (Martha Carson's "I'm Gonna Walk and Talk with My Lord") and pop-country songs like "That's All I Want from You." Sands cut the title track on three occasions. There was a version for the sound track with Lionel Newman's orchestra in November 1957 and a faster (unissued) rendition accompanied only by drums, and the single. The song was written by Sands and Rod McKuen, the actor and best-selling poet who also penned the title track for Universal's *Rock Pretty Baby* in which he starred.

Next came Sands' R&B album, *Sandstorm*, recorded over five days in April 1958. It demonstrates a real affection for the verities of black popular music. In an interview with British deejay Stuart Colman, Sands elaborated on the importance of R&B during his high school years: "All the kids were switching off the country channels and the pop music stations that played 'Oh! My Pa-pa' and stuff like that, and we were looking for something else, and we found race music, R&B. We used to go out at lunch and sit in our cars at the back of the school and listen on the sly to the black music. It wasn't accepted in our homes, and you couldn't hear it anywhere else so we'd get radios and get off in the woods someplace and listen to the R&B stations. Elvis was doing the same thing in Memphis, James Burton's doing the same thing in Shreveport and out in Lubbock, Texas, Buddy Holly's doing the same thing. We're all about to come together with these black roots combined with our country and western roots."

127

Tommy Sands came closest to perfection in the summer of 1958. By this time he'd met up with the Raiders, a rockabilly band led by Scotty Turner who played guitar like a virtuoso and wrote material that stimulated Sands' finest instincts. Sands' best recording, "The Worryin' Kind" (written by Turner and Diane Lampert under the pseudonym of Allison Dewar), featured Turner's matchlessly pure rock 'n' roll riffs. His short solos do little more than restate the melody but they shine with power and authority. Sands and the Raiders featured "The Worryin' Kind" on the "Milton Berle Show." Berle liked the beat so much he asked the band to play it again while he adlibbed some lyrics about the show's sponsors.

Turner is almost a story within a story. Born Graham M. Turnbull in Sydney, Nova Scotia, on August 23, 1931, he received a track scholarship from Dubuque University in Iowa where he ran 100 yards in 9.6 seconds. In 1957, while completing an advanced degree at Texas Tech in Lubbock, he wrote a clutch of songs with Buddy Holly. The year before, he'd been introduced to fellow student, Hal Goodson, leader of a group Goodson had formed in high school. The pair quickly formed a new band with Turner on guitar and Leon Bagwell on bass. Renamed the Raiders, they trekked to Norman Petty's studio in Clovis where they cut a rockabilly single with Goodson on vocals. This emerged on a Hollywood label and the band left Texas for California taking a rhythm guitarist, Eddie Edwards, with them. There, according to Turner, "we starved until Tommy Sands heard us and then we traveled with him all over the world."

It was Sands who insisted that the Raiders should get a drummer. Ted Wick hired Hal Blaine who was playing the Garden of Allah, a Hollywood jazz lounge, with the Carol Simpson Quartet. A smart Jewish kid who moved out West at 14, Blaine was quick to admit his strict jazz background: "These Texas fellas immediately started training me and I found I was very fond of this country music. Songs like 'My Bucket's Got a Hole In It,' songs which I'd never even dreamed existed." Blaine, a few years older than Sands, doubled as road manager and kept the boys in line.

Texan desert blues-rock could have been Sands' new direction but the hour was getting late and "I Ain't Gettin' Rid of You" didn't catch on. Capitol pulled "I'll Be Seeing You" off a smoochy album with Nelson Riddle and it bisected the Hot 100 in October 1959. That, in effect, put paid to Sands' rock 'n' roll releases. One unreleased rocker, "Wicked Woman," got an airing on the other side of the world. Sands and the Raiders (now renamed the Sharks) toured Australia, and the band took an interest in local artists and played on a number of their records. "Wicked Woman," written by Hal Blaine, was released on the Teen label by New Zealand rocker, Johnny Devlin. Turner and Blaine played on the record.

When Sands stopped rocking, Turner and Blaine remained in Hollywood as sessionmen. Turner played on Gene Vincent's *Crazy Beat* album, and worked for Guy Mitchell and Eddie Fisher. In the mid-1960s he worked for the fledgling A&M Records, where his tunes got the Baja Marimba Band off the ground. He's written for Wynn Stewart, Dean Martin, Tennessee Ernie Ford, and Eddy Arnold. "Shutters and Boards," a smash hit for Jerry Wallace, was cowritten by Turner and his good friend Audie Murphy. He and America's most decorated war hero also penned "When the Wind Blows in Chicago" for Roy Clark. After a brief stint as manager of Central Songs, Turner was invited to

128

head Liberty-United Artists' country music department where he produced Slim Whitman, Del Reeves, Penny DeHaven, and fellow guitar maestro, Jimmy Bryant.

Hal Blaine became the Rolls Royce of drummers, with a carefully kept log book numbering many thousands of sessions. If you've got any kind of record collection, Blaine's in it somewhere. He's the light touch behind John Denver and the thunder behind Phil Spector. Anonymity beckoned the other Raiders, Leon Bagwell and Eddie Edwards.

Sands stayed with Capitol and the tuxedoed supper-club circuit until his contract expired. There were more movies (eight in all) and a lot more records. He was on Vista, ABC-Paramount, Liberty, Imperial (Scotty Turner producing), Superscope, and Brunswick. Following the breakup of his much-publicized marriage to Nancy Sinatra (1960–1965), he worked out of Hawaii for 20 years. Hal Blaine again: "Tommy more or less quit the business. Rumors had it that Frank Sinatra put out the word that Sands was not to work anywhere, but insiders knew it was total hogwash. Tommy called me just prior to his move to Hawaii and told me he didn't really want to work anymore. He wanted to find himself and get back on the right track. He just had to get away and what better place than Hawaii...."

There were a nightclub and a clothing business, a second marriage and another divorce. Eventually, promoter Paul Barrett, who'd never forgotten Sands' gospel-shouting entrance in *Sing Boy Sing*, brought him to England for a rock 'n' roll festival at Brean in 1990. For one so long regarded as an opportunist teen idol, he proved eminently capable of unbuttoning rock 'n' roll's raw spirit. "Y'know," he told Stuart Colman, "Capitol could have gotten a lot more out of me if they had let me do what they let Gene Vincent do. It wasn't called rockabilly then but that's what I was singing when Ken Nelson first heard me in Houston. 'Teenage Crush,' 'I'll Be Seeing You'. ... that kind of middle-of-the-road sound was a sound that I just never really liked. It wasn't really my thing. The thing that I grew up with, what I really felt comfortable doing, was the kind of stuff your kids here found twenty or thirty years later. *Sandstorm* was not a big hit but it's my favorite album. And 'The Worryin' Kind' is the only song I ever did in one take, that's my favorite record. But people over 25 thought rock 'n' roll was a passing fad. Nobody realized it was the birth of the new American music."

For all that he wanted it otherwise, Tommy Sands is little more

129

than a footnote in rock 'n' roll history, famous mostly for bedding Nancy Sinatra. If he's cited in any other context, it's usually as a prototypical manufactured teenage idol. There was more to Sands than that, but just as there are no prizes for *almost* hitting the game-winning run out of the ballpark, so there are no prizes for *almost* making it.

These notes accompanied The Worryin' Kind, *a single CD "best of" Sands' Capitol recordings (BCD 15643).*

10

Springfield, Missouri:
Bop A Lena
Ronnie Self

Colin Escott

Springfield was another of the cities that might have been Nashville. The "Ozark Jubilee" was the focus of the local country music scene. Hosted by Red Foley, the Jubilee was the first networked television country music series. Starting in 1954, it was a magnet for talent in much the same way as the "Grand Ole Opry" and the "Louisiana Hayride," but—like the Hayride—the Jubilee simply became an Opry farm club. Nashville's preeminence was well established by the time the Jubilee folded in 1960, but the country music scene in the Ozarks didn't roll over and die. In the late '80s, Branson (some 60 miles south of Springfield) posed the first pointed challenge to Nashville in 30 years.

Ronnie Self came out of the Springfield scene. He yo-yoed between Springfield and Nashville, all the while dreaming of the record that would make him as big as the artists he wrote for. Most songwriters don't crave the limelight and realize early in their career that they simply don't have what it takes as a singer. Self not only craved the limelight, but knew that he had what it took to make it as a singer. That knowledge probably accelerated the descent into the alcoholism and mental imbalance chronicled here. (C. E.)

If ever there was a record that neatly encapsulated everything that was different about rock 'n' roll, it was Ronnie Self's "Bop A Lena." This *wasn't* a white kid playing R&B; it was something else again. "Bop A Lena" highlighted most of the differences between rock 'n' roll and R&B. The core difference was that R&B was adult music; rock 'n' roll was teenage music. The subject matter was worlds apart. The nonsensicality of songs like "Be-Bop-a-Lula" and "Bop A Lena" owed more to dumb early '50s pop songs like "Hoop Dee Doo" than to any R&B song. The nervous, twitchy energy of rock 'n' roll came from white kids setting out in search of R&B and hopelessly overreaching. In singing their nonsense songs and in overstating the mellow charms of R&B, they found something new. Rock 'n' roll was exaggeration and overstatement. It was hormonally out of control. It was *feel* over everything. The whole point about guys like Ronnie Self and many of the 1950s rock 'n' rollers is that they *didn't* understand R&B, and didn't understand the virtue of laying back. "Bop A Lena" started over the top and built up from there.

Ronnie Self also proved the link between talent and instability. Just as success seemed to be within his grasp, he'd self-destruct. His songwriting eventually gave him a fairly steady income, but, with the exception of the larynx-searing "Bop A Lena," which spent seven weeks in the charts, peaking at No. 63, he was hitless as a performer.

Ronnie Self was born in Tin Town, Missouri, some 30 miles north of Springfield, on July 5, 1938. He was the oldest of five children, and his parents, Raymond and Hazel, ran a farm for a few years before moving to Springfield where Raymond took a job with the railroad. The relationship between Ronnie and his parents is somewhat clouded. "When I first met him," said his wife, Dorothy, "he carried a Bible in his pocket and talked of being able to make enough money to get his folks out of poverty, but as the years went on he showed an increasing hostility toward them that I never really understood."

From the outset, Ronnie was unstable, temperamental, and confrontational. His brother Sammy told interviewer Lloyd Hicks that Ronnie once sawed down a tree so that the school bus could not get to their house. He's also reckoned to have hit a teacher with a baseball bat some years before it became commonplace. Then, when he was 14, he somehow acquired a car, drove to California with a few songs he had written, sold them, and came home.

Since 1954, KWTO (Keep Watching the Ozarks) in Springfield had hosted the "Ozark Jubilee." The Jubilee went out on ABC-TV with hokey, avuncular Red Foley heading the regular cast. Si Siman was one of the producers. "Ronnie was in and out of the station with demos," said Siman, "and showed all kinds of promise as a prolific writer." The train of events that found Self in Nashville cutting his first session for

Ronnie Self

Ronnie Self on the Philip Morris Caravan

ABC Records seems to go roughly like this: Jubilee regular Bobby Lord was in Siman's office, heard Self, and set up a demo session that he took to his manager, Dub Allbritten, in Nashville. "Dub called Ronnie," says Ronnie's sister, Vicki, "and sent him some money to get to Nashville. He rode down with one of the Foggy River Boys who were on the Jubilee. He went and sang some more songs for Dub—he had fifty or a hundred at that time—and Dub called Jim Denny at Cedarwood Music in the middle of the night and they set up a session at eight the next morning for 'Pretty Bad Blues' and 'Three Hearts Later.'"

It could be that Ronnie ended up on the newly formed ABC Records because ABC-TV wanted to cross-promote its records on its television network. One single hit the market but no one noticed. A second record was scheduled and canceled. Allbritten had much stronger ties to Decca, and, after the ABC deal ended, tried to get Self on that label. Allbritten not only managed Ronnie Self, but also managed Webb Pierce (who owned a stake in Cedarwood Music), Red Foley, and another Jubilee regular, Brenda Lee, all of whom were on Decca. It was an incestuous business in those days, but Decca wouldn't bite.

Early in 1957, Allbritten assembled the cast for the Philip Morris Caravan. Apparently the idea for the Caravan began when Philip Morris organized some shows for its employees. Under Allbritten's guidance it became a traveling country music show that offered work to several country acts hit hard by rock 'n' roll. The tobacco company's motives weren't entirely altruistic. The tour was a peace offering to the southern white customers who had found out that Philip Morris had donated money to the NAACP. There were calls for a boycott of the company's products, and the tour was a way of smoothing things over and keeping some of the best customers loyal. The Caravan debuted in January 1957 with a cast that included Carl Smith, Red Sovine, Goldie Hill, Gordon Terry, Mimi Roman, and Ronnie Self. Admission was free to anyone bearing or smoking Philip Morris's product. Self was the token rockabilly. On a live album drawn from the show, his is the only cut derived from a studio session with dubbed applause. The reason might have been that his stage antics made live recording almost impossible.

"He'd start at the far back of the stage," recalled Vicki Self, "throw his guitar over his back and run out to the mic, grab the mic-stand and go right down on the floor with it and sing the first song. That was how he'd start. He'd never stop moving on stage. He'd turn around with his back to the audience and face the band, but he never stood still. He'd never talk to the crowd, just went from one song to another but the band never knew what it was gonna be."

By 1957, Columbia Records had gambled and lost on the bet that rock 'n' roll would go away. Rock 'n' rollers were still seen as mutant hillbillies, so it fell to Columbia's Nashville office to flesh out the label's rather meager rock 'n' roll roster. The task devolved to a debonair 55-year-old expatriate Englishman, Don Law, who had sung with the London Choral Society and probably despised rock 'n' roll every bit as much as his New York counterpart, Mitch Miller. Cedarwood was especially tight with Law, and Jim Denny probably persuaded him that Ronnie Self was just what Columbia needed. Law signed him on February 10, 1957 in a deal that called for a paltry 2 percent royalty. The first session, held on February 16, resulted in one single, "Big Fool"/ "Flame of Love," cut from pretty standard rockabilly cloth circa 1957.

The follow-up, recorded in June, was closer to the mark. "Ain't I'm a Dog" had proto punk snarl and lyrics to match ("Forget about the danger and think of the fun…"). It must have sold enough for Law to shelve the two remaining cuts from the June session and bring Self back in December to cut another song in the same vein. That song was "Bop A Lena." It was pure overstatement, pure abandon. Its brattish immediacy marks it out as perhaps the first garage rock record.

Ten days after the "Bop A Lena" session, Ronnie Self took a bride. "He was dating a friend of mine," said Dorothy Carlton, "and we went backstage at Wally Fowler's 'All Night Singin' show. 'Pretty Bad Blues' had just been released. He looked at me and said, 'I'm gonna marry you.'" On December 26, 1957, they were wed. Ronnie went back to join the Philip Morris Caravan. "They were in Los Angeles," said Dorothy, "and Ronnie was due to have a screen test for 'Rally Round the Flag' to play the part of Opie. I was getting ready to give birth to our first child. I'd talked to him on the phone and told him the contractions were starting. He just left the tour, never attended the screen test, and came home. He'd been with them nineteen months."

"Bop A Lena" was breaking. Ronnie Self should have been on the road hustling television dates, showing his face at record store openings, lip-syncing at sock hops, but he was back in Springfield. He'd wanted a son he intended to name Ronald Jr.; instead, he had a daughter he named Ronna. After going AWOL from the Caravan, he was confined to local dates around Springfield. "I think he appeared on the

135

'Ozark Jubilee' on a few occasions," recalled Si Siman, "but he couldn't be relied upon to turn up and that was no good for a live television show. His unpredictability became a major problem."

There was one more Columbia session in March 1958. Ronnie cut "Big Blon' Baby" (a song that Jerry Lee Lewis cut with no more success a year later), and two awkwardly contrived rock 'n' roll songs, "Date Bait" and "Petrified," that had been cobbled together from the cliché pool by country songwriters who should have known better. Two singles sputtered and died, and Don Law lost no time jettisoning Ronnie Self from the roster.

Allbritten's credibility at Decca was still high and he succeeded in getting Self a three-year deal with the label and its affiliated publishing company, Champion Music. Much as Ronnie Self wanted it otherwise, it was the publishing deal that paid the rent and persuaded Decca to keep recording him. In 1959 and 1960, Brenda Lee recorded two of Self's songs, "Sweet Nothin's" and "I'm Sorry." Both ruled the charts. Little Brenda's phrasing on "Sweet Nothin's" suggests she'd listened very closely to Self's demo. In 1962, she scored a Top 10 with another Ronnie Self song, "Everybody Loves Me but You."

Ronnie and Dorothy moved to Nashville in the wake of all this activity, but soon headed back to Springfield. Ronnie was drinking heavily by this point and not winning any popularity contests by telling artists how to cut his songs. "At one point in my life," recalled Vicki Self, "I went to Nashville and I wasn't even going to tell anyone that my last name was Self because he'd done so much damage with the record companies. He didn't stop at the little people. There was a time when he was big enough to walk in the main office of every record company and tell them exactly what he thought of their cuts of his songs. They would mail him a song of his they had recorded and he'd listen to it and break it in two."

Needless to say, the frustration, anger, and volatility spilled over into the marriage. "Ronnie was torn between his family and his career," says Dorothy. "He loved us but said if it came between me and his guitar, he'd take his guitar. He wanted us to be together but wasn't happy when we were. We were married and divorced three times. Something else controlled him. I think he thought that in order to write his songs he had to go through a lot of pain. At one time he went to Alcoholics Anonymous for twenty-two months and stayed sober. Then he called me one day and said he'd forgotten to stop in at A.A. that day and he was off the wagon."

The Decca contract expired in 1962. Much as he valued Self's songs, Decca's country A&R man, Owen Bradley, had had enough Ronnie Self for one lifetime. Kapp Records offered a one-year deal. The only session was held at Sam Phillips's Nashville studio, and it was probably there that Phillips's guitarist and publishing manager, Kelso Herston, picked up one of Self's songs for Jerry Lee Lewis's last Sun sessions a few weeks later. The song, "Love on Broadway," was unissued at the time but fared well when Shelby Singleton released it eight years later.

Publishing companies placed Ronnie Self on a draw against royalties because he had a tendency to cash a big royalty or BMI check and spend all the money in a few hours. He left Decca's Champion Music and rejoined Cedarwood. Dub Allbritten's death in 1971 unhinged him. "After Dub died," said Si Siman, "Ronnie came back to Springfield again and we started a company called Tablerock Music. I put up the money; he did the writing. We split the company 50/50. Once again, he was his own worst enemy. He wanted to be the manager, artist, producer, and publisher. After about two years, he came in one morning and said, 'It's splitting time.' I said, 'What do you mean? We're still down about $25,000 but everything's going OK. All you need to do is stop jumping around like a Cardinal short stop and stay solid.' He said, 'I'm sorry, it's splitting time,' and he left.

"During that time he got into some crazy stuff. He burned his draft card, stomped on the flag which was kinda in vogue then. He burned his BMI awards in front of the BMI building because he tried to play his gold record and found it didn't have 'I'm Sorry' on it. He loved to create a crisis or action. He was on amphetamines or funny cigarettes back then, and still drinking."

After a long dry spell, Siman got Ronnie a deal with Amy-Mala-Bell Records. "They'd just had a big record with a tune I published, 'The Letter,' [by the Boxtops]," said Siman. "I'd arranged with Larry Uttal that he would take Ronnie, but Ronnie demanded that Larry take his sister too and got mad when they wouldn't. Dale Hawkins was going to produce an album but the deal fell through."

Dorothy left for the last time in 1978 and remarried. Ronnie moved into an apartment building in Springfield. His brother had a room in the same building. It was there that he died on August 28, 1981. He'd called Dorothy a few weeks earlier trying for a reconciliation. "I'd tried and I'd have given anything to see it work," she said. "It was

137

unbearable to see someone so talented destroy himself." Ronnie had burned Si Siman for the last time, too. "He came back to see me after a few more bumps in the road and wanted to start over but I couldn't afford to re-tie that knot. I think he was probably clinically insane then, doing real unusual things. It wasn't safe to be around him although I still thought he was a terrific writer. When he was straight, he was great to do business with. He was a gentleman. But when he got some juice inside him he'd shoot holes in the wall, fire off a bow and arrow, chase people and try to run 'em down with a car. He was in and out of jail God knows how many times. His talent was a curse. When success was real close, he'd have only had to do what people were telling him, but he couldn't handle that—and he blew it.

"He was a perfectionist. He wanted to do it all. He was like the guy who hires an artist then tells him how to paint the picture. I wanted to be his friend but he wouldn't let me. Nobody could get real close to him."

The songs hold up remarkably well. Shortly before Ronnie died, Dave Edmunds revived one of his songs, "Home in My Hand." Five months after he died, Diana Ross placed "I'm Sorry" on the flip side of one of her biggest hits, "Mirror, Mirror." The Ronnie Self catalog is filled with hugely intriguing titles that have never been recorded, or never got much airplay if they were. A few samples: "Bad Girls Don't Have Suntans," "Before I Take It Out on the World," "I Started World War One," "Here Comes Authority," "I Got a Kid by a Woman Somewhere." Or what about these self-knowing, self-immolating titles: "I Always Wind Up Run Down," "A Glass Is a Fool's Crystal Ball," or "The Little Boy in Me." Among the unissued Decca recordings was one entitled "Some Other World" in which Ronnie Self wrote his own epitaph:

> *Down with your theories, down with your conventions*
> *This cat lives in another dimension*
> *You like my sounds, you like my song*
> *I'm guess I'm right and you cats are wrong.*

These notes accompanied Bop A Lena *(BCD 15436).*

11

Diddilly Diddilly Babe
The Four Lovers

Peter A. Grendysa

This is a story of almost Biblical complexity that tells us two things about early rock 'n' roll. First, it was made by performers who had been no further south than Baltimore, and whose roots were in the Italian social clubs of New Jersey, not the honky tonks and bars of Tennessee. Inasmuch as the Four Lovers experienced R&B and country music, it was via radio and records. They incorporated what they picked up into their own music, and the result was barbershop-Italian-social-club rock 'n' roll. Very different from Little Richard, but no less valid. The Four Lovers' career parallels that of Dion, Bobby Darin, and others. Their story also shows the virtue of just hanging in, going for every job and every deal with every no-hoper label. Ninety-nine percent of the time, the dead-end labels and dead-end jobs lead nowhere, but every so often the stars fall into alignment. As we'll see.... (C. E.)

139

If "Chicago Ain't Nothin' but a Blues Band," then Newark ain't nothin' but an Italian quartet. It's a safe bet that the northern New Jersey cities contain more Italian singers, musicians, and show business types than fabled Napoli ever did. The dreary coastal plain that encompasses the cities of Paterson, Newark, Passaic, and Jersey City is relieved only by the Palisades, a natural barrier that does nothing to shield Jerseyites from the bright lights and dark secrets of Manhattan. Singing can do wonders for the environment.

Some things never change, and 40 years ago, as now, singing was an attractive alternative to working in the gray cement-block factories that have swallowed up fathers, brothers, and uncles for generations. The DeVito family of Belleville, a town on the northern outskirts of Newark, knew this fact of life very well. Poppa DeVito had brought his accordion with him from Italy and his five sons were encouraged to do something musical. The baby of the family, Tommy DeVito (born June 19, 1928), thus learned guitar from eldest brother Danny, who had learned that instrument and accordion from their father.

In 1938, when Tommy was ten years old, the country was suffering a relapse of the Depression that had never really been cured, and the family urged him into playing and singing at neighborhood bars for small change. That year, he made an appearance across the river on the "Major Bowes' Original Amateur Hour," a radio talent show that had been broadcast coast-to-coast since 1935. It was not unusual for the Amateur Hour to receive 10,000 applications each week during those desperate times, with hopefuls from all over the country making "one last try" at big show business bucks.

Bowes's organization actually listened to between 500 and 700 artists in auditions, before selecting the fortunate 20 who would appear on the hour-long program that Thursday night. The cacophony was mind-boggling. As John Dunning puts it in his book *Tune In Yesterday*, "And so they came, players of jugs and washboards, tap dancers, foot shufflers, piano players, mimics, tellers of old jokes, duos and trios and quartets and more. There were harpists and yodelers and chime-ringer and harmonica players.... There were flutists and ukulele pickers, fiddlers who wanted more than anything in the world to be violinists; and there were singers—baritones, tenors, and sopranos—singers of 'The Lords's Prayer' and 'This Is My Country' and 'The Battle Hymn of the Republic'."

Dunning also points out that few of the participants ever became real stars. One of those few was an Italian boy from Hoboken, Frank Sinatra, whose Hoboken Four quartet had appeared on the show the year before little Tommy DeVito, shaking in his knickers, mounted the stage. What impression the ten-year-old made, singing and playing "Red River Valley" to a nationwide audience, is not recorded. Just making the show was something to brag about, however, and he returned to Belleville a star. In 1940, older brother Nickie (born September 12, 1924) left high school and formed an eight-piece band of teenagers in which he played bass and Tommy sang and played guitar. Nickie and The Starliters played swing music for parties and wedding receptions until the draft broke them up.

In 1946, Nickie returned home from Europe, where he had served in the Special Services unit, and began playing in a duo with brother Tommy, all the while working "real" jobs and hanging around the street corners. In the background absorbing the aura of being with the older guys was Frankie Castelluccio (born May 3, 1934). By the end of 1949, the DeVito duo became a trio with the addition of Nick Macioci (born September 19, 1927). Macioci, who became better known as Nick Massi, was a singer with a gift for vocal harmony and arrangement. Calling themselves the Variety Trio, the three were reportedly very well received by the customers at the bars and clubs who heard them in early 1950. Tommy DeVito still played lead guitar, while brother Nickie had picked up rhythm guitar and handed the bass fiddle chores to Nick Massi. They harmonized and also took solo turns, doing songs from the current "Hit Parade" and old favorites.

Usually on the scene at Variety Trio gigs was Frankie Castelluccio, now 16 years old, darkly handsome, and not at all self-conscious about his lack of stature, both physically and professionally. Frankie had worked out a little number, a parody of Rose Murphy's hit "I Can't Give You Anything But Love," done in falsetto and faithful to Murphy's breathless, whispery delivery. The group decided to let him on stage one night at the Bellbrook Tavern and the audience seemed to enjoy it. And so did Frankie, as Nickie DeVito recalled to journalist Rex Woodward in 1982, "He started coming in every night because he knew we'd call him up. And he'd always wear the same thing, a pair of dungarees and a tee shirt with a hole in it." Frankie's repertoire was as limited as his wardrobe at that time. "I Can't Give You Anything But Love" was the only song he could do on stage. When the group moved to Newark and a big-time booking at the El Morocco in 1951, he tagged along. The older fellows gave him another song to learn, the hoary "My Mother's Eyes," an unabashed appeal to the mothers in the audience, first popularized by George Jessel in 1929. Lathering on the sentiment and layers of piercing falsetto, Frankie was an instant hit. He was featured on one of the group's live remote broadcasts from the El Morocco during this time, but was not an official member of the Variety Trio, which remained just that, a trio.

In late 1952, the Variety Trio disbanded after Nickie DeVito quit. Brother Tommy got a gig with the house band at The Strand Bar in New Brunswick, and found Frankie had followed him there, too. Notwithstanding the fact that the band at the Strand was strictly instrumental, Frankie got in. He reportedly learned to play bass in a matter of days, auditioned, and got the job. There are musicians out there who take lessons, study hard all their lives, and never get a band gig. Either Frankie was a phenomenon, a musical wunderkind, or you simply didn't have to be very good to play at the Strand, a bar that catered to servicemen from Camp Kilmer.

The bass that Frankie played towered over his pompadour by about 12 inches, but he really just wanted to sing, and before long his big falsetto was trilling out over the bar din. Barely 18 years old, he had been singing so long that he had developed an amazing range, some said three-and-a-half octaves, and there certainly were few like him on the pop music circuit at the time. Through the rhythm guitarist, Jody Vadala, he was introduced to artist representative and publisher Paul Kapp of the famous Kapp family (Jack Kapp founded Decca Records, Dave Kapp founded Kapp Records). Paul Kapp decided to record Frankie on his considerably less well-known Corona Records, a New York–based outfit whose sole reason for existence was to showcase Kapp's unknowns.

Despairing of ever fitting "Frankie Castelluccio" onto a record label, Kapp gave him the name "Frankie Valley," borrowed from the stage name of one of the manager's acts, "Texas Jean Valley," a singer then working with Milton Berle and, incidentally, the sister of Jody Vadala. In the summer of 1953, Frankie and Tommy DeVito recorded "My Mother's Eyes" and "The Laugh's on Me" with a studio rhythm section. The coupling was released on Corona and Frankie immediately became the biggest thing in the old neighborhood. He started calling himself Frankie Valley, although the record sold in such minuscule quantities that collectors pay $200 for it today. A recording star can't stay a sideman in some cocktail band, so Frankie and Tommy left the Strand and formed a new group with Hank Majewski on rhythm guitar, Frank Cattone on accordion, and Billy Thompson on drums. They tagged themselves the Variatones. This new group played much the same venues as before, with long stays at the Silhouette in Harrison and Rendezvous in Newark. In the meantime, Mercury released "Somebody Else Took Her Home" and "Forgive and Forget" in 1954, probably purchased from Corona.

The big break finally came in early 1956. With two New York record men in attendance the Variatones did backup for a female singer who was auditioning, then hit a few licks of their own. Suitably impressed,

The Four Lovers

one of the men, Peter Paul, became their manager. A week later, they were auditioning for RCA Victor. Joe Carlton, who went on to start his own Carlton Records, was the A&R man for RCA at the time and he liked the way the group could blend country music (Majewski had been singing hillbilly songs as half of the Hank and Joe duo and liked to wear fringed jackets) and R&B. The label was starting to have considerable success with Elvis Presley, who did the same thing. Carlton signed them up that day. With the time of playing weddings and bar mitzvahs now hopefully in the past, the group selected a more hip name, the Four Lovers, and recorded for RCA on April 12, 1956. When they entered the studio the top song in the country was "The Poor People of Paris," an instrumental by Les Baxter. It was shortly to be knocked for a loop by Presley's "Heartbreak Hotel," and only the hopelessly out of touch didn't know that a change was gonna come in pop music.

The lineup that swaggered into RCA's rented studio that day consisted of Frankie, now playing drums, Tommy on lead guitar, Hank on rhythm guitar, and Nickie DeVito on bass. Arranger-director Leroy Kirkland also added some guitar licks. Al Williams, star studio pianist, provided his inimitable touch on the ivories, and the *real* drumming was done by Panama Francis. According to fond legend, the Four Lovers were first given "Don't Be Cruel" to rehearse, only to have it taken away and given to Presley. Whatever the truth, they ended up with two other Otis Blackwell tunes, "You're the Apple of My Eye" and "Diddilly Diddilly Babe." Sticking with the white-guys-sing-R&B theme, they also recorded covers of the Cliques' "The Girl of My Dreams," the Drifters' "Honey Love," Faye Adams's "Shake a Hand," and Fats Domino's "Please Don't Leave Me."

For some strange reason, RCA dumped the first two singles by the group on the market at the same time. This was usually the kiss of death in the record business. The pluggers can handle one side, but four are impossible to promote at once. The radio stations settled on "Apple of My Eye," a breakneck, hiccuppy reading that sounded a lot like the sort of parodies the "Three Haircuts" (Sid Caesar, Howie Morris, Carl Reiner) were doing on television. Since the teenagers of that day were parodies themselves, they loved it. It entered the *Billboard* charts on May 26, 1956, inched up to No. 62, and then disappeared after only five weeks. This relatively poor showing puts this—the only chart record the Four Lovers ever had—in the company of such forgettable numbers as Hugo Winterhalter's "Memories of You" and Gogi Grant's "Who Are We," among those records that pegged out at No. 62 in 1956. Yet, the Four Lovers' waxing is rightly considered a classic rock 'n' roll tune today, showing the exuberance and uninhibited flavor of early rock.

"The Girl of My Dreams," written by veteran bandleader and arranger Maxwell Davis and almost certainly not written by the two other names on the credits (record label owners Joe and Saul Bihari), features the obligatory one-finger piano, chimes, and Frankie's flights up and down the octaves, climaxing in a stunning falsetto display. It stayed pretty close to Jesse Belvin's original, recorded under the name of the Cliques, and, unlike the performances of R&B tunes by other white cover artists, it had soul.

That RCA really believed in the group, at least for a while, is demonstrated by the fact that they had the boys back in the studio two weeks later to work on an album. *Joyride* was a weird mixture of R&B covers ("Shake a Hand," "Lawdy Miss Clawdy," "This Is My Story," "Too Soon to Know," "Memories of You") and pop ("Cimarron," "San Antonio Rose," "I Want a Girl Just Like the Girl that Married Dear Old Dad"). The title track was an instrumental, another departure from the norm. Despite effusive liner notes that declared the Four Lovers to be "four Elvis Presleys," the record-buying public remained unconvinced. Today, copies of that album are regularly sold for upwards of $200. Never mind, the group was doing very well despite lackluster record sales. An appearance on the Ed Sullivan Show and representation by the mighty William Morris agency kept them busy for two years. As Nickie recalls, "We were on the road constantly, we didn't fade out. We played the classiest rooms in the United States and Canada, most of which had never booked a rock 'n' roll act before. We played the Fountainbleau in Miami, the first rock group to play the LaRome Room; we played the Chaison Park in St. Louis, the Beachcomber in Wildwood; the Blue Room in the Hotel Roosevelt in New Orleans; the El Morocco in Montreal; we did all kinds of television while we were in Canada. We worked with all the big stars of the time: Nat King Cole, Burt Lancaster, Tony Curtis, Jonathan Winters, Lucille Ball, George Jessel ... we had top billing at the Town Casino in Buffalo, using an unknown comic named Don Rickles as our opening act."

"Jambalaya" and "Be Lovey Dovey" were released in August 1956, while all this frenetic traveling was going on, and "Happy Am I" backed with "Never, Never" appeared in December. Unfortunately, the rock 'n' roll revolution was in full swing and the Four Lovers were not invited. If you weren't Elvis Presley or Perry Como, 1956 was a tough year to be an RCA Victor act. The salesmen could meet their quota off Presley and be on the golf course by noon. Presley had five No. 1 singles that year (six, if you count "Don't Be Cruel" and "Hound Dog" separately) and promotion money was not going to other newcomers, either. The label had given up on finding "another Presley." One was enough.

Perhaps if the Four Lovers had been signed to a hungry little independent label such as Specialty, Atlantic, or King, things would have been different. Their approach to the limelight would have been through the back door, but maybe the fall wouldn't have been as devastating. They went out with some hardcore R&B, anyway. "My Memories of You" was originally done by the Harptones, and the two songs written by the former Four Buddies Larry "Leon" Harrison and Gregory Carroll, "Love Sweet Love" and "Be Lovey Dovey," had been done by the Teen Queens and Rockets, respectively. After one more release on RCA in January 1957, "Shake a Hand" and "The Stranger" from their first session, they were dropped.

The Four Lovers were picked up later in 1957 by Columbia, and that company issued one single on Epic and another (under the name "Frankie Tyler") on OKeh in 1958. By this time the original group had split, with Nickie and Hank leaving. A figure from the distant past, Nick Massi, moved in along with Hugh Garrity, both of whom had been whiling away the time in New Jersey working as the Hollywood Playboys. As the touring continued, the only constant members of the group were Frankie and Tommy DeVito. Massi was in and out, and Charles Calello joined on accordion. The group recorded again for Decca in 1959, and one single was released under the name "Frankie Vally." Later that year the piano player for the Royal Teens (remember "Short Shorts"?), Bob Gaudio (born November 17, 1942) was signed on. The 17-year-old had a bag full of original songs, and the group was soon recording some of them for old homeboy Bob Crewe, a producer and writer born in Belleville, New Jersey, on November 12, 1931. Tommy DeVito recalls Crewe's magic touch, "I think he is a genius in his own right. I don't put him down for anything. He had no ability in music; he doesn't know one note from the next. I still think today he doesn't know C from D, or anything else. It's just that he had such a creative ear and creative mind for a sound. He was a producer who couldn't write a lick of music, but knew what he wanted. When we went into the studio, he knew what he was looking for and that's what he always came out with."

During the next few years, the Four Lovers did studio backup singing and recorded for a number of small labels under a bewildering variety of names: Frankie Valle and the Romans, the Village Voices, the Topics, Alex Alda, Billy Dixon and the Topics, and, for George and Sam Goldner's Gone label, they were the Four Seasons. By 1962, the

Four Lovers were history, and the group was earning $100 per side as backup singers. Frankie was doing construction work to support his family and was contemplating a move to Las Vegas where Nickie DeVito had offered to help him find a job. Bob Gaudio had written "Sherry," a song perfectly suited to Frankie's falsetto delivery, but their employer, Bob Crewe, had eyes for having one of his other acts do the number. Frankie and Gaudio insisted on doing it with their own group and not for one of Crewe's go-nowhere labels, either. When Crewe finally gave in to their demands, the only company he found interested in the tune was Vee-Jay, an operation hitherto featuring black acts, but anxious to make pop inroads.

"Sherry" by the Four Seasons hit the pop charts in August 1962, rocketed to the No. 1 spot on September 15 (replacing "Sheila" by Tommy Roe), and stayed there for five weeks. Their next release on Vee-Jay, "Big Girls Don't Cry," likewise took only one month to make No. 1, also hanging in the top slot for five weeks. No more name changes for the Four Seasons were necessary or desired, except for a frivolous excursion as "The Wonder Who" in 1965. Today, Frankie Valli and his Four Seasons are a pop constant in a musical world of everchanging tastes, giants on record and in personal appearances. The road has been very long for those kids from New Jersey, all the way to the rhinestones and spangles of Las Vegas, but they made it the old-fashioned way; they earned it.

These notes accompanied The Four Lovers, *1956 (BCD 15424).*

147

Ben Hewitt

12

I Heard You Died In '64
Ben Hewitt

Colin Escott and Hank Davis

In 1983, Bear Family was planning an LP to be split between Ben Hewitt and Eddie Bell. Little was known about either, except that they'd both recorded for Mercury in the late 1950s, and their records had become quite collectible. Ben was rumored to be living in Canada, so I called around everyone I knew at record companies and performing rights societies, and the last anyone had heard of him, he was living in St. Catharines, Ontario, near Niagara Falls. I called all the Hewitts in the Niagara Falls phone book and found Ben easily enough.

*   One afternoon I drove down, picking up Hank Davis on the way. It was probably the easiest interview either of us has ever done because it essentially consisted of turning on the tape recorder and saying, "Hi, Ben." We got the feeling that Ben had told his stories about being a Mercury recording artist to anyone who would listen, but no one much was listening. Maybe that sort of thing doesn't carry much cachet with the Tuscarora Indian community around the Falls. Suddenly, he had two people in his living room who were ready to be impressed. Hank brought along his copy of Ben's "Whirlwind Blues" as a token of our interest.*

*   Interviews transcribed verbatim usually make lousy reading. This is one of the few exceptions that comes to mind. (C. E.)*

Ben, let's begin with some of the standard biographical stuff, like when and where you were born.

I was born on September 11, 1935, in a one-room, dirt-floor log cabin on the Tuscarora Indian Reservation in New York State. I wanted a

149

guitar from the time I was nine or ten. I kept bugging my father and finally when I was about 12 he broke down and bought me a ukelele. About a year or so later, I got my first guitar. A $12.50 Stella. That thing would make your fingers bleed and would go out of tune while you were changing chords. An old guy named Clayton Green taught me the basics. He made his own guitar picks out of the ivory on piano keys. Tom T. Hall had his Clayton Delaney. I had my Clayton Green.

What kind of music influenced you?

I loved Sun Records. I was a real nut for that stuff. I have the Prisonaires' "Just Walkin' in the Rain." I used to love "Ubangi Stomp." You ever heard "Chicken Hearted" by Roy Orbison? Great stuff. Remember "Dixie Fried" by Carl Perkins?

And Elvis?

People who saw me performing in a bar somewhere would call me Elvis. Years later, some of them would swear up and down that they had seen Elvis performing in a bar, but when I was up there performing I wasn't doing Elvis, I was doing my hero, Little Richard. I saw him on a package show. Ruth Brown was the headliner. He was hot with "Ready Teddy" at the time. I was awestruck by the drive of that man. About six months later, he came to the Zanzibar Club in Buffalo and I was there on Monday night and I caught every show that week. I even booked off work to go see him. I blew a fortune there. He had a band that wouldn't quit. When I went back to do my act, that's who I was doing. Shakin' my ass, carryin' on, doing flip-flops.

How did you get on Mercury?

I was playing this little bar just over the border, a place called DeFazio's in Niagara Falls, New York. This guy kept coming in and buying the band the odd round. His name was Julian Langford. I swear he looked exactly like Colonel Tom Parker. He was up from Florida working in construction. He asked us what we'd charge to do some demos for him. He thought of himself as a songwriter, but he had the same tune to everything. The lyrics were nothing to write home about either. He'd come to us week after week and sing us the latest song he'd written. For the hell of it, we said, "We'll do it on one condition. You supply the booze. We'd like a bottle of rye and some ice. Plus you gotta pay 20 bucks apiece and rent the hall." Of all the songs he gave us, there was only one I didn't change. That was "Whirlwind Blues." So we made this tape for him. We got to the end of it and I asked if I could stick a song of my own on it. He said, "Sure." He was feeling generous by then. I threw on "You Break Me Up." So he pays us and we took what's left of the bottles over to my apartment and got so drunk we could have laid on the floor and fell off it.

About a week later, there was a banging on the door at six o'clock in the morning. It's Julian and he says, "Hey, get packed. We're going to New York City." I said, "We're going nowhere, especially at six o'clock in the morning." He keeps it up. He says, "Look I got you a record contract." I said, "Sure you do. You want me to go. I'll go on one condition: You hand me a round-trip ticket and it stays in my possession." He says, "Okay." He comes back in a little while and drags me off to a lawyer. He's had a lawyer draw up a management contract and it's a shitkicker, man. I mean, I don't fart sideways without giving him 15 percent of it. I said I'd sign it if he puts a rider on there that says I can play DeFazio's whenever I want and I don't pay Langford nothing. He says, "Okay," thinking I'm gonna be such a star I won't ever play DeFazio's again.

So we go to New York and we're staying at one of the neater hotels. The next day we get up, he marches me off to Mercury Records. I kept thinking, "This man is shucking it through right to the end." This really neat looking receptionist says, "Oh, Mr. Langford, Mr. Otis is expecting you." This was a Tuesday and we recorded on the Thursday night. Years later, I found out that Clyde Otis didn't want Langford's material, he wanted "You Break Me Up." Meanwhile, Langford goes out and gets a New York entertainment lawyer to make a new contract even tighter than the last one.

Did any members of your band come down with you?

That's a story in itself. I called Ray Ethier, my guitarist, on Wednesday night and he said, "I can't make it. I don't get paid until Friday." So anyway I'm in the hotel room, the phone rings and it's Ethier. He says, "I'm catching the first damn bus out." He'd bought a lottery ticket and won a thousand dollars. He showed up the day before the session. I could see his face through the bus window. He gets off with his guitar under one arm, doesn't say "Hi" or "How are you" or anything. He just says, "When do the bars open?" So we found a bar that opened at 7:00 A.M. and had "breakfast." We had breakfast until about three o'clock, went back to the room and fell down. Next day we were still on our backs and we had to sober up for the session at 8:00 P.M. I'm pouring coffee down Ray and walking him around. He got there and he played. About halfway through the session we took a break for coffee and Ray sees this bar across the street. Clyde Otis saw where we were going and he says, "One, Ray. One! At eleven o'clock you can fall over." And he did. Ray was a great guitar player. He could play chords he didn't know the name of.

Where's Ray now?
Ray was from St. Catharines. Still lives there, I think. He married Patricia June. Pat told Ray it was either her or the guitar. Ray chose her. At that time, Clyde Otis wanted Ray to be a staff guitarist for him in New York. At a minimum he could have made seven or eight hundred dollars a week. He said, "No." I said, "Why?" He said, "I don't know anybody here." I said, "For 700 a week I could become a recluse." This was back in '59. I said, "Stay here. In a few years you can go back to Canada, buy yourself a house, marry the girl of your dreams." Anyway out of that first session came a 45 of Ray doing "President's Walk" and "Slave Girl." I tried to get Ray to do my last Mercury sessions, but he told me "No." I see him every couple of years or so and ask him if he wants to sit in with the band, but he still says "No." He says it's been too long, but I think he wants to. It was a hell of a waste when he quit.

So Clyde Otis produced your sessions?
All of my stuff for Mercury was produced by Clyde Otis in New York. I remember the first time I went in there. Scared???? I mean what do you do when you have someone like Brook Benton standing on the side-lines watching you. Freddie Parris and the Five Satins are the backing group on that first session. At that moment "In the Still of the Night" was a smash. Half of the band was from Roy Hamilton's road band and part of it was Brook's outfit. God, you've got to be kidding. What's a little hick doing in this studio.

Who arranged your bookings?
Shaw Agency. I was the only non-black artist booked out of Shaw. They had me working some places I shouldn't have, like the Flame Bar in Detroit. You could see the guys in the audience saying, "What's *he* doing here?" I was doing my usual material…and it ain't going over

too well. Now I was an R&B fan from way back and that's what saved me. I started doing Jimmy Reed and John Lee Hooker songs. Stuff by Lowell Fulson and B. B. King. It went over so well I got picked up for a second week.

I used to be a big fan of George "Hound Dog" Lorenz. He worked out of WKBW in Buffalo. He used to play my records on his R&B show. He wanted to be my manager. He offered me this deal where he'd get 80 percent and I'd get 20. He said, "I'll guarantee you'll be a millionaire in two years." I said, "George, I can't live on 20 bucks a week."

What was it like touring in those days?

Some of it was unreal. I went down on a promotion tour to Dayton once. I got off the plane and there was a couple of hundred kids behind this fence, 'cept at that time it looked more like ten thousand. All of a sudden they run through the gates and across the tarmac. I turned around to see who got off the plane and the stewardess said, "They must be for you. You're the only one getting off here." It turned out that I had the biggest record in Dayton at that time. I did some other touring, but you know that us little guys didn't get to sit on the same bus as the big stars. Brenda Lee had her own little bus, even her band didn't ride with her. There was no glory in those tours. The bus would pull into the gas station and we'd have five minutes to go to the john and hopefully they had running water. As soon as you got to the auditorium everyone would run for the showers. You'd say, "God, my right nut for a bed." I worked with Bobby Vinton. He didn't even sing in those days. He was just a bandleader. I worked a show with Jape Richardson [the Big Bopper] and Ritchie Valens.

What were the circumstances under which you left Mercury?

In 1961 or thereabouts, I was with Clyde and we were going over material for a session. A phone call came from Irving Green, the president of Mercury, and I didn't need a phone to hear him. He was livid, screaming, mad, hot, hostile. "What the hell kind of people are you signing to my label? You know what that son-of-a-bitch Hewitt did last night? He raped a 14-year-old girl. I just sent the money to get him out of jail in Florida. He played a record hop down there last night, and he offered some little teenybopper a ride home. When she wouldn't come across, he forcibly raped her. She called the cops, the cops hauled

153

**Ben Hewitt at DeFazio's
with Ray Ethier (left).**

him in, and he called me up first thing this morning asking me to send the money." Clyde says, "Irving, you're going to tell me that Ben was in Florida last night? I don't want to break your heart, but I think you've been had. Ben has been here in New York since Monday. We've been together every day and most every evening, and he sure as hell wasn't in jail in Florida this morning. He's been with me since 8:30."

Turns out that Langford in a need to grab some fast money had got some guy to pantomime to my records in Florida. The guy started thinking he was me and he had the nerve to phone Mercury, and they gave him the money. Mercury started to cool on me after this. They got involved in suing Langford. I looked at the contract and there was no way I could get out. The only thing I could do on my own was to play DeFazio's. I told Langford I wanted out. He said, "Fine, give me

$10,000." I told him I wasn't worth it. He said, "Well, Mercury's got it. Ask them for $10,000." I said, "Mercury ain't gonna give me that kind of money." I think Langford was really pissed off because he wanted to see a product out with his name on it. After that first session, we were mostly using other peoples' material. He wanted to go up to someone and say, "Hey look at that record. I'm Julian. I wrote that." He got pissed at Mercury and me both. Maybe that's what that whole thing in Florida was all about. Later, Langford wrote a really nasty letter to Mercury. You couldn't print it.

After Art Talmadge left Mercury to set up Musicor, he wrote to me and said, "When you get free of Langford, you can come record for me." Belford Hendricks went on from Mercury to Capitol, and he said the same thing. Clyde went over to United Artists, and he told me, "Get rid of that mad southern person, and when you do, get in touch." But by then I'd lost interest in making records.

Did you record after leaving Mercury?

Not really. My buddy Bob Cammidge and I put out a live album on B-A-B Records. After that, I went with Broadland Records in Toronto. They put out one single, "Border City Call Girl," that they leased to Shelby Singleton's Plantation label. Shelby had been with Mercury and he remembered me. He was really taken with that song. About a week after it was issued, Singleton lost a major lawsuit from Johnny Cash for all the Sun material and my single went down the tubes. That record was fated to do nothing. When it came out in Canada and was starting to move, we had a postal strike and that killed the promotional work behind it.

You're known by quite a few names.

I'm probably known to most people as "Smoky." I played over 13 years at DeFazio's. A guy from CBC [Canadian Broadcasting Corp.] Radio called me and wanted me to do a show for him. I said, "Why? I'm just a honky-tonk player. I hang around barrooms." He said, "You'd be surprised how many people know who Smoky is." I was playing on a stage in Okinawa, and a note comes up on stage. It says, "Smoky, you're a hell of a long way from DeFazio's." When I toured, at least one person in every country we were in walked up and made some reference to DeFazio's. Sometimes, people say, "Hey Ben, where you been? I saw you 30 years ago at DeFazio's. I heard you died in '64."

155

There are a number of postscripts to this story. Right after the LP came out, Hank called Ben and asked him what he thought. "It's fine," said Ben. "No problem." A pause. Finally, "Aw shit, there's no use pretending, I cried when I saw it. It just felt so good. After all this time, to see something like that. It's beautiful. I just couldn't believe it." A year or so later, Ben went to Europe to perform at Bear Family's Tenth Anniversary Show. He was drinking but he was a happy drunk. He went over really well, and recorded an album of new songs for Bear Family. After that, we lost touch, and then, sadly, we got a note from Ben's daughter that he had died on December 8, 1996.

Finally, you might remember that Ben's Mercury recordings were to be on an LP shared with Eddie Bell's Mercury recordings. By using Ray Ethier's Mercury single and a few unissued recordings we had just enough for a complete LP by Ben. Then, a year or so later, Hank Davis and I interviewed Eddie Bell with the idea of doing a complete LP of his Mercury recordings and a few records he'd made for diddly labels. The years had been much kinder to Bell, as his ample girth betrayed. He had reverted to his real name, Eddie Blazoncyzk, and had become one of the kingpins of the polka business. Laugh not. Polka is huge across the northern United States and central Canada. Eddie and his entourage tour Polish community centers, and he's reckoned to be second only to Frankie Yankovic. One numbingly cold night, Hank Davis and I sat in his bus, off in the corner of a motel parking lot in one of the bleaker areas of Toronto. Eddie tried to remember his short, inglorious life as a rock 'n' roller for us. We then had trouble licensing the other recordings we needed to fill up the album, and the project went on a back burner, where it's been ever since.

Ben Hewitt's Mercury recordings are on You Got Me Shook *(BCD 16199) and his Bear Family recordings are on* The Spirit of Rock 'n' Roll *(BCD 16200).*

13

A Boy and His Guitar: Twangin' from Phoenix to Los Angeles

Duane Eddy

Rob Finnis

Let's not talk about guitarists who can play circles around other guitarists. Let's talk instead about guitarists who influenced kids, tens of thousands of kids, to pick up the guitar. In that regard no one succeeded like Duane Eddy. For would-be musicians, rock 'n' roll offered a populist, democratic ideal in which attitude was treasured over adroitness. Duane Eddy extended a sense of the possible to kids sitting on their beds cradling their first guitar. After a week or two, they could pick out a few bars of "Shazam!" or "Rebel-Rouser." At the same time, they'd come to appreciate the finer points of tone and dynamics that would take them years to master. With his commanding simplicity, Duane Eddy could plant a seed, whereas someone like Les Paul or Bill Haley's Danny Cedrone would make a young picker want to heave his instrument into the yard.

Duane Eddy also made the first true rock 'n' roll instrumentals. Even on the smallest record player, they were big *records. They had a rock 'n' roll sensibility—and rock 'n' roll titles like "Rebel-Rouser," "Stalkin'," and "Forty Miles of Bad Road." Duane Eddy was a rock 'n' roll name, and he had a rock 'n' roll look to match. Unlike previous generations of performers, he rarely cracked a smile in his publicity photos.*

Every now and again, the world relearns Duane Eddy's little credo: simple is best. "I read the greatest thing in Reader's Digest *that summed it all up for me," Duane once said, "They talked to this oriental painter who painted vases, and he would paint this pottery with intricate designs. Just beautiful. Then over here he had one with just an 'S' design. Very simple. Now the intricate one was priced much lower than the one with just the one line on it, and they ask him why. He says, 'When I paint the intricate things, I do so much, you can't tell where I've made a mistake. When I do one simple line, it has to be perfect. Any mistake I'd make would glare tremendously and stick out, and I'd have to start over again.' That stuck in my mind. It was a great way to explain simplicity."*

In this piece, British writer Rob Finnis not only covers Duane Eddy's career, but explores the changes in the industry in the wake of rock 'n' roll. He looks at how out-of-the-way places like Phoenix, Memphis, and New Orleans became recording centers thanks to the vision of one or two men. He also explores the beginning of rock 'n' roll production and the fascination with the studio and its capabilities that became very much a part of rock music in the 1960s and beyond. We also learn about the bitter pills that Eddy had to swallow. Finnis tells us how Duane accommodated the lack of success more readily than the realization that music, which had started out as fun, was a matter of dollars and cents. (C. E.)

158

It's 2:00 A.M. at the Sun Studio on a summer's night in 1957 as a group of careworn musicians under the direction of Sun's in-house arranger Bill Justis prepare to record an instrumental to go on the B-side of a vocal novelty. The band comprises Sun's regular rhythm section, augmented for the occasion by Justis himself on sax and Sid Manker, the guitarist in Justis's Memphis dance band. A schooled musician playing below his capability, Manker has sketched out an infectious guitar riff over which Justis weaves a mildly off-key countermelody on his tenor sax. Justis later overdubs additional sax parts, creating a generation loss in the sound and emphasizing the mildly chaotic feel of the record which he titles "Raunchy."

Though barely remembered today, "Raunchy" was a hugely influential hit, launching a chain of events that led to the birth of the rock 'n' roll instrumental. In Los Angeles, Lee Hazlewood, a 28-year-old former deejay who had gone into business as one of the first indie producers, planned to exploit the "Raunchy" phenomenon. Hazlewood had made his mark in 1956 when he wrote and produced "The Fool" by Sanford Clark, an atmospheric rockabilly lament which came out of left field to soar into the Top 10. It was produced in Phoenix, Arizona, and it paved the way for other local acts, including one destined for in-ternational stardom, Duane Eddy.

Duane Jerome Eddy was born on April 26, 1938, the eldest of three children, in Corning, New York, far upstate close to the Canadian border. He grew up there and in other small upstate New York towns like Bath and Penn Yan. No one in the family was musically inclined but when Duane was about five, his father taught him a few chords on an old guitar and later bought him a cheap Kay.

"I learned a few chords but frankly I was never infatuated with it," he later remarked. An aunt bought him a lap steel for his ninth birthday and Duane says he did his first radio show about a year later playing "Missouri Waltz" on the steel. In 1951, when Duane was 13, his family moved west and settled in Tucson, Arizona, where he learned to ride and shoot out in the desert. A year later, the Eddys moved to Coolidge, a small town on the edge of the Gila River Indian Reser-vation. His father opened a grocery store while Duane attended the local high school.

"In Coolidge, the other kids were dressed well," he recalled, "and I wore Levis and patched shirts. I was not invited to parties. I didn't care because I was popular with girls anyway." Distracted by the excitement of the move and his new surroundings, Duane suffered a temporary lapse of interest in the guitar and it was only after the Eddys were permanently settled that he took a more determined interest in the instrument, picking up a lot by ear. Not long after, he met Lee Hazlewood.

A lifelong maverick, Barton Lee Hazlewood was born the son of a wildcat oil driller in Mannford, Oklahoma, in 1929. His family was constantly on the move and it was not until Lee's high school years that the family finally settled in Port Neches, Texas. He later attended Southern Methodist University in Dallas, where his education was interrupted by the draft. After his discharge, he married Naomi Shackleford and tried to settle down, but the outbreak of the Korean War led to his reenlistment and a spell as a deejay with the Armed Forces Radio Service in Japan.

Encouraged by friends who remarked on his rich voice and laconic manner, Hazlewood moved to California to study broadcasting, then to Coolidge, 60 miles north of Phoenix, to work as a nighttime deejay on a small country station, KCKY. There, he assumed the alter ego of Eb X. Preston, a grizzled old-timer who sat on the sidelines exchanging

159

jokey on-air banter with Hazlewood himself. It was in Coolidge, in 1953, that Hazlewood first encountered Al Casey, a stocky, myopic 17-year-old musical prodigy then playing steel guitar in a country band fronted by vocalist Jody Reynolds, who later recorded the morbid hit "Endless Sleep." He also met another musician, Donnie Owens, who was, like Hazlewood, a new face in town.

"My friend Donnie Owens got me my first radio job," Hazlewood remembered. "I was on a station in Coolidge that was playing Bing Crosby and Perry Como and we were about fourteenth rated. And there was one other station in town, about a 12-watt, and all night all the kids listened to this station, which had a black deejay who wasn't very good but he played people like Howlin' Wolf, Little Willie John and even some white guys like early Elvis Presley, and I knew that some of the college kids were listening to him. So in the morning I started slipping in records like 'Annie Had a Baby' by Hank Ballard after a Bing Crosby record, if you can imagine. That's kind of an odd combination and the station manager got very mad. I put my job on the line but the ratings went up because college kids from Arizona State started listening, and I stayed there for two and a half years."

By 1954, Duane had met Ed Myers, a guitar-playing friend who served as his musical sparring partner. More outgoing than Duane, Myers made the rounds of radio stations between Coolidge and Phoenix with the aim of landing a deejay job. "Ed was wantin' to be a deejay so he went and talked with local jocks in Arizona," Duane told Wayne Jancik. "Lee had not long been in the job and Ed went out and got to know him. Ed said, 'You must get to meet this guy.' So, one night I did. We hit it off and he gave me a few records the station had extras of, and he made a friend for life. He was much older than me but we hung out together."

Lee Hazlewood: "Duane used to come around the station to pick up the country records because we never played most of them, and for the first year or so my wife and I used him as a babysitter so we could go to a movie occasionally. Duane was playing Chet Atkins at this time."

Duane: "One Saturday afternoon when I was about 16, I cut a tape of a Chet Atkins song, 'Spinning Wheel' or something, at the station in Coolidge. They would play it over the air and a guy named Jimmy Dellbridge heard it and got in touch and we started performing together." Dellbridge, a tall, big-limbed local boy the same age as Duane, had a local gig as a singer-pianist and needed a group. Both

160

Duane and Ed Myers on rhythm guitar were co-opted into Dellbridge's loosely knit group.

Quick to determine each others' musical strengths, Dellbridge and Eddy were soon woodshedding as a duo with Dellbridge's vocals supported by Duane's increasingly confident guitar playing and less-than-confident vocal harmonies. By mid-1955, they were going out as Jimmy and Duane—The Coolidge Kids, playing weekend dances for a few bucks. Lee Hazlewood was their manager. Keen to increase his income since he had two small children to support, Hazlewood turned his hand to songwriting, figuring he could write material as good if not better than the songs he was playing every day.

"Suddenly, records that people never heard before started selling in town and the kids were asking for them. The record stores used to call us and ask, 'What label is it on for chrissakes?' because labels were a big thing in those days. You had Decca, Capitol…whatever, then all these little labels no one had heard of before like Sun and Fortune and Abbott. And [I] thought if I can play this stuff I can record it. So I started Viv Records."

Toward the end of 1955, Hazlewood approached Ray Odom, a deejay on KTYL, Phoenix, who presided over the "Arizona Hayride," a country barndance broadcast every week from the stage of Phoenix's Madison Square Garden. The first hour of the show was reserved for amateurs, and in February 1956 Jimmy and Duane made their debut on the show backed by its resident band, Al Casey and the Arizona Hayriders. It was here that Hazlewood and Eddy made the contacts that were to have a profound influence on their lives. Falling in with a coterie of local musicians whose number included Casey and his guitar-playing wife Vivian (professionally known as Corki Casey), drummer Conway Crunk (known as Connie Conway), and Lee's jack-of-all-trades pal, Donnie Owens, Hazlewood and Eddy were quick to realize that Phoenix promised infinitely greater opportunity than sleepy Coolidge. Within a few weeks, Hazlewood had moved to Phoenix.

Now operating at the hub of a very parochial scene, Hazlewood took Jimmy and Duane into Ramsey Recording, a small studio behind a barber's shop at 3703 North Seventh Street and had them record two of his songs, "Soda Fountain Girl" and "I Want Some Lovin' Baby," which he pressed up on a one-off logo, jokingly named after his radio alter ego, Eb X. Preston. Sales were low and local. The songs, performances, and recording fidelity were all poor, but Hazlewood

161

found that the studio was a conduit for his ideas. His radio experience had given him a basic grounding in audio technology and his local reputation as a deejay enabled him to dominate, if not control, those around him. Pretty soon, he was cutting other local folk and country acts at Ramsey's studio using Al Casey's group as the backup.

"I kinda sponsored Duane and a lot of the other guys around Phoenix," said Hazlewood. "It was mainly cowboys and we were trying to get something going locally that you could compare with the stuff they were doing in California or maybe the 'Louisiana Hayride,' only we had to do it on a smaller scale because we had less people to work with and no big names except for the ones who came through town. It was a strange time. We had cut two singles by Jimmy Spellman for Viv. Decca or Columbia covered one of them, which didn't help. Then I wrote a country song—at least I meant it to be a country song—called 'The Fool' and I asked Al Casey if he knew anyone who could record it, and he suggested this tall, good-looking kid who thought he could sing, Sanford Clark."

Clark, lifelong friend of Casey's, was stationed at an Air Force base in Phoenix, and—when off duty—occasionally sang in clubs in a deep faltering tenor. Casey got him on the "Arizona Hayride" and introduced him to Hazlewood. In May 1956, they went into Ramsey's to cut "The Fool." "When we cut 'The Fool,' Ramsey's had a four-pot board," says Hazlewood. "It took a day to do the track. Connie Conway played drums with one brush that we found in the studio and a Campbell's tomato soup box over a drum stool. That was the afterbeat on 'The Fool.' The guitar was Al Casey, and Jimmy Wilcox played a bull fiddle. I meant it to be a country song, then Al Casey came up with a riff out of an R&B record [Howlin' Wolf's 'Smokestack Lightnin'"] that he liked to play and put it against this cowboy song. I only owned half the record because I didn't have enough money to pay for the studio. It took a day to do the track but nearly three weeks, on and off, to get Sanford's voice on it. It wasn't his fault, it was just me trying to get a sound on it 'cause we didn't have echo chambers so we tried all kinds of combinations of 7½ and 15ips tape echo on little machines, stretching them and plugging them into each other 'til we got something like I wanted it. I didn't know what I wanted but I had loads of time to do it 'cause it was only eight bucks an hour. Everybody went crazy when they heard the sound, people used to come in and listen to it.

"We put 'The Fool' out on a little label called MCI, which I owned a part of with Jimmy and Connie and Floyd Ramsey, and sent out our usual two or three hundred records to all the distributors and stations in the South. And we waited for our orders because on a Jimmy Spellman record, we'd sell thirty or forty thousand. I told everyone we had a No. 1 country record but our distributors didn't order at all. Then about six weeks later, after we'd forgotten about the record, some strange man called me from Cleveland, Ohio, and said 'You got a hit.' And I said, 'Do they play country music in Cleveland?' He said, 'No, it's a pop hit.' That was Bill Randle who was the number one record-breaking disc jockey in the States—there was no Dick Clark then—and I thanked him very much. He got it to Dot Records and it just took off from there. Then some idiot from New York called me up and said if I didn't give him the record he was gonna' cover it. I said, 'I've just sold it to Dot, now screw off.' We never did get into New York with 'The Fool' because he had New York City sold out with The Gallahads' cover version which knocked us out of about 200,000 records, while Sanford got up to 800,000."

"The Fool" elevated the ambitious Hazlewood to a different league. Although he had no track record other than his solitary hit, Dot had sufficient faith in his potential to place him on a retainer in return for first refusal rights on his productions. In February 1957, Hazlewood gave up his radio job in Phoenix and moved his family to a small house in Topanga, California. None of Sanford Clark's follow-ups made a serious dent in the charts, though, nor did other Hazlewood-produced Dot singles. His failure to consolidate was tempered with the knowledge that he was gaining valuable studio expertise and making useful contacts at Dot's expense, although he knew the gravy train would soon come to a halt if he didn't produce another hit.

Between August and December 1956, when local excitement surrounding "The Fool" was at its height, Duane was finishing his education and beginning to ponder his future. He and Jimmy Dellbridge were still working together, only the billing had gradually changed in Dellbridge's favor to reflect the changes wrought by Elvis. Every city needed an Elvis, and Jimmy Dellbridge was ready and primed to assume the role in Phoenix. A poster announcing an appearance by the pair at the Coolidge Armory on June 28, 1956, reads: "Buddy Long and all the TV Hit Paraders featuring rock 'n' roll sensation Jimmy Dellbridge with Duane Eddy and Guitar." In a photo taken around this

Duane Eddy

time, Sanford Clark is shown center stage, looking every bit the local hero; he's flanked by Duane, the earnest young sideman marshalling the band with his Les Paul gold-top. Another photo of Duane taken no more than a few weeks later has him wearing fancy western threads and sporting an immaculate Elvis ducktail and sideburns. His guitar is now a brand new Gretsch 6120—the instrument with which he would shortly generate, in posterity's colorful phrase, "$1,000,000 of twang."

"When I first got it," he told Dan Forte, "here was this new toy [the tremolo arm] to play with. I played Chet Atkins and Merle Travis stuff and, of course, later on I used it in my own way!" Duane was still playing in the fingerpicking style of Chet Atkins as late as 1957, until Casey advised him to broaden his scope by concentrating on flatpicking, but, as Casey explained, Duane was reluctant to change. "One night we were playing and Duane always played with the thumbpick. I couldn't get him to do anything but that. So I asked him if I could borrow his thumbpick for a second, and I broke it and gave him back a flatpick."

When Hazlewood moved to Hollywood, Duane felt as if he'd lost sight of his career hopes. Al Casey's departure added to his sense of isolation. Phoenix now seemed like desolation row. Duane's morale suffered a further blow in the fall of '56 when Jimmy Dellbridge annulled their partnership, claiming to have been diverted by religion. "Jimmy was always religious," said Duane, "it was a long involved story but once we made that first record, Jimmy came to us saying he'd been saved and couldn't sing with me anymore, not worldly music. So that was the end of us."

Duane may have been a little ahead of himself in his recollection for although Dellbridge did indeed become a minister, it was not before he succumbed to the temptations of secular music with RCA for whom he recorded three rock 'n' roll singles in 1957–1958. He also played piano on a couple of Duane's early Jamie cuts in the fall of '57. In March 1957, Duane lit out for Los Angeles hoping to make a career in the music business by staying within Hazlewood's orbit. "When I got there," he said in a 1959 interview, "I was sick the first three weeks. I felt depressed. I got a job at an office from nine to five. After work, I went home and went to bed. I did not know anybody in town and all the people at the office were married. I was lonely."

Hazlewood hadn't much to offer. He let Duane play on some of his Hollywood sessions. It wasn't much, but enough to encourage Duane to quit his job as a gas board clerk and scrape by on the few bucks he'd managed to save. Duane also took a handful of lessons from veteran Western Swing guitarist Jimmy Wyble, a former member of Bob Wills's Texas Playboys.

Meanwhile, Hazlewood was indulging in a little side deal. He issued a pair of singles on Ford Records, a nonunion label named for his wife and run from his home in Topanga. Hazlewood knew that the bigger labels were eager to snap up or cover records on smaller labels. The trick lay in convincing a larger label that you had a potential hit on the evidence of a little airplay in some far-flung state. Neither of the two Ford singles—one by Jerry Demar and the other credited to Duane Eddy and The Rockabillies—happened, nor did a third by a lady called Alvie Self. The few hundred copies pressed languished in Hazlewood's carport. However, within the grooves of these stillborn curiosities lay the germ of the Duane Eddy sound. Hazlewood had gone into Goldstar studios to cut the track on "Lover Man" (one of his lesser songs) and "Cross-eyed Alley Cat," a Leiber and Stoller discard. He had already produced a version of "Alley Cat" by Sanford Clark back in March only to have it rejected by Dot. Someone called Jerry Demar was listed as the rhythm guitarist on the session logs for Clark's version and his name reappeared on the Ford single about three months later. Demar then vanished, leading to speculation that it was, in fact, Al Casey.

166

Whether or not he was Demar, Casey turned in powerful performances on the Demar record, coaxing single-note licks and grungy twangs in a frantic attempt to fill the holes in the sound, creating a prototypical Duane Eddy style in the process. With the levels still set, Hazlewood then had Casey reprise the same licks in the form of a brief, repetitive instrumental which Hazlewood titled "Ramrod."

It's possible that Duane played rhythm guitar on three of the four sides and Hazlewood had been promising to record his 19-year-old protégé, so Duane's name appeared on the Ford release of "Ramrod" with the consent of the good-natured Al Casey who was bound by a Dot contract. "For one, Duane was a lot better looking than Al who wore glasses and was so fat at that time that I once bought him logs to put under the seat of his Ford to hold the springs up," joked Hazlewood, adding, "Duane wasn't even around on 'Ramrod.' For posterity and prosperity it was Al Casey all the way."

Homesick and disillusioned, Duane packed his bags and went back to his folks in Phoenix not long after the Ford single was issued. Three years later when asked to describe his "biggest career disappointment," he replied, "Flopping on first try at breaking into show business in Los Angeles."

In September 1957, Hazlewood went into partnership with Lester Sill, a local music entrepreneur with a proven track record in R&B. Earlier that year, Sill had helped Hazlewood to set up a music publishing company and promised him the office space vacated by Leiber and Stoller. Sill had started in 1945 as a salesman for Modern Records. During a brief spell running his own distributorship, he hired two aspiring songwriters named Jerry Leiber and Mike Stoller as his shipping clerks. They formed Spark Records, a one-desk-and-a-filing-cabinet indie that released a series of imaginative R&B discs like "Riot in Cell Block No. 9" and "Smokey Joe's Café," by the Robins, a group which later metamorphosed into the Coasters. Spark folded when Atlantic Records bought the Robins's contract and hired the services of Leiber and Stoller on a nonexclusive basis.

"I didn't want to go back east," Sill explained, "I didn't feel like uprooting. The competition was a little heavier in New York and I didn't like the weather. We had a long thin office at 7407½ Melrose Avenue and when Jerry and Mike moved to New York, I took it over. The rent was all paid up and it was up to me to sub-let it. About three weeks later, I met Lee Hazlewood through a mutual friend and he moved in with me. We formed a music publishing company called Gregmark Music named after one of my sons, Greg, and Lee's son, Mark. So I was doing the same thing only with a new partner. I managed the Coasters who had broken big with 'Searchin'' and 'Young Blood' and that provided the income to keep us going." To tide him over, Sill continued working with an old friend, George Mottola, and they leased two singles to Jamie Records, a Philadelphia label run by a distributor named Harry Finfer. "This was the first Jamie label," he pointed out, "not the one they reactivated later that had all the Duane Eddy hits."

With his experience and extensive contacts, Sill was the administrator and money man, a diplomat with the knack of bringing the right people together and clinching deals. For his part, Hazlewood pledged his writing and producing skills to the partnership. They were leasing finished masters to record labels long before it became common practice within the industry.

Sill's first move was to drive Hazlewood down to the offices of Modern/RPM Records to meet Saul Bihari, Sill's old employer. Although 1956 had seemingly been a good year for Modern with hits by The Cadets ("Stranded in the Jungle"), and the Teen Queens ("Eddie My Love"), the company had tried to overcome its poor representation in the rock 'n' roll field by converting its existing roster of R&B artists into would-be rock 'n' rollers. The results were mixed, and Hazlewood sold Bihari on the idea that there were a dozen Elvises out there in the sticks waiting to be discovered and that only he had the savvy to make it happen. Keen to ride the bandwagon, Bihari stumped up an $800 advance, and Sill and Hazlewood hightailed down to Phoenix to cut some masters on the cheap.

Hazlewood: "The first thing we did was 'Snake-Eyed Mama' by Don Cole with Al Casey playing the piano 'cause we wanted to make it sound like Jerry Lee Lewis and we put Al's name on the label like we did on 'The Fool.' That thing was cut in a garage in Glendale, Arizona, 'cause I didn't want to spend any money. It was a two-car garage converted into a little studio. If I remember, we had a dirt floor in that garage. They sound hungry. That's why it sold."

Lester Sill: "After I'd done a deal for Lee with Saul Bihari, I went down to Phoenix with him to produce some things for Modern and that's when he introduced me to Duane. Al Casey, a very, very fine guitarist, was part of his group. We talked to Duane and arranged to come back to Phoenix shortly after."

Determined to record an instrumental in the "Raunchy" mold, Hazlewood instructed Al Casey and Duane to work up some ideas in time for his next trip to Phoenix in three weeks. "I spent a few weeks working on it," said Duane. "Al Casey played bass. He was also a great guitar player and taught me a lot about the guitar. Al and I worked up some things, Lee joined in and between the three of us we came up with the idea of playing songs on the bass strings."

Lee Hazlewood: "The idea for the sound came from the Eddie Duchin Piano, the low piano where he played melody down on the bass. I always used to like that. I guess I was a little square because it made no difference what went on in the background, you always heard a little melody. Since I liked the guitar, we tried the idea with Al. The only trouble with Al, poor Al, is that he could play so good, he could play anything. We tried it for about a year with Al, we had records on Liberty and Dot, then we quit and went over to Duane Eddy."

Don Cole's "Snake-Eyed Mama" had cost less than fifty dollars to record, enabling Hazlewood to turn a good profit on the deal with Saul Bihari, so Sill and Hazlewood returned to Phoenix in late November to pick up where they'd left off. Hazlewood had a special affection for Ramsey's studio. The musicians were friendly and compliant ("he bullied us," said one) and the cost of studio time was always open to negotiation. Better still, there was no local musicians' union to hamper the recording process.

"I went to Phoenix to cut just a group—any group," Hazlewood explained. "We wanted a group called The Rebels. It wasn't a Duane Eddy record, we were cutting a group record. But then Duane worked so hard on it. He was fooling around with the wang bar of his guitar bending the notes on the bass strings just for the heck of it 'cause it made a nice twanging sound. That was the start of it, the wang bar. And, of course, Duane's tone and phrasing which he developed."

At the same time as he was experimenting with the tremolo arm on the low strings, Duane was fooling with the opening lick of Chuck Berry's "Brown-Eyed Handsome Man" on the top strings. "I played the high part," he said later, "and I had this riff that I liked on the low strings, and I said to Al Casey, 'I don't know where to go.' And Al just leaned over his guitar and said, 'Well, man, put 'em together, do 'em both.'"

Lester Sill: "We cut 'Moovin' 'n' Groovin'" for ninety dollars! It was silly. The musicians got five dollars a side because there wasn't a union there and we worked out of our back pockets. But we looked after them and told them that if it was a hit we'd cut them in on certain royalties."

Hazlewood cut the tracks hot with ample presence and clarity on the drums and guitar. "At the end of the date," he remembered, "I said to Duane, 'Hey it's your record, we're gonna use you.' So instead of putting 'The Rebels' on that record, we just put 'Duane Eddy and His Twangy Guitar.' People laughed at the word 'twangy.' We got a lot of laughs. It was my idea. Duane didn't like 'twangy'—he thought it sounded awful and corny which it was. But it worked."

"When I first went into the studio in the '50s," Duane said, "I learned that the bass strings recorded better than the high strings. They were more powerful and more gutsy, so that's how I came up with that sound. It was just a process of logic and elimination. We did some experimenting but basically it came out right the first time. I had to be careful not to overplay. It takes away a lot of feeling and direction. I had this amp that was more powerful than any on the market at the time. It didn't actually make it louder, but it made the sounds clearer."

169

Lee Hazlewood: "At that time there was a bunch of guys in Phoenix experimenting with sound. Buddy Wheeler was the one who started messing about with sound. He started rebuilding his amps and other people's too. He could really pump power into them and they wouldn't break up. That 'click' cowboy sound on 'Rebel-Rouser' came from the hyped-up amp he had. He'd take the smallest little Fender amp and make it sound like the biggest in the world."

Duane: "Buddy Wheeler was a steel player by trade and he used a Magnetone amp he'd rebuilt with two 15-inch JBL speakers and a tweeter in it, and he'd get a great clicking sound which was sort of a forerunner of the Danelectro sound they used a lot in the '60s. I used a similar Magnetone amp which Buddy boosted to around 100 watts with one JBL 15-inch and sometimes a tweeter and sometimes not. It was more powerful than any on the market at the time."

Back in Los Angeles, Sill's pal, George Mottola, had gone into Goldstar studios to cut an instrumental by veteran sax man Ernie Fields, using a studio band led by another saxophonist, Plas Johnson. The A-side, "Annie's Rock," a hepped-up version of "Annie Laurie," attempted to plow the same furrow as "Raunchy." Once they'd finished, Hazlewood asked Plas Johnson to lay down some raunchy blasts onto Duane's "Moovin' 'n' Groovin'." All Sill had to do now was place the record.

Hazlewood played a dub of "Moovin' 'n' Groovin'" to Randy Wood at Dot Records who took a pass on it. Wood was something of a genius at picking lease deals, but no one hits a home run every at-bat. He passed on Ricky Nelson's first record, the Royal Teens' "Short Shorts," Danny and the Juniors' "At the Hop"…and Duane Eddy. In January 1958, Sill pitched "Moovin' 'n' Groovin'" to Dick Pierce at RCA (who'd already signed Duane's pal Jimmy Dell) but Pierce passed, too. He then contacted Harry Finfer in Philadelphia. "I had got to know Harry when I was selling product on Spark," he said. "Harry and Harold Lipsius had a distribution company called Universal on Girard Avenue in Philadelphia. I told him what we had and sent him dubs and they thought the records were tremendous. At that time they were going to reactivate Jamie Records with Dick Clark and we did a deal."

Sill lucked into a deal that was not so much a last resort as a free pass into every living room in America. With the growing influence of *American Bandstand*, Philadelphia was fast becoming the focal point of the record industry. Syndicated nationally, it shaped the tastes of its after-school audience and rapidly turned Clark into the single most influential figure in the American record industry. Clark was candid about the formation of Jamie Records: "Harry Finfer, Harold Lipsius, Sam Hodge and I each owned 25 percent of Jamie," he wrote. "Harry was a promotion man, Harold was a lawyer, and Sam Hodge the owner of a record-pressing plant. A young west coast producer named Lee Hazlewood approached us with Duane Eddy.... A talent manager named Al Wilde and I eventually formed SRO Artists to become his manager." Clark also owned a 50 percent stake in Hodge's pressing plant which pressed for Jamie and many other local labels. Lee Hazlewood later claimed that he and Sill were also partners: "Lester, myself, Lipsius and Clark each had 25 percent," he says. "I sold out my share before the payola investigations so I'm not in the congressional record."

In February 1958, "Moovin' 'n' Groovin'" was one of the three inaugural releases on the new Jamie label. Duane's disc didn't rate a mention in *Billboard*, but got an early boost when he flew into Philly to make his first appearance on *Bandstand*. By late March, "Moovin' 'n' Groovin'" was on the charts, peaking at No. 72 and selling about 90,000 copies. Sill sent Duane out on a brief tour with Al Casey on bass guitar.

"Al was a drivin' ass bass player," says Hazlewood. "He'd never played bass before Duane's first tour so he stopped by Donnie Owens' house to borrow Donnie's bass 'cause Donnie was playing bass at the time. When Duane was at his top, a good percentage of the bass sound was Al Casey—only Al didn't like touring much and he'd drop in and out of Duane's group and we'd have to find someone else. Duane was always nervous to play around Al. He loved to have Al in the band but didn't like for him to play guitar because Al could play incredible. But he couldn't play like Duane, and seven million people tried, but they couldn't play like Duane. It was on the beat and then it stumbled right in front of the beat and then he'd get back on the beat and all the time he played with a lot of feeling. It wasn't mechanical like a lot of the super slick guys and that's why he sold."

Duane's first tour consisted of a week-long show at the Paramount State Theater in downtown Los Angeles on a bill with the Clovers, Roy Hamilton, Don and Dewey, Thurston Harris and the Sharps and some local acts. "Lester managed the Sharps and the Coasters," says Hazlewood. "He 'owned' the Coasters and I 'owned' Duane and that was the basis of our corporation. So the Sharps kind of took Duane under their wing. He was a young white kid, no experience, and we managed them both."

There were few blacks living in Phoenix in the mid-1950s and R&B was rarely played on local radio except for crossover hits such as Bill Doggett's "Honky Tonk" and "Fever" by Little Willie John. "I was country," says Duane. "I never even heard much blues until early '58 when I did that show in L.A. for a week. That one song was all I did. I came out and did that and someone would yell, 'Next!' Well, the Sharps, for some reason, started taking a liking to me, and I started hanging out with them. They took me down to Watts. 'Get your guitar,' one of 'em yelled. 'You can sit in with the group.' I said, 'Oh God, I can't play like that.' I drank a little Thunderbird wine with 'em and pretty soon it sounded right and I said, 'Well, like maybe, I can do that.' I could see what they were doin'. By this point, I could feel it. So, I got up there and just jammed with 'em. And that's how I learned to play the blues.

"After that week in L.A. I was called back to cut some more. I got to the studio and we didn't have anything to cut. Lee said, 'Write something. We'll just throw it together.' It comes easier when I'm under a little pressure. I wrote 'Rebel-Rouser' at the session that day. I had the drummer play a backbeat and I fooled around with the melody until I got it where I wanted it. I'd worked a week on this show so now I knew what I wanted. That's why the intro of 'Rebel-Rouser' is like it is. I thought it would be cool to do the first bars by myself. I pictured this spotlight with me moving out on stage, then the band started moving out. The mood and atmosphere I saw and felt was like a 'West Side Story' scene with guys walkin' toward you in this dark alley. The melody was based on 'Who's Gonna' Shoe Your Pretty Little Feet,' an old public domain song I once heard on a Tennessee Ernie Ford album."

Hazlewood had sketched out a guitar riff, which Duane and the band worked into a menacing instrumental, titled "Stalkin'." "On 'Rebel-Rouser' and 'Stalkin','" he says, "we used an upright bass played by a guy named Jimmy Simmons. Buddy Wheeler picked an electric bass that clicked like the cowboys did." The drummer was Bob Taylor. "He was a cowboy drummer with a bad eye who never drummed in his life since, before or ever," says Hazlewood. "He just played cowboy drums—boom-di, boom-di. I wanted him to play other things and he just couldn't do it. He was six foot three and I'm five foot seven and I used to stand there and scream at him, threaten to kill him and he'd just stand there and look at me and shake. Then he'd go back and play his ass off. Then it wouldn't be right and I'd yell at him again and he'd think I hated him. Then I'd take him out and buy him a drink then take him back into the studio."

172

Back in Hollywood, Sill and Hazlewood asked Gil Bernal (a Mexican saxophonist who'd gone to school with Mike Stoller and later recorded for Spark) to come in and overdub sax parts. He then brought the Sharps to the studio to do the rebel yells that became an integral part of Duane's records. Each was enveloped in a swathe of Goldstar's famously deep chamber echo—a device Phil Spector would use to breathe life into his Wall of Sound in the early 1960s. Long before him, Hazlewood used the same echo to layer the sound on Duane's early hits by feeding the backing voices and sax solos, and sometimes the entire track, through the chamber to create an illusion of unfathomable depth.

Both "Stalkin'" and "Rebel-Rouser" were sophisticated productions which transcended the limitations of contemporary studio technology to make a near physical impact on the listener. The Phoenix engineer, Jack Miller, cut the bed tracks hot with extra presence to allow for both the generation losses caused by the anticipated overdubs and the dissipation of the sound through the addition of echo. But there were crucial refinements. Duane was now plugged into a DeArmond outboard tremolo box that made the signal from his guitar pulsate variably. And the Phoenix studio had recently acquired a makeshift echo chamber.

"After we had a chart record with 'Moovin' 'n' Groovin'," says Hazlewood, "they sent us a check from Jamie for about three or four thousand dollars. So I went to Phoenix and told Floyd Ramsey, 'We gotta have an echo chamber 'cause we needed it for "Rebel-Rouser."' And he says, 'Well, they cost a lot of money, blah, blah.' I said, 'I'll tell you what, let's not bother with an echo chamber, I want some kind of huge barrel, you know—we'll put a microphone at one end and a speaker at the other.' So we went out all day and yelled in grain storage tanks. I yelled in 'em all day, going from this lot to that lot, yelling, Hah! Hah! and when I finally got one where the yell came back to me, I said, 'Right, we'll buy that one.' We paid two hundred dollars for it and we put this big cast iron grain tank sitting up in a corner of the parking lot with a four dollar mike at one end and a sixty cent speaker at the other and that's not exaggerating too much about the value of it. We almost meant to bury it or house it in some way but we were afraid we'd ruin the sound, we were cutting too many hits. When it rained, which wasn't too often, we couldn't record, or a bird would get in and we had to stop and shoo the birds away. And every now and then we even had to get the kids away from it because they used to go out and listen to what we were recording."

173

Although it was only Duane's second record, "Rebel-Rouser" pretty much defined the classic Duane Eddy sound. "In those days," said Hazlewood, "I thought, my God, there's nothing that's bigger or sounds better, and that's what people could not believe, that Duane wasn't playing on telegraph wires, let alone guitar. And for a while we achieved that. Phil Spector came along later on and did something to his records, I don't know what, to make them sound even bigger."

Incidentally, the label on the initial pressings of "Rebel-Rouser" bore the false legend: "From the Production Rebel-Rouser Starring John Buck," a jokey subterfuge on the part of Hazlewood to draw attention to the song. According to Duane, Hazlewood thought "Stalkin'" was the hit side. Dick Clark thought so too. He played it every day for two weeks on *Bandstand*. The reaction was negligible, but Clark got a better response when he started spinning "Rebel-Rouser" and, as Duane says, "Then the radio stations started playing it."

Once Duane achieved the big breakthrough, Sill and Hazlewood's covert relationship with Dick Clark began to work to everyone's advantage. On July 24, 1958, Duane appeared on *Bandstand* miming to both "Moovin' 'n' Groovin'" and "Rebel-Rouser," and followed through by appearing at a Philly record hop hosted by Dick Clark. "He really liked what I'd done," says Duane. "He said 'Come to our Saturday night show next weekend. We're gonna be in Miami.' I drove down to Miami. Just before the dress rehearsal, Dick said, 'Would you mind opening with "Moovin' 'n' Groovin'," just doin' it live?' They had us on a fork lift takin' us through the audience down to the stage, and then we'd finish up 'Rebel-Rouser' onstage in this big auditorium. Dick said, 'Now, I need something to close with. Have you something else? "Stalkin'" is too slow.' I said, 'Well, we got this thing we cut last summer called "Ramrod."' He said, 'Let me hear it.' So, we worked it out on the spot. Dick said, 'That'll be a great closer.' So when Dick signed off, we started 'Ramrod' while the credits rolled. Monday morning Jamie has orders for 150,000 copies. And it didn't even exist yet. Jamie panicked and called Lee. Lee called me and I told him I'd really like to cut that thing again, that I had some other ideas on the song. He said, 'We don't have time and can't afford to fly you back here. So I'll just overdub the Sharps and Plas Johnson on it. I saw what you did on the show and I'll try and keep it as close as I can.' By the next day, he had the Sharps whoopin' and yellin' and Plas wailin'. He sped the original track up a little so Plas could play it in B-flat, 'cause we had played the thing in A."

In fact, Hazlewood was apoplectic when he saw Duane resurrect "Ramrod" on prime airtime. "I sat right at home and I thought, 'That's the most awful thing they've ever done to me, the sound is terrible.' They probably only had one mic. That Clark show was done for twelve cents. There goes my artist down the tubes. Here we go, you've just ruined it. Away we go back to the radio station for fourteen bucks a week. Next morning Harry Finfer called me from Philadelphia. He said, 'What did he do last night, where's the record?' And I said, 'What record?' He says, '"Ramrod."' I said, 'That's not even his record, it's the only other song he knows, Al taught it to him.' So that's the reason why 'Ramrod' was his third release. And he played it live and, boy, it sounded bad. We didn't even have a backside so I took the instrumental track off an old vocal record we'd done with Al ["She Gotta Shake" on Liberty] and put the Sharps on it and that went on the back of 'Ramrod' as 'The Walker.'"

"Ramrod" gave Duane his third consecutive hit, peaking at No. 27. Hazlewood was determined to compensate for this comedy of errors with Duane's next release. "The Lonely One" was a melancholy ballad similar to Jack Scott's then-current smash, "My True Love." Then Dick Clark decided it was too soon for a ballad and sent the producer scurrying back to the studio to cut a suitable rocker. In a 1959 interview, Hazlewood hinted at the pressures created by the relentless demands of the singles market: "The most trying time we have had came at our next session. Duane had been doing one-nighters for three months and was very tired. We had been working night and day and were equally tired. But we needed a new record. We recorded for five days, and Duane didn't like a thing he had done in that time. We didn't either. He left Phoenix more disturbed than we had ever seen him and we didn't feel so good either. Two days later Duane called from New York to say he had a great idea for his next record; could we meet him in Phoenix."

Duane picks up the story. "So I said I had an idea, and they booked me on a flight. We had to go to Phoenix to do it, so they flew us all back on a DC6 prop plane on a Thursday night, which took all night. On Friday we were in the studio all day and recorded 'Cannonball.' We mixed it down Friday evening, got back on the airplane, got to New York Saturday morning to rehearse all day for the Dick Clark TV show that night. He was so big that if he played your record it would almost automatically become a hit. If he didn't, it would be very difficult."

Like all Duane Eddy classics, "Cannonball" incorporated subtle production touches that were vital to the arrangement—in this instance, the use of shakers overdubbed and put through deep echo to fill out the sound and underscore the rhythm. Five years later, Phil Spector would use shakers in exactly the same way. Again it's likely that the entire track was put through Goldstar's chamber before being mastered for release.

"Cannonball," which charted at No. 15 at the tail end of '58, was the last of Duane's singles to be recorded in Floyd Ramsey's original studio in mono. Ramsey subsequently installed a new studio with multitrack capability. The price went from eight to twelve bucks an hour. "Nobody knew why we went over there," said Hazlewood, "'cause there were no musicians. Guys used to call me: 'Where do you cut those damn records?' And I'd say, 'Phoenix, but honest-to-goodness I don't think you should go there.' And guys would come over from Capitol and Decca and come back and say 'You're insane, you're nuts, you're crazy, you can't cut over there.' But they didn't know that we'd start at nine in the morning and we worked 'til we collapsed at night and maybe we didn't get one take all day that was any good. I worked those guys 'til they dropped. Nobody had cut any hit records out of Phoenix before. In fact, they laughed. I'm glad they laughed."

The deceptive simplicity of Eddy's records enticed experienced session pros like Billy Mure and Al Caiola into the studio to cut copycat instrumentals that sounded like weak travesties. They failed because as Lee Hazlewood remarked, "It was fifty percent the sound production which was me and fifty percent Duane because [of] the way Duane played, and God knows what that way is. I don't understand it yet today. But whatever it is, the way he played worked. The sound worked too, because I don't think anybody had heard a guitar played that way or that big."

Duane's success also induced envy on the part of his backing musicians, especially saxophonist Steve Douglas who often had as much solo space on the records as Duane himself. Before leaving the Rebels in March 1959, Douglas played on half of Duane's second LP, *Especially for You*, and a version of Ray Anthony's then-current hit, "Peter Gunn" (a TV theme written and originally recorded by Henry Mancini). "Steve had learned it," Duane told Dan Forte, "and I said, 'OK, we'll play it [live] but I don't want to record it. There's nothing for me to do in it.' We needed one more song for the album and Steve kept suggesting 'Peter Gunn.' 'There's a lot for you to do; that riff goes all the way

Duane Eddy and his peers. (*Left to right*) George Hamilton IV, the Kalin Twins, Frankie Avalon, Paul Anka, deejay Milt Grant, Annette Funicello, Duane, Ray Peterson, and Gary Stites.

through the song.' So we worked out an intro and stuck a break in the middle. We really started rocking out."

Lee Hazlewood: "Duane didn't want to cut 'Peter Gunn' and we had a little argument over it. The next morning he came into the studio and said, 'Let's do it.' I said, 'How come? You passed on it yesterday.' And he says, 'Well I didn't know it too good and now I've got it worked out so let's cut it.' We usually ended up doing what the old producer wanted, although sometimes we had a little ... I won't say artistic dispute ... because neither of us was artistic—we were both commercial as hell!"

Following Australia's lead, London Records in England pulled "Peter Gunn" off the LP and issued it as a single backed with "Yep!"

A valuable TV plug on *Juke Box Jury* prior to release created an immediate demand which swept "Peter Gunn" into the British Top 10. Duane Eddy had a huge impact in England, as much for his intimation of the unknowableness of American culture as for his records. He appeared on his LP jackets as the cool loner armed with the Big Guitar under the Big Sky. The effect was reinforced by cryptic song titles: "Theme from Moon Children," "The Secret Seven."

In truth, the image wasn't so phony. Duane Eddy was every bit as cool as he seemed. He was intelligent, articulate, but essentially an extreme introvert cursed with the obstinacy of a determined perfectionist. "He's really a very quiet guy and so shy we have to speak for him," Hazlewood told a reporter from the British movie magazine, *Picturegoer*, in March 1960. *Photoplay* also noted that Duane's shyness had proved something of a handicap. "When I go on stage," he confessed, "I look out at the crowd with terror. Somehow, I overcome it, and for the performance I change my personality completely. But as soon as the show is over I become an introvert again." It helped that Duane was handsome and could compete with the Frankies and the Bobbies for space on bedroom walls. To underscore this fact, all of Duane's Jamie singles after 1959 were issued in full-color sleeves.

Duane was still touring ceaselessly. It was hard to assemble a complete show built around instrumentals so he tended to go on package tours organized by his booking agency in conjunction with a sponsor such as Alan Freed (before his fall from grace) or Dick Clark. "When the hits started coming," Duane recalled, "I did 'em all and, to start with, I'd have six to eight minutes on a show and then, as the year wore on, I had eight to ten or twelve, and the second year I was up to about half-an-hour. There were eight to ten acts on the show and my favorite spot was second to closing because, even though I might head the show, it's better to close with a singer. So that was my spot, and I'd just go out and do those bus tours. Toured around a lot by ourselves, too. Just us in the back of a station wagon with our gear, just pile in and drive."

There were none of the luxuries associated with modern-day touring. "It wasn't that thrilling," said Steve Douglas. "Also, very recently, Buddy Holly and those guys had been killed. The last gig I did with Duane was in Toronto, Canada. It was snowing and freezing, and I remember I slipped on the ice in the parking lot and hit my head, and I said to myself, 'What are you doing here?' It was time to go home."

Duane was now approaching the apex of his career, touring

constantly, putting out a single every two months and two albums a year. "Forty Miles of Bad Road" was released in time for the summer season of 1959, and it gave him his highest chart placing since "Rebel-Rouser." The melody came from a tune Al Casey had taped for Hazlewood in 1958 when Jamie's Canadian licensee had put in a request for filler to pad out Duane's first LP. Hazlewood paid Casey $50 to run off four instrumentals which he then tried to pass off as Duane Eddy cuts. The Canadians weren't fooled and the tracks were shelved. Casey later played one of the tunes for Duane who wrote a bridge and cut it as "Forty Miles of Bad Road," an expression he'd overheard a stranger use to describe a girlfriend's face. A soothing melodic ramble set to a midtempo shuffle, its very simplicity disguised Lee Hazlewood's meticulous production touches. It marked the first time that a bass drum, deadened and properly miked, was heard to proper effect on a rock record (studios and producers had hitherto ignored this component of the drum kit other than for novelty effects). Hazlewood also had the drummer slacken the snare to obtain a thin, tissuey sound for the contrasting shuffle beat. Duane's guitar had noticeably less reverb than usual, emphasizing the tranquil summery feel of the record.

In 1959, as the profits rolled in, Sill and Hazlewood moved from their office on Melrose to 1610 North Argyle in what was then Hollywood's record row. "We had a string of offices there on the second floor," Sill recalled. "One day in the fall of '59, Phil Spector came up to see me. The Teddy Bears had broken up and he said he'd like to write again and get back in the business." Spector had come to the fore in late 1958 when "To Know Him Is to Love Him" by the Teddy Bears, a group he'd formed at Fairfax High School, went to No. 1. When the follow-ups flopped, the group fell apart and 19-year-old Spector cut a one-off guitar instrumental as Phil Harvey for Imperial records in 1959. One side featured Steve Douglas who'd recently come home after his year-long stint with the Rebels. Douglas, Mike Bermani, Spector, Marshall Leib of the Teddy Bears, and some of their friends held jam sessions at each other's homes and Spector was intrigued by the techniques utilized on Duane's records. Lester Sill: "When Phil came in, we took him to Phoenix with us while we were producing Duane Eddy. Phil would just sit in the studio. Lee really was a master at sound at that time, particularly with tape reverb, and for hours he would sit and experiment in that studio with sound. Phil would just sit and watch and listen for hours and hours, all the time he was absorbing, wouldn't

179

utter a word. On occasion he would lean over and ask me a question, 'Why are you now using 7 1/2 echo or tape reverb?' Or 'Why are you just using plain echo rather than tape echo?' and so forth and so on. Also, we began to record Phil, he did a couple of things on his own down there."

Lee Hazlewood: "The combination of echoes we used would drive Phil crazy. He wanted to know what everything was. I used to beg Lester Sill to get him out of the studio."

In the Fall of '59, the record industry was bracing itself for the forthcoming congressional investigation into payola. It was the talk of the town at the annual DJ convention held in Miami that October, and Sill and Hazlewood, forewarned, quietly negotiated the sale of their stock in Jamie to Harold Lipsius. They were also scheduled to accompany Duane on an overseas tour taking in England and Australia over a period of ten weeks that they hoped would keep all of them out of the country for the duration of the hearings.

Dick Clark was called to testify before the committee. He parried pointed questions with inverted logic and a tangle of statistics. "With about a week to go before I took the stand," Clark wrote, "Harry Finfer, one of my partners in Jamie Records, was called. Harry was a nervous man with black slicked-back hair, and his mustache quivered as he spoke in rapid bursts. I'm sure that to the congressmen he fit the role of the dark, sinister record man. He admitted paying payola to Tom Donohue, Lloyd 'Fatman' Smith, Joe Niagra, Hy Lit, and others. The subcommittee called Bernard Goldstein of Computech Inc. He arrived with half-a-dozen suitcases stuffed with 300 pounds of information. Computech was a data processing organization I hired to analyze the record plays on *American Bandstand* from August 5, 1957, to November 30, 1959. I spent six thousand dollars creating the biggest red herring I could find, something that would shift the sub-committee's attention away from my scalp. In those days, I was the only guy in the world that kept lists of the records played....The result was an argument that lasted for several days and wasted a good deal of the time they might otherwise have spent flailing my poor carcass."

Alan Freed and others took the fall but Clark escaped unscathed. Freed was loud, vulgar, and an alcoholic. Clark looked like a decent young man who had maybe stretched the limits and wouldn't do it again. In the end, the committee chairman pronounced Clark "a fine young man," and he was allowed to divest himself of his companies and walk

180

away. He had already sold his stock in Jamie to Lipsius the previous November.

On March 11, 1960, Duane recorded his biggest hit of all, "Because They're Young," at United Sound studios, Hollywood. He was playing his new Danelectro in front of a live string section and a stellar crew of Hollywood musicians. The number titled a Dick Clark movie designed for the summer crowd. Five days later, Duane's entourage flew to England to participate in a three-week package tour with Clyde McPhatter, Bobby Darin, and a domestic star, Emile Ford. While they were away, "Because They're Young" broke. "We were sure 'Because They're Young' wasn't gonna be a hit because of all the strings on it," said Duane. Lee Hazlewood was equally surprised. "[It] was his biggest record and I think that one time we sat down and counted that he'd only played 32 notes on the whole record!"

Cynics might argue that Duane's affiliation with Dick Clark gave him an unfair advantage over many of his contemporaries and it's true that Duane never wanted for airtime. This, though, only served to encourage Duane and Lee to try harder with each new release because they both knew that airplay alone wouldn't fool the kids into buying a record they didn't like. Sill and Hazlewood produced around 30 singles by artists other than Duane for Jamie, and its sister label Guyden, yet only one, "Linda Lu" by Ray Sharpe, ever became a hit. Furthermore, Dick Clark's sphere of influence did not extend beyond the States yet Duane's Jamie sides were hits in England and through-out the Continent.

The upheavals precipitated by the payola row had created fissures in the relationship between Sill-Hazlewood and Jamie Records. Duane had sold five million records and his two mentors now demanded an increase in their royalty rate commensurate with the income they generated. Under the terms of his original contract, Duane's recording costs were deducted from his royalty of 5 percent, and Sill-Hazlewood received a 2 percent override. In June 1960, Duane signed a new deal which stipulated that Jamie was to pay all future recording costs as well as an increased royalty rate of 8 percent to be paid directly to Duane, thus casting Sill and Hazlewood adrift. "They wanted more money for their production work and Jamie wouldn't give it to them." Duane explained. "They wanted me to go on strike and I said, 'I can't.' I had just signed a new contract and my manager was telling me that they'd sue me and my whole career would be over. Lee said, 'I don't care.

You've got to stick with us or we won't get any more money.' I had my manager approach them and they came up with this thing where they'd give 'em a penny and I'd give 'em a penny off my royalties. And Lee said, 'No, I don't want it that way. I want it all from Jamie or I quit.'"

Hazlewood's stand would prove more costly to him than to Sill who went on to work with Phil Spector and eventually form Philles Records with him. Sill was wary of fighting with Jamie because Jamie's affiliated manufacturing and distribution companies made them potentially useful allies, and it was Sill rather than the obstinate Hazlewood who backed down when Jamie refused to return the master tapes of Eddy's sessions. An extraordinary and potentially ruinous impasse followed whereby one of the nation's most popular recording stars did not cross the threshold of a recording studio for nine months.

"It hurt my feelings," Duane said. "Here's my old friend from since I was 15 years old and to me it was all a lark and like, ain't we havin' great fun and hit records and makin' money and success. And it was all a bringdown to realize that to them it was just strictly business. If they didn't get the money they weren't goin' to do it. And even when they were offered the money it wasn't offered the way they wanted it so they still quit. I never did understand that."

Unlike most labels, Jamie lacked an in-house A&R department, preferring to purchase masters and rely on its distribution clout. The owner, Harold Lipsius, was a lawyer, not a music man, and couldn't offer the close support and career guidance Duane needed in his hour of disillusionment. The omens didn't look good. "Kommotion," released in the middle of the stalemate, bombed. It was one of Hazlewood's last productions for Jamie and may not have been intended for single release because it lacked an identifiable hook. Duane himself admitted that it hadn't quite come off.

Quick to recover, Jamie rushed the 18-month-old "Peter Gunn" onto the market and retrieved the position with a No. 28 showing. Forced to contemplate producing his own sessions, Duane set up Linduane Music and Twangy Music in order to publish his own material and on November 20, 1960, he took his road band into Audio Recorders to make "Pepe"/"Lost Friend," his first new recording since "Because They're Young" back in March. Strings were overdubbed on the tracks the following day, and ten days later, Duane wrote to Jamie's office manager, Paul Fein, in Philadelphia:

Dear Paul,

Would you please send all the checks to my house and I'll see that all the musicians are paid. The reason for this is that if they're sent to the Union, it takes longer for some of the guys to get their checks. And some of the guys need their money sooner. Also send me $200 for the vocal group.

My address is 2301 West Butler Drive, Phoenix, Arizona.

Thank you very much. I hope this record is a smash. I don't think we did too bad without Lee and Les.

Best Personal Regards,

Duane

"Pepe" was inspired by a film starring the Mexican comic actor, Cantinflas. "It came out before the movie," said Duane, "so I was like advance publicity, although my recording had nothing to do with their movie." Any doubts Duane might have felt about going it alone were temporarily dispelled when "Pepe" rose to No. 18 in the States and was only prevented from making No. 1 in England by Elvis's "Are You Lonesome Tonight." Crisp and melodic, "Pepe" didn't obviously lack the Hazlewood touch (and it's unlikely that anyone noticed a change in the sound) but Duane modestly conceded that without Lee things weren't the same. "I couldn't do it all," he said. "Be in the studio and in the booth, too. Jack Miller was a great engineer but without Lee we couldn't get it the same. Things were left out."

Duane himself was beginning to wind down a little. He married an 18-year-old Phoenix nightclub singer, Mirriam Johnson, who, as Jessi Colter, later married Waylon Jennings. He came off the road and did a movie, taking a minor role in *Thunder of Drums*, an M-G-M western shot in the Arizona desert in the spring of 1961. Duane found that he was no more comfortable talking on-camera than singing on-mic, though. He knew his limitations, and, as a result, there aren't any clunkers to come back and haunt him on late night TV.

With the end of his Jamie contract coming into view, Duane didn't want to leave any unreleased material in the can and sat it out. In the absence of anything new, Jamie issued an edited version of an album cut, "My Blue Heaven," as a stopgap single, and generated enough sales to push it to No. 50. With Jamie threatening to put out more album cuts as singles, Duane went back to the studio to cut a final single for

183

the label. Two sides were recorded, an emotion-wracked "Londonderry Air," which matched some of the earlier Hazlewood-produced standards, and "The Avenger," essentially an aggressive riff repeated from start to finish with very little light and shade in the arrangement. Some see it as one of the first surf instrumentals, but it was somewhat monochromatic and made a poor showing. It missed the Top 50 in England and pegged out at 101 in *Billboard*.

Duane's relationship with Jamie was now at a low ebb. Looking back, he said, "I'd get some royalties, just enough to make me think we were doing great. I found out later it was about half of what I should have gotten. I didn't know it at the time but [in 1960] I signed away my royalties to Jamie for all the early records. I thought I was signing something saying that I wouldn't audit them. A lot of the business people when I was starting out thought rock 'n' roll was a fad. They thought, 'Why should we give the money to these idiot kids who come out of the sticks when we're in the business to stay.' There'd be these big sacks of mail for me that they'd put in the back room of the record company and I never knew about it. They'd go through it, or burn it, and it was my mail. I'd get bags and bags of fan mail. I guess they didn't want me to see it for fear that I'd start thinking I was a big star."

The record industry of 1962 was very different than the one Duane had entered in 1957. Independent labels were finding it increasingly difficult to compete against the majors who were using their financial muscle to bid for acts whose contracts were up for renewal. Paul Anka, Ray Charles, Ricky Nelson, Fats Domino, and the Everly Brothers were among the big names who made news when they signed major label deals. Duane's managers, Al Wilde and Mort Garson, mulled over offers from Warner Bros., ABC-Paramount, Columbia, and RCA before negotiating a deal with the latter in a convoluted licensing arrangement with Paul Anka's production company. Anka had recently signed with RCA himself.

Even as he pocketed RCA's handsome advance, Duane knew it wouldn't be easy to sustain the momentum of his career without an infusion of fresh ideas. RCA's corporate approach made no allowance for artistic idiosyncrasies, and Duane knew it the moment he stepped into the studio with staff producer Al Schmitt. Schmitt had been engineering sessions for nearly a decade before he joined RCA in 1960. He'd cut a lot of jazz LPs, Elvis's *G.I. Blues*, and some of Sam Cooke's Hollywood sessions. Coincidentally, it was Schmitt who coengineered

Henry Mancini's original recording of "Peter Gunn" back in 1958. Feisty and ambitious, Schmitt pushed for a producing role and received his first assignment when RCA paired him with Duane.

As an engineer, Schmitt was used to working with sessionmen who breezed through three or four sides in the allotted three hours, then went home. Duane liked to bide his time waiting for his muse. Schmitt lacked the virtue of patience, preferring the brisk journeyman approach. "Duane was a difficult guy to work with," he recalled. "He's a really nice person and easy to get on with but very shy and it would take a lot before he would say anything and when he would finally say something, you would have to change everything around, you know, work it out, whereas if he had said it earlier, it would have made it a lot easier. That was the one problem, his problem of communicating. He was young and impressionable and shy. Lee was very, very definitely the main force. The sound was Lee's. He got something out of Duane that no one else could."

Schmitt's first session with Duane on February 15, 1962, was aborted. When they tried again a few days later on the 19th, there was a surprise guest in the control room. Lee Hazlewood.

Duane: "I had run into Lee a few weeks before I went with RCA and he said, 'Well, if you ever need me, just give me a call. I've split up with Les and I'd love to work with you again.' So, I called him up and asked him if he was working. He said, 'No. What are you doing?' I told him I was trying to get through this session. 'I got another one in the morning. Do you want to come to it?' He said, 'I sure do.' He came and we did the *Twistin' and Twangin'* LP. Lee stayed with me that first year with Victor and we had hits again."

Duane was obliged to use RCA's studio in the corporation's building on Sunset Boulevard, a concrete encasement renowned for its thin, unfocused sound and conservative engineering staff. Originally designed for orchestral recording, it was almost impossible to record a proper bass sound there, a sonic deficiency that also affected the drums. RCA engineer, Dave Hassenger, was thought to have worked miracles when the Rolling Stones recorded "Satisfaction," "Paint It Black," and "Get Off My Cloud" there a couple of years later.

As an interloper, Hazlewood wasn't yet in a strong position to make significant changes to the album in progress, and *Twistin' and Twangin'* was compromised by politics. No producer credit appeared on the finished product. Once it was in the can, Lee and Duane

185

collaborated more closely on "Deep in the Heart of Texas," a some-what overproduced single which brought Duane back into the charts at No. 78 at home and No. 19 in England, paving the way for "Ballad of Paladin"/"The Wild Westerner," which marked a return to the standard of the Jamie period, and sold accordingly (No. 33 in the U.S.A.; No. 10 in the U.K.).

In July 1962, Lee and Duane sneaked down to Audio Recorders in Phoenix to try and recapture the old groove. Girl groups were a now popular chart attraction and Hazlewood suggested a new slant on the girl-group record. "Lee said, 'Let's try something different,'" Duane recalled. "He said, 'I got this idea with this line of girl singers and then [you] playing.' He sang me the lines. We put a little melody to them and I worked out the rest. It needed a couple of verses. We cut it ['Guitar Man'] in Phoenix and he took it back to L.A." No sooner had the Blossoms recorded "He's a Rebel" as the Crystals for Spector than they became the Rebelettes on Duane's "(Dance with) The Guitar Man."

"Guitar Man" brought Duane back into the international lime-light, charting at No. 12 in the United States and No. 4 in England, and gave him his third million-seller. They went back to Phoenix to record the follow-up, "Boss Guitar." Its funky drum and guitar sound was impossible to reproduce in RCA's auditoriumlike studio. Duane decided to go for broke by making "Boss Guitar" his twangiest record yet—an insane rollercoaster ride of wang bar manipulation with some fabulous hot treble licks thrown in as relief. It got to No. 28.

Then, just as things were looking good again, Lee left the fold to oversee some other projects including a record label, Eden Records, and a hootenanny group, the Shacklefords, fronted by his wife, Naomi (Shackleford), and Marty Cooper. The group had a minor hit with "Stranger in Town" in June 1963. Lee also produced Al Casey's "Surfin' Hootenanny," a Duane Eddy soundalike record which charted on the Stacy label in the fall of '63. At the same time, Hazlewood was supplying Al Schmitt with instrumental themes for Duane and other RCA acts like the Astronauts.

When Duane went back into the studio in April 1963, Al Schmitt was in the producer's chair. Persevering with the tired Rebelettes concept he sidetracked Duane into making what were essentially girl-group records. Losing his sound and on the point of losing direction, Duane's career began to falter. The badly mixed "Lonely Boy, Lonely Guitar" nearly put paid to Duane's career at a time when he needed another hit to consolidate his recent successes. The error was compounded by another Rebelettes-led single, "Your Baby's Gone Surfin'" (one of Hazlewood's weaker songs) which confirmed the impression that Duane seemed to be playing a marginal role on his own records when he should have been center stage competing with the Surfaris or the Ventures or countless other instrumentalists who had cut their teeth on his records and were now setting the pace.

There's a case to be made for saying that Duane Eddy virtually invented surf guitar. One only has to listen to the undubbed outtakes from the "Yep!" session where the hugely amplified guitar is suspended in echo or go back to 1957's "Moovin' 'n' Groovin'," which can claim to be the first surf record, to appreciate that surf bands weren't doing anything that Duane Eddy hadn't touched on years earlier.

The very week Duane's seventh RCA single, "Son of Rebel-Rouser," crept into the lower reaches of the Hot 100 in February 1964, the Beatles made their U.S. chart debut with "I Want to Hold Your Hand." Duane continued to record under Al Schmitt's direction right through '64 without much success. Lee would occasionally come to the studio to supervise the odd session or contribute the occasional song but now that British bands were monopolizing the airwaves, Duane was no longer receiving the airplay he had once enjoyed.

Duane was philosophical enough to realize he'd had a good run. "Yeah," he said, "[The Beatles] changed the whole scene, but that was fine with me. I was tired. I'd been on the road for five years, nonstop, only coming home to record new albums. I was mentally weary of it and I just wanted to settle down and relax and enjoy some of the fruits of my labors. So I was not unhappy when it stopped. It's still that way: five or six years you're hot and then you cool off for awhile. The records weren't doing as well and there was a whole new thing happening. I just sat back and enjoyed it."

Of course, the story doesn't really end here. Duane was no longer at the cutting edge but he confounded time and fashion by making isolated chart comebacks with "Play Me Like You Play Your Guitar" (a No. 9 hit in England in 1975) and as a guest on Art of Noise's techno-pop revival of "Peter Gunn" in 1986. His influence and importance in the scheme of things was finally recognized when he was inducted into the Rock 'n' roll Hall of Fame by his peers in 1993.

Andy Starr

Rockin' Rollin' Stone

Andy Starr

Wayne Russell

Andy Starr was a country singer who leaped into rock 'n' roll with both feet—and both fists—flying. In this, he was typical of many young country singers who felt constrained in what they perceived as the straitjacket of early '50s country music. Country music, like R&B, was profoundly adult music. Andy Starr was young and almost out of control. Rock 'n' roll was his kind of music. It was teenage music. It held the tantalizing promise of a career outside the beer halls and schoolhouses of the midsouth. You could go nationwide with rock 'n' roll. Andy Starr epitomized the blind, wayward enthusiasm of the first generation of young country boys who declared themselves for rock 'n' roll in the wake of Elvis. His fate, too, was typical. (C. E.)

Joe M. Leonard, Jr., was the owner of radio station KGAF and Lin Records in Gainesville, Texas. His greatest commercial success came with the pop-rock ballad "Pledge of Love" by Ken Copeland, a record he leased to Imperial Records where it became a No. 17 hit. Leonard's success with Copeland encouraged him to take a chance on other rock 'n' rollers who came through his door. Enter Andy Starr.

Andy Starr was born Franklin Delano Gulledge on October 21, 1932, on a farm near Combs, Arkansas. His father, Grover Cleveland Gulledge, carried on the now-discredited tradition of naming sons for politicians by naming his son after the thirty-second president. FDR was elected for the first of four terms the year the future rockabilly was born. The world was still in the grip of the Great Depression and the

Gulledge family was in direst poverty. Frank grew up tough and mean, pulling a gun on a teacher (yes, that happened in the '40s) before dropping out of school at the tender age of 14. He rode the rails and slept rough, but was saved from his dead-end life by two things: the guitar and Korea. He had learned to play music on the old family guitar and the Korean conflict needed young men with some anger to vent.

Frank was sent to Korea in the Special Services where he formed the Arkansas Plowboys with friend Sonny Barker. After his hitch in Korea he worked in a factory with his brother, Chuck, before inducing another brother, Bob, to leave Wichita, Kansas and move to California. There the three brothers formed another Arkansas Plowboys, with Frank playing lead guitar. When his brothers proved less serious about music than him, he sold his home in California and headed for Texas. After a drunken night in Las Vegas, he woke up married to a woman who had aged noticeably overnight. He skipped town, still heading for Texas.

"In 1954 I started playin' a mile-long stretch of small clapboard beer joints called the Oklahoma Strip. It was just across from the Red River which separates Denison, Texas, from Oklahoma. All down the road were these hastily put up shacks that had been turned into clubs to accommodate the personnel from a nearby Air Force base. These places were wild rip roarin' joints full of female hustlers and lunatics." There are plenty of beer-joint jokes that begin "This joint was so rough that...." Ronnie Hawkins used to say, "This joint was so rough you had to puke twice and show your razor just to get in." Frank says that the joint he played on the Oklahoma Strip was so rough that they would take your weight at the front door, so you wouldn't fight out of your weight classification. He also remembers ducking behind the jukebox to fend off airborne beer bottles. Most nights, he was lucky to clear two bucks.

After securing his own daily radio show on KDSX in Denison, the station manager suggested he approach Joe Leonard in nearby Gainesville. Joe was impressed and an early 1955 session produced four songs. Mietzl Miller and Bill Baker were Dallas songwriters with an eye on Broadway, which meant they weren't getting much work in Dallas. Joe Leonard commissioned some upbeat songs from them, and they came up with "Dig Them Squeaky Shoes" and a novelty country rocker "The Dirty Bird Song (You Can't Hardly Get Them No More)." The latter was based on the expression "I'll be a dirty bird" used by guitar-playing comedian George Goebel. Frank had no faith in the song, but found it opened doors for him. Suddenly, as a recording artist, he was guesting on shows with Porter Waggoner and Grandpa Jones. Then Leonard heard that an altogether different "dirty bird" song by a different artist had been released in California only to be slapped with a million dollar lawsuit by George Goebel. He let Starr's record die quietly in Texas.

There was a second release on Lin, which did very little business. The two records to this point had been under the name Frankie Starr, but there was another Frankie Starr in Phoenix who was slightly higher up the scale of anonymity, so Frank became Andy Starr. (To confuse matters, there was another Andy Starr who recorded even less successfully for Arcade Records.) It was now late 1955. Andy had shared the stage with Elvis Presley on a Gainesville date in 1955 and a vision of the future had opened up for him. Incidentally, Joe Leonard had promoted Elvis's Gainesville date and had actually lost money on it. Elvis promised on more than one occasion to come back to Gainesville and play a concert for the original $300 fee. For some reason, Joe never took Elvis up on this offer.

By late January 1956, Elvis was with RCA, and was selling records by the carload. He was the talk of the industry and every label was in the hunt for their own Elvis. Joe Leonard hoped to emulate Sun Records' Sam Phillips and place his contender for the Presley crown with a major label. He saw the Aberbach brothers, who had helped engineer Presley's move to RCA, as the means to this end. The Austrian-born Julian and Jean Aberbach owned Hill & Range Music, a company that competed with Acuff-Rose to lock up country airplay. Leonard approached them, played some Andy Starr tapes and hoped they would bite. He knew other labels wanted their own Elvis, and Joe thought Andy "…had everything it took, and the Aberbachs thought the same." The problem was that they took Andy to the wrong label. As an experienced radio man, Joe knew which labels were the best at promoting a new artist, and MGM was not among them. MGM was high on Andy Starr, though, and waved its checkbook under Joe's nose. Joe had his doubts, and they proved well founded, as MGM sent out just 200 promo copies of their first release on Andy Starr. In contrast, Randy Wood at Dot Records routinely sent out 5,000 promos. MGM wanted their own Elvis. They just didn't want to pay the price.

Andy Starr's defining moment on record came with his first MGM single. Joe Leonard took him to the Cliff Herring studio in Fort Worth and cut four songs, including "Rockin' Rollin' Stone," a record that routinely commanded a week's pay among rockabilly fans at one time. It had all the ingredients of classic rockabilly, with an especially strong debt to Elvis's recording of "Good Rockin' Tonight." Leonard tells of an Associated Press story about Andy hitting the wire when they were in Nashville for the 1956 deejay convention at the Andrew Jackson Hotel. He and Andy made the mistake of walking from their hotel to the Andrew Jackson. Andy was in his stage outfit of red and white jacket with red shoes, and on hearing screams turned around to see who was causing the commotion. Before he realized it, his clothes were being torn off. The cops rescued him, taking him up in a freight elevator, but not before an aggressive female managed to slip him a note saying "I slept with Elvis last night in Oklahoma City and want to sleep with you tonight."

Joe Leonard took Andy back to the Herring Studio on September 9, 1956, and put his faith in the hands of his new discovery, the Strikes from Graham, Texas. The Strikes were one of the few white rockabilly vocal groups. They, too, had their moment and it came with their song "If You Can't Rock Me." Leonard leased their recording of it to Imperial Records. It did no business, but another Imperial act, Ricky Nelson, liked it enough to record it. The Strikes played on Andy's second MGM session and wrote two of the songs. One of them, "Give Me a Woman," was a big hit on the influential California country station, KXLA in Pasadena. TV and stage shows were set up to promote the record in California. The record didn't take off from there, though, and, after his fourth MGM record, Andy got his termination notice.

Andy landed a daily radio show on KWAL in Wallace, Idaho, and cut a one-off record for Kapp in 1957. Then the owner of the Hi Hat club in Anchorage, Alaska, bought him a T-Bird and booked him for six months. Andy ended up staying for five years. He brought rock 'n' roll to the forty-ninth state. He was back playing the honky tonks where the patrons participated in the shows in their own inimitable way. Clubs were open 23 hours a day with an hour to sweep out the refuse and any horizontal patrons. As Frank Starr again, he played the Hi Hat seven nights a week with his band, the Blue Notes. There were a few side trips to Nashville to record with Joe Leonard.

Sam Phillips, an early investor in the Holiday Inn chain, had convinced founder Kemmons Wilson to start his own booking agency and his own record label. A vice-president was hired to oversee the operation. Joe Leonard read about it in *Billboard* and leased completed sessions to the label. On the last session for Joe Leonard in Nashville, Frank revived the Ken Copeland hit "Pledge of Love." He had now gone full circle from anonymity to Lin Records, to MGM, back to Lin, and back to anonymity—at least in the Lower 48.

While playing Anchorage in 1959, a spirited mob of screaming females got carried away and ended up with Frank's stage clothes. This went over so well that he incorporated a stripper segment into his show. It became an integral part of his act for five years along with singing. Frank finally cruised out of Alaska in his T-Bird for good in 1965. Someone had offered screen tests so he tried Hollywood, and when that didn't work out he cooled out in Mexico. Then it was off to the Rockies trying to dry out from all the booze and drugs that had fueled his life for so many years. He claims to have suffered from post-traumatic stress since Korea, but it's unusual for someone in Special Services to have post-traumatic stress disorder. The honky tonks had represented a bigger threat to his life.

A relatively peaceful period saw him working in a sawmill and releasing country music on his own Starr label out of Kingston, Idaho. Frank then got religion and started working and recording with lifers in prison. He recorded *In Concert at the Idaho State Penitentiary* for his own Starr label. There was a religious album and some X-rated cassettes *Good Stuff (Rated XXX)* and *Uncle Sam Sucks*. Starr then tried his hand at politics and religion. He ran for Idaho State Senator in 1974, and, after failing, ran for president of the United States in 1978 and again in 1992, when another guy from Arkansas won. FDR Gulledge promised that he would be trying again in '96, but early polls suggested that he wasn't going to make it.

These notes accompanied Dig Them Squeaky Shoes *(BCD 15845)*.

Conway Twitty

15

It's Only Make Believe
Conway Twitty

Colin Escott

In many ways, Conway Twitty was the precise opposite of Andy Starr. Like Starr, Twitty was from Arkansas, and, like Starr, Twitty was inspired by Elvis, but Conway Twitty pursued success like a heat-seeking missile. Whatever it took, he would do. Starting with an arsenal of warmed-over Elvis mannerisms, he worked tirelessly at his music and his image until he became one of the biggest recording stars of the '70s. Certainly, it was calculating, but there's no denying Twitty's feel for an audience and instinct for a good song. He was a notoriously secretive man, and it's unlikely that a full picture of him will ever emerge. This piece concentrates on the early days when he was trying with his usual grim determination to make it as a rock 'n' roll singer. (C. E.)

During Conway Twitty's last years, he might well have reflected that country music had become very similar to rock 'n' roll as he remembered it. New faces, impossibly young and good looking, coming and going so quickly. Twitty probably knew that—in all likelihood—there would never be another career like his. Almost 30 years in the country charts, and another five years in the pop charts before that. All told, there were five decades with a Conway Twitty record somewhere in the charts.

Twitty's greatest gift was probably his intuitive understanding of his audience. When rock 'n' roll changed in the mid-1960s, he realized that neither he nor his fans were listening to it any more. Country music spoke to him and his audience in a way that rock didn't. He followed a generation as it made its often awkward way into and through adulthood. Whether rockin' on *Bandstand* or playing to the RV crowd in Branson, Conway Twitty knew his audience.

The details of Twitty's early life have been fairly well covered. There's a semiofficial biography and comprehensive notes accompanying an MCA Records boxed set. Very briefly, Harold Lloyd Jenkins was born in Friars Point, Mississippi, on September 1, 1933. His father worked in WPA crews and on the riverboats. Harold spent his early years in Friars Point and across the river in Helena, Arkansas. Music, baseball, and preaching were all considered as potential careers, but when he went to Chicago in 1953 it was to work at the International Harvester plant. He'd gotten a woman called Ellen pregnant, and they'd married, although they never lived together. He was still working in Chicago and sending money back home when he was drafted in 1954. We pick up the story on March 14, 1956. After two years in Yokohama, Harold Jenkins arrived back in Helena. As soon as he switched on the radio, he realized that Elvis Presley, who hadn't so much as made a record when he left, had changed the rules while he'd been away. Now there were bands in northeast Arkansas led by guys like Billy Riley, Sonny Burgess, and Ronnie Hawkins, who were playing this new, mutant strain of country music. Harold Jenkins wanted in.

196

"I still had some thoughts of baseball, but Elvis Presley stirred me up," he said later. "Elvis knocked me out, and the first time I heard him talk it sent cold shivers up my back. Later, when I was compared with Elvis, it made me proud and still does. He's the ultimate. Of course I was influenced by Elvis. Hundreds were. The only difference is, I admit it. I picked up a guitar, and decided to get with it."

Sitting on his porch at 1011 Poplar Street in Helena, Jenkins was playing his guitar when another wannabilly, Bill Harris, heard him. Harris traveled for Quaker Oats, knew some other pickers, and assembled a rockabilly band called Harold Jenkins and the Rockhousers. By this point, Jenkins and Harris had figured out that all the local bands were either on Sun Records or wanted to be. The Rockhousers drove to Memphis.

Harold had written a theme song for his group, and "Rock House" allowed him to leapfrog the line of Tex Nobodies that hung around Sun day and night. Sun president Sam Phillips liked the song and acquired it for his publishing company. Roy Orbison, just coming off his first hit, "Ooby Dooby," reworked it, took half the composer credit, and made it his second Sun single. Much as Harold Jenkins wanted it otherwise, "Rock House" was the only Sun record with his name on it. "I knew I wanted to be around that label," he said. "The studio was like a hole in the wall, but it looked like Radio City in New York to us. You used your own band and you played. We were trying to create in the studio. We'd start at say 10:00 A.M., and Sam would say, 'Have you written anything?' and I'd say, 'Yes, I've written this and this'… mostly country stuff. Sam would say, 'We can take good country songs and put a new beat to them. Do a new vocal thing.' But the only vocal licks you had were what Elvis had done. You had to create. Take the old songs and change 'em around. We'd write songs in the studio. We'd play for four or five hours without a break. We were so wrapped up in it."

Bearing those words in mind, you'd think that the Rockhousers' Sun recordings would be among the great undiscovered jewels of rockabilly music. Not so. They're limp, warmed-over Elvis records. The best thing left at Sun was a spare haunting country song called "Just in Time" that Harold wrote and demo'd for the Browns.

While he was trying out at Sun, Harold Jenkins's management was taken over by Don Seat. A former big band pianist, Seat had become an agent (he says a partner) in General Artists Corporation (GAC), one of the largest artist management companies in the United States. He worked with Johnnie Ray, Nat "King" Cole, Desi Arnaz, and many others. In one sense, Seat typified the old-line New York music business that had been shaken to its roots. He wasn't an A&R man, though; he handled booking and management, and, at some point, the new artists needed him every bit as much as the old ones.

Seat signed Harold Jenkins and renamed him. Their accounts differ, as they differ on almost everything. "Everybody's recording," Twitty said later, "and deejays are getting 30 or 40 new records a day, and they can only play so many. I figured that 'Harold Jenkins' would get lost in the shuffle. I decided that I'd better get an unusual name so that when deejays were flipping through all those records, they might say, 'Hey! I wonder what this sounds like.'" It's part of Twitty folklore that he picked "Conway" from Conway, Arkansas, and "Twitty" from Twitty, Texas.

Rubbish, says Seat. He had already coined one memorable name, Something Smith and The Redheads (a no-hoper harmony group that scored one big hit in 1956), and insists that his girlfriend had come up with the name "Conway Twitty" long before he ever found Harold

197

Jenkins. There's correspondence, says Seat, in which Twitty is insisting that his stage name be Harold Lloyd.

Twitty asked Seat to force the issue with Sun, but Seat wanted a major label deal. He took Twitty's demo tape to Bob Shad, Mercury Records' New York head of A&R. Mercury had only been in business since 1945, but was a *de facto* major label. As such, it needed a Memphis rock 'n' roller, and Seat seemed to have one. Contracts changed hands and a session was scheduled in Nashville for March 13, 1957. Twitty uncorked his entire arsenal of vocal gimmicks, and applied them to songs that were so like other songs that lawsuits would have flown if anyone had heard them. It was sterile, paint-by-numbers rockabilly. Twitty thought otherwise. Thirty years later, he still remembered the giddiness of that first break.

"It was a gala occasion," he said. "They had a photographer in the studio. We left Nashville at midnight driving back to Memphis. I had just bought a 1957 Mercury automobile, two-tone orchid and white. The worst car I ever owned. I thought all my problems were over. Then the car broke down. It started smoking. I just put my foot to the floor and drove it 'til the engine just ate itself up. Then we all got out and sat by the side of the highway talking about the session. We didn't care about the car. We thought we'd be able to afford a hundred of them shortly. Finally, I found a telephone, called the man in Arkansas who sold us the car and he came and picked us up. But that night I thought I'd be as big as Elvis in two or three weeks. I thought that was all it took. Put a record out."

The first single pegged out at No. 93 on the Hot 100, about 90 places shy of what everyone had hoped. Mercury sprang for one more session, then decided that Conway Twitty wasn't going to make it. Seat wasn't discouraged. He found Twitty a booking at the Flamingo Lounge in Hamilton, Ontario, Canada—a steel town on Lake Ontario halfway between Toronto and Niagara Falls. It was the late summer of 1957.

"We left Marianna," Twitty said later. "It took two days to get to Hamilton. None of us knew what to expect—we thought it was all igloos. We pulled up in front of this club, and we were late and the owner, Mr. Gunn, was standing outside. He saw this old Mercury with black smoke belching out of the back and a bass fiddle tied on top. And, of course, we hadn't shaved in two days. He started screamin' at us and said 'Get on that bandstand right now!' The Flamingo Lounge was a jazz club, and we had been booked there by Don Seat and a guy named Harold Kudlets. Rock 'n' roll hadn't made it into Canada yet, but we thought it was all over the world. Meanwhile, Don Seat had told the agent that we could play anything. So we got up on-stage wearing black shirts, black pants, white belts, and white buck shoes. We thought, 'Well, everything's starting off bad, but as soon as we hit 'em with a few rock 'n' roll licks everything will be alright.' We cut loose with that down-home stuff and within 15 minutes every person in the place was gone—including the bartenders! The owner looked in, shook his head and told us to turn that racket down. Finally, Harold Kudlets came down and said, 'Well, you can let them go, but if they go you've got to pay them for two weeks.' The club owner said, 'If I've got to pay them, they're gonna stay.' I was hurt and mad. We were in a strange place and country. We agreed that if they were going to throw us out they would throw us out playing what we wanted to play, so we turned it back up. That was Monday night. On Tuesday night people would drift in and out. On Wednesday night a few would stay. By Friday night it was full, and it stayed full."

Twitty booked a return engagement at the Flamingo Lounge in the Fall of 1957. By then he had a new band. Two men came from Sonny Burgess's Pacers. Jack Nance had played trumpet with Burgess, but switched to drums; Joe Lewis played guitar. "We had never played a note together before we went to Canada," said Nance. "They were remodeling the Flamingo while we were there. Like most clubs back then, it had two sides. One for men by themselves, and one for couples. The band played in the middle. We had to put dropcloths over the instruments at night because of the remodeling. They had moved the piano upstairs, and I'd go upstairs between sets, monkey around on the piano, and that's when I started 'It's Only Make Believe.' I went and told Conway, 'Hey, I got a good song going.' He came upstairs with me after the next set, and we finished it. He didn't want to take it up that high. He wanted to bring it back down. I told him it needed to keep building."

Don Seat says that Twitty sent him a tape from Canada with "I'll Try" and "It's Only Make Believe." As soon as he heard "It's Only Make Believe," he remembers thinking, "Oh shit, it's lifted straight off '(All of a Sudden) My Heart Sings.'" The two songs were indeed close, although unintentionally so, according to Nance. Seat pitched the new demos around town and found a taker at MGM Records. It couldn't

199

have been easy to land the deal. Rockabilly was more or less finished, and inasmuch as Twitty was known it was as a rockabilly.

Jim Vienneau looked after rock 'n' roll and country music at MGM, and he scheduled a session in Nashville for May 7, 1958. They recorded four songs, including "It's Only Make Believe" and "I'll Try." "The record was out for three months, and I knew they were plugging the wrong side," Twitty said later, forgetting that he'd gone along with the decision to plug "I'll Try." "Tommy Sands was working harder on the record than MGM. When he was out visiting stations, he would say, 'Have you heard "It's Only Make Believe" by Conway Twitty?' We were successful in Canada, but I didn't want to spend the rest of my life playing clubs, so I quit and went home."

"It's Only Make Believe" broke out of Columbus, Ohio. A deejay called Doctor Bop flipped "I'll Try" and found "It's Only Make Believe." Suddenly, Conway Twitty had the biggest record in Columbus. He quickly reassembled his band. "We drove from Cincinnati to Columbus," said Jack Nance, "and we were hearing the record on the radio all the way. We stopped at a place to eat, a drive-in. A guy and his girl were sitting in a car, and 'It's Only Make Believe' was on the radio. I said, 'Do you like that song?' He said, 'Yeah, that's our song.' You wouldn't believe what that meant to us."

"The radio station treated us like we were Elvis," said Twitty. "That night Doctor Bop did a show from the top of a drive-in restaurant, and we were supposed to pantomime to the song. So we got into this broken-down Mercury and headed toward the restaurant. When we got about two miles from the restaurant we found people everywhere—walking in the road, walking in yards—and we couldn't drive but one or two miles per hour. We had a big rack on top of the car and it had 'Conway Twitty' and 'MGM Records' painted on it. The people saw that, and there's no way I can describe what we went through going that last two miles. I'd never seen that many people in one place. Hell! I'd never seen that many people! They were just wild, they were grabbing the car, rocking it and screaming. Scared! I was petrified. I didn't know how to react. I could see the guy on top of the drive-in restaurant, but we had a l-o-n-g way to go. The police finally got up to my car, and they said, 'Roll the window down.' I said, 'No way.' Finally, I rolled it down, and the noise was just tremendous. We got through the window, and the police physically carried us—laying flat—over this sea of people. I thought it was all over.

"From the top of the drive-in there were people as far as you could see. I remember hearing this Doctor Bop saying that 'It's Only Make Believe' was going to be the record of the year. He was a big black man, and he was hugging the mike and announcing in a booming voice, 'Yonna he come. Yonna come that big man. Yonna come Conway Twitty!' When they played the record, it was like one giant explosion. There's no way to explain something like that. You have to experience it. That was the day Harold Jenkins became Conway Twitty."

Don Seat offers a little more detail. He insists that he didn't have much faith in "I'll Try," but went on the road promoting it anyway. "I got to Columbus, Ohio," he says, "and I paid this Doctor Bop $100 to play 'I'll Try.' He played the shit outta it. I went on to Chicago. I had an act at the Chez Paree. I got a call at midnight one night. It was Doctor Bop. He said, 'Try that "Only Make Believe" song.' Then Dick Clark calls. He's telling me that 'Only Make Believe' was the side. Then everyone got with it."

"It's Only Make Believe" entered the charts in mid-September, and then—on November 10, 1958—it was the biggest hit in every man's town. That was the date it hit No. 1. As Don Seat sagely observed, "You can't stop a hit, and you can't make a hit." Leeds Music, the publisher of "(All of a Sudden) My Heart Sings," got in touch, and as part of the settlement Twitty had to record several Leeds copyrights including a camp rock 'n' roll version of "C'est si Bon."

The best deal that Seat could get when Twitty was signed to MGM was a lowly 2 percent royalty—less even than Sun Records paid. MGM tore up the contract and re-signed him to a more lucrative deal. Twitty not only had a worldwide hit, but he'd cowritten both sides. He always held himself up as a model of financial probity, proud of his investments and his money management, but Seat insists that Twitty was as dumb as all other rockabillies when the money came in. "He had one hundred thousand dollars coming," he said, "and he'd spent two hundred thousand before he'd got it."

It was a chance encounter in Memphis that gave Twitty his next shot at the charts. Cecil Scaife was hired as promotion manager at Sun in mid-1958. He was hanging around the studio when a band turned up from Jackson, Tennessee. Carl Mann was the pianist. The featured artist didn't show, and Mann started noodling around with a goosed-up version of the 1951 Nat "King" Cole hit, "Mona Lisa." "Carl was faking a lot of it," said Scaife, "but I turned the machine on and I

Conway Twitty with Bill Harris (bass) and the Rockhousers.

remember thinking, 'This ole boy has a potential of cutting a hit if we can get it right.'" Sam Phillips wasn't interested, though. Weeks and months went by, and then Twitty breezed through town on his way to Nashville from Marianna, Arkansas. He was short a song or two for a session and called in to see Scaife. They'd grown up together in Helena, and Twitty asked if there was anything sitting in the publishing catalogs he could use.

"I told Conway we didn't have anything we owned," said Scaife, "but we had an arrangement on 'Mona Lisa' that sounded great. I played him Carl's arrangement and he got real excited. He said, 'I don't believe you're gonna give this to me.' I said, 'You can borrow the arrangement if you put it on an LP. I still have hopes of putting it out on Carl as a single.'" Twitty memorized Mann's arrangement and taught it to the pickers in Nashville. He was, more or less, true to his word; he didn't put out "Mona Lisa" as a single, but it was pulled from the album for the lead cut on an EP, and it started getting good play in several markets. Scaife quickly goaded Phillips into releasing Mann's version. Mann got to No. 25, and Twitty to No. 29.

The lead guitarist on "Mona Lisa" was Al Bruno, who had joined Twitty a month earlier. They had first met in Toronto in 1957. "There was a lady came into a club we worked," says Jack Nance. "Her name was Loretta Martin and she later went to work for Don Seat, and married Dick Clark. She said that one of her friends was married to a guitar player and she wanted us to go hear him. It was Al." Born Al Bruneau in Sudbury, Ontario, Bruno had grown up in Toronto, and had worked with Opry and WWVA acts that came to town. Twitty kept Bruno in the back of his mind. Then, in late 1958, Don Seat was pressuring Twitty to assemble a nightclub revue with a 17-piece band. Seat still thought the legit route was the passport to longevity in the business. Bruno was hired to do some of the arrangements and play lead guitar. He stayed four and a half years. "While Al was waiting for his Green Card, we hired Fred Carter [father of country star Deana Carter] from Ronnie Hawkins," said Nance. "For a while, we had both guys working with us, and to watch these two playing together was amazing. There was probably no better rock 'n' roll band at that time." For several years, Twitty led a double life. He mounted his revue for the older crowd at venues like the Steel Pier in Atlantic City and at big supper clubs in Buffalo and Washington; at the same time, he was playing one-nighters for the teens. Meanwhile, Twitty's thoughts were heading in an altogether different direction: He was starting to think about going back to country music.

There were two more Top 10 hits. The first was a rock 'n' roll version of "Danny Boy," now mostly of interest to connoisseurs of the absurd. Then came Fred Wise and Ben Weisman's "Lonely Blue Boy." Twitty was probably the fifth singer to take a shot at it. Weisman's career virtually revolved around writing songs for Elvis; by his count, he wrote 57 of them—mostly movie filler. "Lonely Blue Boy" was written as "Danny" for *King Creole*, but was dropped at the last minute. Elvis cut it, but his version wasn't released until 1978. Gene Bua recorded it in the United States and Cliff Richard and Marty Wilde cut it in England, but it blanked out everywhere. Wise and Weisman rewrote it as "Lonely Blue Boy" and pitched it to Twitty. It entered the charts just before the end of 1959, eventually rising to No. 6.

By the time "Lonely Blue Boy" was a hit, Twitty was in the movies. Like the local beauty queen who goes to Hollywood intending to get major dramatic roles but ends up half-naked in sub-B movies, Twitty went to Hollywood with Elvis's example in mind, but ended up in movies that made *Kissin' Cousins* look like *The Seventh Seal*. In the summer of 1959, he started work on *Platinum High School*. The studio put him on a diet, and paired him with a cast of has-beens and wannabes under the direction of Albert Zugsmith. To visualize Zugsmith's style, think of Ed Wood at a major studio. The plot, inasmuch as there was one, centered around Mickey Rooney investigating the suspicious death of his son in an Alcatraz-like school. Yvette Mimieux was a bikini-clad nymphet inexplicably residing at an all-male school. Presumably, Twitty didn't see the reviews because he made two more movies.

In 1960, there was another execrable Zugsmith movie, *College Confidential*, a follow-up to Zugsmith's *High School Confidential*. This one gave Twitty a chance to star alongside that old habituée of the casting couch, Mamie Van Doren. Costars included Steve Allen, Jayne Meadows and a down-on-his-luck gossip columnist, Walter Winchell. Allen played a sociology professor who ignited the nation with an intimate campus student survey. Twitty and Mamie Van Doren played students who touched each other more often than they touched a book. There was one more movie with Mamie Van Doren, *Sex Kittens Go to College* (a.k.a. *The Teacher Was a Sexpot*). Brigitte Bardot's sister, Mijanou, was in that one. All three movies tortured the art of the film until it screamed for mercy.

Interviewed in 1960, Twitty said, "You can bet I'm going after a real career in the movies. I never realized before what a kick acting is. Now I know I'll never get enough." He even talked about moving to Hollywood. Incredibly, Twitty looked back on his movies with something approaching pride. "They were real movies," he said late in his career. "Not rock 'n' roll movies. I enjoyed the challenge. They weren't silly movies. Hell! I was a killer in one of them. In fact, Sal Mineo said that my performance in *Platinum High School* was the best by any singer/actor he'd seen." Sal Mineo lied.

Twitty's band went through some changes in 1960 and 1961.

Blackie Preston had been playing bass since the Flamingo Lounge days. He'd slap his bass and look good, but never really mastered the instrument and drank way too much. Finally, Twitty fired him. Around this time, Joe Lewis wanted to go out as a front man. He hired Blackie Preston, and rounded out the group with Tommy "Porkchop" Markham on drums and Sonny Burgess on bass. Lewis's band played a few stints in Canada, but it didn't work out. The two bands met somewhere out in the Midwest, and Lewis toured with Twitty as a supporting act for a few weeks. He then returned to Twitty's band as a bass player.

Late in 1960, Jack Nance quit. He had kids that were growing up, but hardly ever saw them. "Conway's career was slipping," said Nance. "Don Seat wasn't the greatest manager in the world, but he was a great agent. He could keep you working. I was still making money, but I just wanted to be with my family. I remember playing a ballroom up in Iowa, and after we got through it was still early enough to go out and have a drink. There was a band playing at a bar across the street, and we went in. There was this elderly guy playing drums. I looked at Al, and I said, 'That's my future.' I wasn't going to be a sideman when I was fifty, sixty years old. Conway handled the absences better because it was his career. I'd had enough." Porkchop Markham took over on drums, and stayed 30 years. Nance went out as a roadie for Dick Clark, Rusty Draper, and Paul Revere. Later, he staged some of Michael Jackson's shows. Al Bruno stayed until June 1963. He went to Philadelphia to work as a staff guitarist at Cameo-Parkway Records, then went to the west coast with Dick Clark in 1964 to become a hugely-in-demand sessionman.

205

The hits tailed off in the early 1960s, and some good records were ignored. Dan Penn wrote his first hit, "Is a Bluebird Blue," for Twitty, and Roy Orbison cowrote "I'm in a Blue, Blue Mood" for Twitty while his own career was in neutral. If Twitty is to be believed, though, he was coming to the realization that he was a country singer who had sold his soul to rock 'n' roll—and now wanted a refund. He insists that he was thinking about switching back to country music as early as 1960, and Al Bruno bears this out. "There was a little studio in Marianna," he says, "and Conway would go there to record country demos. We'd listen to country music on the radio all the time."

Twitty had a convoluted and not entirely convincing explanation of why it took him so long to get back to country music. "I didn't think I was good enough for [it]," he said later. "Rock was a young kind of music and it was something I thought I could do and compete....After seven years, though, it began to cross my mind that maybe I'd lived long enough and experienced enough of the things that a country song is about to be able to do it justice." This conveniently ignores the fact that he was singing country music when he had considerably less maturity—when he was 11 years old. There's no doubt, though, that Twitty now found country music speaking to him in a way that rock 'n' roll didn't.

It was mid-1963 when Twitty's MGM contract was up. He tried to convince Jim Vienneau to re-sign him as a country singer. Not doing so was an epic mistake on Vienneau's part in light of what happened. Justifying himself later, Vienneau said, "As a company, we did not have the department to handle country acts at the time. He had a great desire to cut country which we could not accommodate." This wasn't entirely true. MGM had an active if not especially large or stellar country roster that included the Osborne Brothers, Hank Williams, Jr., and Sheb Wooley. On top of that, the company was still churning out two LPs a year on Hank Williams. Within two years, Vienneau himself would be posted to Nashville to oversee the destruction of Roy Orbison's career and to build up the Nashville roster. The truth is probably that Vienneau thought—with some justification—that Conway Twitty was washed up.

Part of the reason that Twitty was eyeing a career in country music was that country music had given him the only hit of any substance in several years. Around 1961, he got acquainted with Harlan Howard, writer of songs like "Pick Me Up on Your Way Down," "Heartaches by the Number," and "I Fall to Pieces." Twitty hung out with Howard in Nashville, and Howard took him off to Muscle Shoals, Alabama, one night to record an album's worth of country songs. He placed one of those, "Walk Me to the Door," with Ray Price, who cut it without Twitty's knowledge in September 1962. "I was in a hotel room in Toledo, Ohio," Twitty said later. "My phone rang. The voice said, 'Is this Conway Twitty?' I said, 'Yes, it is.' The voice said, 'This is Ray Price. I've got a song I want to play for you. See what you think about this song; it's going to be my next single.' I said, 'Okay.' He put the song on, and it was 'Walk Me to the Door.' There was no way to explain what that meant to me. I was just thrilled." It got to No. 7 on the country charts right around the time that Twitty's MGM contract was up, but even that wasn't enough to make Vienneau take the plunge.

In years to come, former rockabillies would be forsaking rock 'n' roll in droves, declaring that they had always been country. To that point, very few had made the switch. Ed Bruce had been an unsuccessful rockabilly at Sun and was then an unsuccessful country singer on RCA. Others who later made the switch, like Jerry Lee Lewis, Charlie Rich, and Narvel Felts, were still vainly trying for the big rock 'n' roll hit.

Twitty was not merely out of the charts in 1963, but out of pocket. He had bought some land on Moon Lake in Mississippi with the idea of turning it into a recreation area. His father would run it. "No reasonable man would have given a dime for this land," Don Seat said. "He wanted cabins, riverboats. He wanted to get rid of the yellow mud and put sand in. It cost $400,000, as best I can remember. Then there was a big rainstorm and the yellow mud covered the sand. He came to New York. He needed $25,000. He had the sheriff's department on his back. It was one day before Christmas. I called Sam Clark [the president of ABC Records]. He had to come in on Christmas day from somewhere in upstate New York, get a bank officer to make up a wire transfer to the sheriff." Jack Nance claims that part of the money that Seat forwarded to Twitty was money that was owed to him. Twitty only ever spoke of the deal in guarded terms.

The involvement of Sam Clark in bailing out Twitty probably accounts for the fact that when Twitty quit MGM, it wasn't to go to a country label, but to ABC, a label that had even less of a presence in country music than MGM. According to Seat, it had been agreed that Twitty would pay back the $25,000 by letting the company recoup the amount from royalties. It was a one-year deal that saw two singles hit the market without making much of a splash. The second ABC single, "Such a Night," was a gloriously lewd song that Clyde McPhatter and the Drifters had recorded in 1954. Twitty had high hopes for his record, but found himself scooped by Elvis. Twitty believed that Elvis had recorded the song in response to his version, but Elvis had actually recorded it in 1960. RCA hadn't dared release it as a single, and it was probably the good initial response to Twitty's single that convinced them to try it. Elvis's record got to No. 16; Twitty's got nowhere. Ironically, Twitty's record was produced by Elvis's future producer, Felton Jarvis.

Twitty always insisted that he was still at the top of his game in rock 'n' roll when he switched to country music in 1965, but this simply wasn't so. He hadn't seen a Top 10 hit since early 1960, and he hadn't

207

seen any kind of hit (except "Walk Me to the Door") since early 1962. The Beatles had broken through in the United States in January 1964, underscoring the fact that he was washed up. Twitty, though, deserves all the credit in the world for recognizing that times had irrevocably changed, and for having the courage to follow his heart back to country music.

In 1965, he moved from Marianna, Arkansas, to Oklahoma City. Don Seat hints darkly that Twitty was in trouble in Marianna, though Twitty insisted that he moved for logistical reasons. There was a big park in Oklahoma City that he often played, and most of his show dates were in the Midwest and prairies, so Oklahoma City was central for touring. During the spring of 1965, he walked out half way through a show at a kids' vacation spot in Somers Point, New Jersey. He went back to Oklahoma City and started booking himself into nightclubs at $200 a night. In June, he signed with Decca Records as a country singer. Owen Bradley, Decca's head of country A&R, recalls that Twitty first approached him with the idea of recording rock 'n' roll as Conway Twitty and country as Harold Lloyd or Harold Jenkins. Bradley correctly nixed that idea, took a chance on him as a country singer, and sat back to reap the rewards.

This scenario was played out against a background of mutual disenchantment between Don Seat and Twitty. Seat insisted that Twitty had reneged on their agreement by booking himself and not handing over a share of the proceeds. He also saw little or no future in country music. Even without hits, Seat thought he could continue to get bookings for Twitty as a pop singer. In the end, lawsuits flew. Seat says that part of the settlement gave him a share in Twittybird Music for 15 years with a guarantee of $35,000 a year. L. E. White, the one-time Bill Monroe sideman who ran Twittybird Music, says that there was no such deal that he knew of. If Seat indeed participated in Twittybird, it would have been a very lucrative participation. Twitty went on to write many of his big hits as a country singer and publish many others. "The one thing he could do," says Seat grudgingly, "is write lyrics." That concession aside, Seat's opinion of Twitty as a person is no more charitable than Twitty's opinion of Seat that emerges from the semiofficial biography.

Chart statisticians rate Conway Twitty's country career as one of the top five of all time. He ruled the late 1960s and 1970s, staying close to a hard-core, unreconstructed vision of country music for most of that time. He played to a predominantly blue collar crowd, and seemed to have an intuitive understanding of what they wanted. It was only in the 1980s that his career started slipping. In 1990, he decided to simplify his life, divesting himself of many of his business holdings, including Twittybird Music and its affiliates, which were sold to Sony-Tree Music. In the end, Twittybird was the only one of Twitty's business ventures that had prospered. His stake in Nashville's Triple A baseball club, the Sounds, had netted him little, and, according to Seat, his mobile home business in Dallas lost spectacular amounts of money. Twittyburgers ("Tweet yourself to a Twittyburger") were long gone by 1990, but not before draining Twitty of hundreds of thousands, perhaps millions of dollars.

By the end of his life, it really didn't matter how good Conway Twitty's songs and records were. His moment had passed. His run had been among the longest. He was still in good voice until the end, though. His last recording was "Rainy Night in Georgia," with Sam Moore, once half of Sam and Dave. It was wrapped up on May 3, 1993. On June 5, Twitty was returning to Nashville from Branson when he was taken ill at a truck stop. He died in Springfield of an abdominal aortic aneurysm, three months shy of his sixtieth birthday. He left behind few words, but a lot of music.

209

Twitty's personal epitaph on his rock 'n' roll years was rife with mixed emotion. "It was almost like a dream," he said later. "Like it happened to someone else. I'd be gone four or five months at a time, then home for two weeks, then gone again. I wasn't home when most of my kids were born. I was told I had contracts to fulfill, but back then I wasn't master of my own ship. It was like a merry-go-round, like a whirlwind. Everything happened so fast from the first day I walked into Sun Records until way after 'It's Only Make Believe.' Sometimes when I see videotapes of those old shows, I say, 'Who was that guy?'"

These notes accompanied an 8-CD box, Conway Twitty: The Rock 'n' Roll Years *(BCD 16112).*

Bobby Lee Trammell

16

New Dance in France
•
Bobby Lee Trammell

Ian Wallis

Back to the nutters for a portrait by British journalist Ian Wallis of legendary wild man, Bobby Lee Trammell. Here is yet another twist on what is becoming a familiar story: the power of rock 'n' roll to channel the reckless energy of youth. Unlike Conway Twitty, Bobby Lee Trammell was never going to do whatever it took to be successful. It wasn't that he didn't want to; he just couldn't. The bit of DNA that would have told him what to do in a crucial situation simply wasn't there. By Wallis's account, Trammell even blew an opportunity to stage a belated late career comeback in Europe (the word comeback *being used loosely, as Trammell hadn't got anywhere in the first place). For many aging rockers, Europe is a cross between an elephant's graveyard and a home away from home. They can tour there once a year, sometimes more often, on the basis of nonhit records that they made 40 years ago. As far as we know, Trammell hasn't returned since his one disastrous appearance. (C. E.)*

I was much wilder than Jerry Lee Lewis or Little Richard. My family always told me that I was ruining the family name by singing rock 'n' roll but I never knew that the family even had a name. My mother loved me very much but she never gave in as far as rock 'n' roll was concerned. If I had sung religious music she would have listened to me all day long. She liked country, but in Arkansas the preachers were preaching about me in church; not just me of course, everything to do with rock 'n' roll." Bobby Lee Trammell sat with his elbows on the table and a coffee cup in one hand while the waitresses scurried past with the congealed remains of a dozen or more breakfasts. The year was 1984, and Bobby Lee had traveled from Arkansas to Eindhoven in Holland, where he was booked to headline the 22nd International Rockhouse Festival. Now he had visions of a new career in Europe, where so many of his contemporaries still tour once or twice a year on the strength of half-forgotten records they made 30 or 40 years ago. Trammell's most recent career as a country singer was dead in the water by 1984. In his mind at least, he was ready to give rock 'n' roll another chance.

Wiley and Mae Trammell raised their family on a small cotton farm near Jonesboro, Arkansas. Wiley had been a professional fiddle player before he married, and Mae played the organ at the Baptist church where they worshipped. Their four children were encouraged to sing in church, but it was Bobby Lee who was most taken by music. He would tune the family radio to the "Grand Ole Opry" and memorize the words to every new Hank Williams record. Then there were other nights when he would sneak out to the black Pentecostal church in Jonesboro and marvel at the uninhibited looseness of the worshippers as they danced and sang. "I would slip off as a kid to those festival meetings. They'd get so carried away that they'd be rolling in the dust. I just felt the music and would be there shakin' and havin' fun."

By the age of 14, Bobby Lee was singing country songs at school and dreaming of the Opry. One night, Johnny Cash and Carl Perkins played a date at Nettleton High School auditorium, and Carl, always the gentleman, allowed the youngster to get up on stage and sing with his band. "Carl is not jealous of anyone, and he invited me up to sing with him. It was a big night for me. He had one of the hottest records in the country with 'Blue Suede Shoes,' but I went over pretty good, and Carl told me I should go and see Sam Phillips at Sun, and if I'd had a little bit more patience I probably would have been on Sun Records." Bobby Lee went to Memphis with a tape of songs he had demo'd at a radio station in Jonesboro. He wasn't shown the door, just told to keep rehearsing and come back later.

"I didn't have time to wait for Sun which was very stupid of me, so I went to the west coast and worked for the Ford Motor Assembly Plant out there for about six months in Longbeach, California. One place we used to go had a big carnival thing called Hollywood On The Pike, and there was a little club there. I was too young to go in but sneaked in with another feller one night when Bobby Bare was singing."

Bare was almost totally unknown outside the hillbilly bars of greater Los Angeles, and was usually welcoming when someone wanted to get up on stage and do a few numbers. Trammell sang a couple of songs, shook his hips, and set about getting noticed. Lefty Frizzell came by and invited him to come out to the Jubilee Ballroom in Baldwin Park to audition for a residency there. "The night I tried out at the Jubilee Ballroom, Johnny Cash, Freddie Hart, and Lefty Frizzell were playing. I opened the show singing rock 'n' roll and afterwards the man asked if I'd like to work every Saturday night and offered me seventy-five dollars a night. God, I would have sung in a place like that for nothing."

Before long, Bobby Lee was drawing crowds of kids to the Jubilee, and the industry started sniffing around. Fabor Robison, owner of Fabor, Abbott, and Radio Records, came calling. Like Bobby Lee, Fabor was from Arkansas, and his oily ways and his genuine ear for talent had led him to Johnny Horton, the Browns, Jim Reeves, and others. All of his acts had wanted to kill him at some point, and rumor has it that Reeves actually got as far as driving to Fabor's house with a gun.

Although he pretends otherwise, Bobby Lee was suckered in by Fabor's opening gambit. "He came over after I'd done my show and asked if I'd like to make a million dollars. I told him that I wasn't interested as I was earning $225 a week at the Ford Motor Company and a further $75 a week at the club, which was $275 more than I could have made in Arkansas, and I couldn't even spend what I was getting now. He just laughed and told me that when I came down from where I was at, I should come and see him. He gave me his card and later I asked Ralph Hicks, the owner of the Ballroom, about him, and Ralph told me he was one of the biggest promoters in country music."

The following day Trammell traveled out to Robison's house and studio in Malibu. After just two verses of his self-penned "Shirley Lee," he was offered a contract and within 30 days "Shirley Lee" was out. It was November 1957. "Shirley Lee" had been cut at Fabor's studio with Bob Luman's band. Luman, James Burton, Jim Kirkland, and a drummer had just arrived from the "Louisiana Hayride," and were paying the rent by working for Fabor. On "Shirley Lee," Burton once again showed his gift for combining rock 'n' roll excitement with exquisite taste. Within a few weeks, Ricky Nelson would co-opt the band, leaving Luman stranded in California.

Fabor got Bobby Lee on some shows. "It all happened too fast. It was unbelievable. From nothing, there I was on the 'Louisiana Hayride.' This was when I really started to tear up on all the shows." Then, just

213

as "Shirley Lee" started to break, Fabor did what he so often did: He leased the record to a larger company, in this case ABC Records. ABC promptly lost whatever momentum Fabor had built, and the only consolation came when James Burton recommended "Shirley Lee" to Ricky Nelson for his second album. "I was asked to be on Ricky's show," insists Bobby. "All his family were nice people, but his father decided I was too rock 'n' roll for a family show. They asked me to write some other songs for him but I told them I was too busy. I made a lot of bad mistakes and I should've known how hot Ricky was and how much money was involved, 'cause I remember going down with Dorsey Burnette when he picked up his royalty checks. He would pick up, like ten thousand dollars at a time. I was having too much fun, but now I look back and wonder how much money I could have made by writing some more songs for Ricky Nelson."

By the Spring of 1958, sales on "Shirley Lee" were tailing off, and Bobby Lee was back in the studio to work on a follow-up. Another of his own songs, "You Mostest Girl," was the new single, but the session at Western Recorders in Hollywood did not run smoothly. "They took me down to Hollywood and wanted to make me into something that I wasn't. Fabor hired a big band and a choir to do 'You Mostest Girl' with a proper arranger, but I didn't even know when to come in. It looked to me like a whole building full of musicians, with violins and everything. All I did was cut a five thousand dollar flop. Eventually they asked what was wrong and I said that I can't sing like that. After five hours we'd got nothing."

Three days later, Robison tried again at his home studio in Malibu. Bobby Lee was given a free hand to produce the session using only a five-piece band led by Roy Lanham. The tune was modeled quite closely on Elvis's "Baby I Don't Care," but a four-man black harmony group gave the record a ballsier sound than any of Elvis's records with the Jordanaires. This one could have made it, but once again all the right factors went into the equation to produce the wrong answer. Bobby Lee was not one to take the lack of success lightly. His frustration led him to ever more outrageous acts on stage. There were riots and property damage. There was overexuberance in the wrong places, like the "Louisiana Hayride." The Hayride manager, Tillman Franks, told Bobby Lee he was "downright vulgar—ten times worse than Elvis Presley." Needless to say, the "Grand Ole Opry" wasn't returning phone calls.

214

Other rock 'n' rollers bear out Trammell's remembrance of himself as the wildest of the wild. Texas rockabilly Mac Curtis recalled that, "He'd jump up and down, scream and holler, grab the microphone, and throw off his clothes; yeah, the whole works. He'd jump up and down on the piano, a real fire and brimstone cat." Fats Domino played a show with Bobby Lee and took him to one side with the advice, "You know your trouble, don't you, you don't know how to stop."

On another occasion, Bobby got into a dispute at KFWB in Los Angeles with a disc jockey who reneged on a promise to play his record. Urged on by Johnny and Dorsey Burnette, Bobby Lee decided that a protest was called for, and wearing a red suit and white shoes and with a guitar slung around his neck, he proceeded to climb the radio station tower. As he neared the top it started to collapse, and he had to cling on for his life while Johnny and Dorsey ran around below telling everyone that it was a suicide attempt. A big crowd built up and the stunt became a major news story in the Los Angeles area. The Burnettes ran home leaving Trammell still hanging on from the tower, and it was only after his guitar had fallen on a policeman below, and after no less than six hours on the tower that he finally came down and was escorted to jail. Dorsey Burnette posted $250 bail.

Around 1959, Fabor Robison gave up on the business and moved to Brazil for a few years. He sold most of his assets to Jamie Records in Philadelphia (including some he'd already sold elsewhere). Bobby Lee says that Fabor sold his contract to a Hollywood movie company, which led to another single, this time on Warrior. By now, though, bookings were getting scarce, and Bobby Lee moved back to Arkansas. He toured Oklahoma with a recently humbled Jerry Lee Lewis. Here were two men denied the acclaim they believed was theirs, and they struggled every night to outdo each other. Jerry Lee wrecked a piano in every town, and on one occasion Bobby concluded his act by pouring a bucket of water into the piano in an attempt to stop Lewis following him on stage.

There were more records on diddly labels like Santo, Alley, and Vaden, but Trammell was now out of control—an outlaw operating outside the system. Deejays wouldn't spin his records and even beer halls were starting to think twice about booking him. He went to Canada and pulled his usual antics. One night he whipped a crowd into such a frenzy that a girl nearly throttled him with his tie. He passed out and needed electric shock treatment at a local hospital.

215

"I can't even remember all the records that I made. If I had been on a regular schedule releasing two records a year okay, but some years I had ten, it seemed like a different record each month. It was ridiculous. Every one of them was selling to the jukebox operators. At one point in Mississippi there were twenty of my records playing on one jukebox. Dot, Warner Bros., and Columbia tried to buy my masters, but I figured that I'd only make 2½ cents. I could make 55 cents a record doing it myself. I could get rich selling $100,000 worth in Memphis alone, but now I know different. They might have sold ten million, while I was just selling out of the trunk of my car."

By the mid-1960s, the British had arrived, and the teenagers who had made him something of an underground legend in the mid-South were moving on. Nashville looked inviting. Bobby Lee had country roots as deep as anyone's, so he got in touch with Fabor Robison's cousin, Russell Sims, who ran a maverick little label, Sims Records, that recorded soul, western swing, and country. Sims decided that Bobby Lee would be better off sticking with rock 'n' roll. He dubbed him "The First American Beatle," and set about taking on the British. "I changed and grew my hair right down my back and that was a shame and a disgrace to my family and all the people who knew me, but I kept working and these Beatles helped me one hundred percent. I would lease a hall and put on shows myself because nobody would book me, and so I survived."

Sims released five singles by Trammell. The first was aimed at the British beat market. "Give Me That Good Lovin" and "New Dance in France" were cut in Memphis with Travis Wammack on lead guitar. The producer was Jerry Lee Lewis's former guitarist, Roland Janes. The sound was right up to date. There was an organ and some obtrusive canned applause *à la* Johnny Rivers. Sims continued to ring the changes in an attempt to find a winning combination. The final session held in Detroit in November 1965 found Trammell cutting a best-forgotten soul version of "Long Tall Sally." Over the next few years there were records on Country, Atlantic, and Hot Records. With all other options exhausted, he finally committed himself to country music and scored the only charted hit he ever saw, "Love Isn't Love ('Til You Give It Away)." It climbed to No. 52 during nine weeks on the country charts in 1972. Capitol bought his contract, but quickly tired of him. He even got a record out on Sun, although by this time Sun was owned by Shelby Singleton in Nashville.

Bobby Lee Trammell's career hasn't been especially well documented so it's not easy to separate the hyperbole and fabrication from the truth. Everything he said led one to believe that the crowd at Eindhoven was in for a special evening, though. Bobby talked confidently about his return to rock 'n' roll, but his eyes lacked the blazing self-assurance they must have once had. He had not been well lately, but he assured his listeners that he was still the wildest of them all and would show this audience what rock 'n' roll was all about.

It all went horribly wrong. Bobby Lee came out in a white jumpsuit and cloak to be met by hoots from an audience that didn't want ringside seats for a Fat Elvis imitators convention. The band was inadequate, and although Bobby opened strongly with "Shirley Lee" he was clearly in poor physical shape. Halfway through he seemed to suddenly remember that he'd promised to jump on the piano, but he lost his balance and fell, breaking his wrist in the process. There was to be no new career in Europe and, instead of a line of autographs, he finished the evening standing in line at Eindhoven Hospital. On another day it could all have been so different, but that's the story of Trammell's life.

Little was heard of Bobby Lee Trammell after the Eindhoven debacle until a small news item from the *Jonesboro Sun* in March 1994 found its way across the Atlantic. Bobby Lee had become a politician and was contesting the District 6 seat in Craighead County with road and bridge work foremost on his agenda when elected. He expressed deep concern about the drainage problems in the Nettleton area.

These notes accompanied You Mostest Girl *(BCD 15887).*

217

Frankie Lymon

17

Why Do Fools Fall in Love

Frankie Lymon and the Teenagers

Peter A. Grendysa

The final piece draws together many—maybe all—of the themes covered so far. It emphasizes that rock 'n' roll was different from any earlier form of music in that it was for and by kids. Others had made that implicit; Frankie Lymon and the Teenagers made it explicit. In terms of poetry, "Why Do Fools Fall in Love" was no "We'll Gather Lilacs in the Spring" or "Violets for Your Furs," but it spoke simply and directly to kids tormented by that first teenage crush.

In order for other kids to hear their music, the Teenagers had to make their little Faustian pact. They had to sell their songs and themselves to the music business. Peter Grendysa writes knowingly about the cast of outsiders, losers, and out-and-out criminals who made the Teenagers into stars. The tragedy lays not only in the fact that the Teenagers were robbed, but also in the fact the handlers failed to appreciate the changes that the Teenagers symbolized. They thought in the old ways, applied the old rules and rubrics. Rock 'n' roll was just a craze to them, like calypso or Davy Crockett hats; soon, the industry would come to its senses. Lymon must be groomed to be an old-time star. Greed not only came into the picture; greed drove it, greed dominated it. Greed and stupidity. At the same time, youthful jealousies and antagonism set in among the group. Who was whispering into Frankie Lymon's ear? "You're the star; the others are holding you back." Within months, the Teenagers were—to all intents and purposes—finished. The entire drama played itself out in a year.

Peter Grendysa gives us a rock 'n' roll parable, and follows the cast of characters in their sad struggle to accommodate the loss of success. Tragedy not only befell Lymon but virtually everyone else around him. The heirs and successors are still squabbling. As recently as 1996, the case surrounding "Why Do Fools Fall in Love" was still making its tortuous way through the courts, and the surviving Teenagers (now in late middle age) seem likely to lose.

Frankie Lymon and the Teenagers meant nothing in 1955; they were stars in 1956; washed up in 1957. Lessons could have been learned, but weren't. It's true that the industry has gotten a little smarter lately, but the history of rock 'n' roll over the last 40 years still calls to mind Karl Marx's clumsily expressed but dreadfully true dictum: "Hegel says somewhere that all great events…in world history reappear in one fashion or another. He forgot to add: the first time as tragedy, the second as farce." Lymon, like those spat out by the industry later on, might have failed to see the joke. (C. E.)

It left the impression on me that this new music called rock 'n' roll was strictly for young people. Sitting there listening to it, I felt like an old man—at twenty-three!" This was the reaction of Jimmy McGowan, leader of the Four Fellows, when he first heard "Why Do Fools Fall in Love" in January 1956. McGowan and his group, like many others, had ridden the crest of the R&B revolution in the early 1950s and had seen their music become widely accepted by enthusiastic hordes of teenagers, white and black. Now the fans were taking control of the music they loved; molding and shaping it into something all their own. Some of the originators of the music would survive by conforming to the new rules, but most would be swept aside by teenagers singing teenage songs. It is appropriate that the group which shook the foundations of the music world was named the Teenagers, and 13-year-old Frankie Lymon was the sensational new voice of a generation. Music historian Jeff Beckman, writing in 1974, recalled the magical effect of hearing this music for the first time.

"He was singing about our juvenile, just-reached-teenage way of life. Transistor radios, candy stores, dances, girls, going steady, making out, hanging out after school—all came under the purview of the lyrics. There was a certain intangible quality—partly the beat, partly the lyric, partly the harmony, partly the lead—that made the whole greater than the sum of the parts, and made listening to those records the exciting, all-encompassing experience it was. More than mere songs, they welded a bond between us, our friends, and others of our generation in the same way that mystical handshakes and code words help bind together the members of secret societies. Here at last was a music of our own. That's what it meant for me to see Frankie up there on stage. He was representing me, my friends, and our whole generation, singing about things only we could relate to, and in a style only we could understand."

Beyond all the mystic teenage-bonding were some cold economic facts. Teenagers had become the largest group of buyers of single records (virtually no rock 'n' roll was available on LP at the time) and their increasing reluctance to lay their money down for the same type of songs that had pleased their parents had driven them into buying surprising numbers of R&B records. Rhythm and blues, the music of urban blacks, had the high-energy earthiness that brought teenagers to the dance floors. It also had the allure of forbidden fruit, since few radio stations would play the records and few stores outside of those in large cities would carry them in stock.

The only drawback R&B had in the eyes of its new young fans was its lyrical content. While the beat was irresistible, and screaming horns and shouting vocalists lured youngsters to the record stores, it was hard for white teenagers to identify with messages of drinking, failed marriages, and ghetto despair, and those white teenagers comprised the pot of gold at the end of the sales rainbow. The canny independent record makers, used to surviving by virtue of quick reaction, wits, and occasional chicanery in a market dominated by megacorporations, took notice of this potential audience in 1954 and 1955, when songs such as "Gee," "Sh-Boom," "Ko Ko Mo," "Earth Angel," and "Hearts of Stone" commanded huge sales figures in both original and cover versions. These simple songs, once categorized as "rhythm novelties," were easy to write and easy to sing, and there was no lack of young voices willing to sing them.

"Why Do Fools Fall in Love" was not only unethnic, the lead voice on the record was asexual—a more democratic record would be hard to find. Teenage boys and girls of all races could identify with the singer and his message. The song itself was touted at the time as having been written by its 13-year-old singer—a big selling point even though one crusty Tin Pan Alley publisher grumbled that it sounded as if it had been written by a six-year-old. The right song, the right singer, and the right time set in motion one of those phenomenal rags-to-riches show business stories that fuel the dreams of countless would-be stars even today. No matter if, ultimately, the rags-to-riches dream often turned into a nightmare of riches-back-to-rags. The dreamers became strivers, and some of the strivers made it. In 1955, $200 would get a record mastered and ready to press—another $500 would have a thousand copies pressed. The result in those days could be a million-selling, No. 1 nationwide hit with writing and publishing royalties flowing into the coffers. For the performers there could be fame, personal appearances, cars, hordes of admirers, and even a little money. Hundreds of youngsters answered the call and found willing record companies waiting for them.

Frankie Lymon was born in Harlem on September 30, 1942, to truck-driver father Howard and mother Jeanette. His father, an amateur singer, sang with a church group, the Harlemaires (not the vocal-instrumental combo that recorded for Atlantic) and soon had his young sons, Howard, Jr., Frankie, and Lewis, working in a junior version of his group. By 1954, Frankie and Howard, Jr., were playing bongos and congas, respectively, in a lively mambo group called the Esquires. Besides appearances at Frankie's school, Edward W. Stitt Junior High in Washington Heights, the Esquires made at least one showing at the Apollo Theater's Amateur Night.

Like all schools in the Greater New York area in the early 1950s, Stitt had its share of amateur singers. The vocal group explosion ignited by the Dominoes in 1950 had motivated black youth to harmonize in school gymnasiums, hallways, and on street corners throughout the big cities. Among those would-be stars at Stitt were Jimmy Merchant and Sherman Marlow Garnes. Merchant, born February 10, 1940, had been singing since he was nine years old. On his first day at Stitt in 1954, he found Garnes, a lanky basketball player born on June 8, 1940, in his homeroom, and the two struck up a fast friendship based on a mutual love of harmony singing.

After an abortive attempt at holding together a group called the Earth Angels (after the big hit by the Penguins, high-schoolers from Los Angeles), Merchant and Garnes hooked up with two neighborhood friends, Joe Negroni, born September 8, 1940, and Herman Santiago, born February 18, 1941. They called their group the Coupe DeVilles, with Santiago taking the first tenor parts, Merchant as second tenor, Negroni doing baritone, and Garnes holding down the bass voice role. Since they all lived within a few blocks of each other, they rehearsed at each other's homes.

Scheduled for a talent show at Stitt, the Coupe DeVilles shared the bill with the Lymon brothers' Esquires, already somewhat celebrated in the neighborhood by virtue of their sole Apollo appearance. Garnes and Santiago already knew Frankie, who worked in a grocery store across the street from Santiago's home. After a dress rehearsal at the school, Frankie asked if he could sing along with the Coupe DeVilles on a few of their songs, a repertoire that consisted of versions of current R&B hits by the Spaniels, Feathers, and Valentines. The 12-year-old slipped into the harmony routines quickly and had a natural exuberance and show business flair. Both the Lymon group and the Coupe DeVilles did well at the amateur show at the school and Frankie began rehearsing with the older guys from that point.

Sometimes calling themselves the Ermines, and finally the Premiers, the quintet honed their singing skills and techniques with constant rehearsals in school and in convenient apartment hallways, the latter much favored by budding harmony groups over street corners because of the acoustics and natural echo. Frankie had insinuated himself as a high tenor voice in the harmony parts and occasionally did duets with Santiago. The songs they worked and reworked included the neighborhood favorite "Lily Maebelle" (done with some Latin touches all their own), and the Dominoes' "That's What You're Doing to Me," originally a hit in 1951 with lead singer Clyde McPhatter.

At this point, there was little to distinguish the Premiers from many other aspiring vocal groups. The harmony techniques they all employed had been developed years previously by the Ink Spots, Ravens, Orioles, Charioteers, and, most significantly, the Dominoes. They had some on-stage experience and considerable rehearsal time under their belts. Even the presence of a 12-year-old was not unusual. The music business had always had a sizeable number of preteen and "kid" stars: Teresa Brewer, Sugar Chile Robinson, Little Esther, Toni Harper, and others, and there were numerous gospel groups composed of "junior" members. The Premiers even had a few original songs to sing, a definite requirement for success in the business.

The mythos of early rock 'n' roll has the participants in this revolution divided into two categories: exploiters and exploited. On the one hand are the semiliterate, mob-connected, payola-paying, rapacious and greedy independent record producers (and, indeed, many of them were all this and more) and on the other are the artists: creative, innocent, starry-eyed, unschooled geniuses who created a new music. Reality, as usual, laughs at simplicity. An objective look at both sides is needed.

223

The record producers had strong survival instincts in a cruel business. They had to have contacts in all phases of the industry: recording, printing, pressing, publishing, distribution, and promotion, and an uncanny sense of what records were going to sell enough to at least recoup their modest investments and—at best—make them a lot of money. The young artists had talent in varying degrees: youthful and pleasing (if untrained) voices, the ability to write songs that fit within the simple framework of R&B and rock 'n' roll, and a natural energetic enthusiasm that played well in personal appearances.

What the artists of that period lacked was knowledge of contracts, copyrights, accounting practices, royalties, and all of the mechanics of the record business. If common decency would suggest that the record entrepreneurs would safeguard the interests of their artists by informing them about all of those things, the sad truth is that they did not. The producers, these days always on the defensive, say that's the way business was done back then and everybody was doing it. "It" translated into ruinous recording contracts that charged all promotion and studio costs to the artist's low royalty, expropriated the songwriting credits and publishing rights, allowed for "creative" accounting, and generally disregarded the artist's future livelihood.

Out of this quicksand of deceit the artist got some money or an automobile, a record that was played on local or (if they were lucky) national radio and jukeboxes, great notoriety in their home neighborhood, plenty of girls, alcohol or drugs, and the chance to travel around the country in uncomfortable buses playing one-nighters with other unfortunates. Few passengers on the tour buses ever found a lasting or lifelong career in show business.

Still, the producers and the artists needed each other, and many artists of the time will admit the importance of the men who launched their careers, even if those careers weren't all that could be hoped. Larry Chance of the Earls says of his producer, Hy Weiss, "He was one of a kind. He had a great ear and knew a hit when he heard it. He also had the gift of gab. He could sell a song to a program director even though the song wasn't that great. He knew his way around a studio and around the industry. It never ceased to amaze me how many friends he had and still does have. We've been friends since 1962."

Besides Weiss, the pantheon of the independent record producer includes Herb Abramson, Syd Nathan, Bess Berman, Lew Chudd, Leonard Chess, Art Rupe, Herman Lubinsky, and George Goldner.

Goldner was the archetypal New York record man; a character that is inconceivable in today's music business. In a world of MBAs and CPAs, the fast-talking high school dropout wouldn't be permitted; nor would he be happy. One survivor of those feverish days is Bob Krasnow, who told journalists Dorothy Wade and Justine Picardie what it took to make hit records in the music business of the mid-1950s. "In those days no one gave a shit whether you had a college degree, or what kind of tie you wore, and whether or not you had Gucci shoes on. This was a tough business and you had to be tough. You had to be funny too, because everybody was tough. So, you could lighten up the slap on the hand when they didn't pay you on time—because nobody paid you on time. You had to be a juggler, you had to be a magician, you had to be an artist, you had to be a painter, a con man, a high-wire walker—everything to everybody. You had to do everything: you gotta make the record, you gotta sell the record, you had to promote the record."

Born in 1919 in Manhattan, George Goldner left a career in the wholesale garment trade to operate a string of mambo parlors—dance emporia opened to satisfy the demand of a rising tide of Latinophiles swept up by the rhythm of the mambo and other dances from south of the border. Goldner spoke fluent Spanish, married a Latin girl, and immersed himself in the salsa culture. His Jewish background was not an impediment. Jerry Wexler recalls in his autobiography, "When the Palladium [a ballroom operated by Goldner] went salsa, the conflagration reached into the boroughs and started the historic bridge-and-tunnel trek to Broadway. Young Jewish hipsters were especially attracted. Seduced by the sensuality of the music, nubile Jewish chicks flocked in droves to the Latin dance halls. They came to be known, with lubricious irony, as bagel babies."

A good dancer himself, Goldner recognized a need for recordings of the music and in 1948 started Tico Records with his cousin Sam to compete with the major labels and their old-line Latin artists. Goldner's records featured the hottest young stars, including Joe Loco, Tito Puente, Tito Rodriguez, and Machito. Always, the rhythm was king and their pronounced beat and simple arrangements made Tico records the favorites at dance studios and with learn-at-home devotees. By the early 1950s the mambo craze was at its peak and had moved into the black communities in the larger cities. R&B records with Latin beats joined dozens of similar pop tunes in vying for a share of the market.

225

In early 1953, Goldner launched the Rama label to specialize in jazz and R&B. The first release on this "New R&B Label with the 3 Dimensional Sock" was in February and his fifth release, "Gee" by the Crows (a group he had discovered at the Apollo amateur show), appeared in June 1953 with little response in the market. At this point, another character entered the scene. Morris Levy, a Bronx-born former hatcheck boy, had built an empire of nightclubs, publishing, and talent management in New York City starting with his Birdland club in 1949. Levy was like Goldner in many ways, only more so. His connections both above and underground were numerous and recordings of the jazz artists he managed were pushed through a network of disc jockeys all across the country.

When Tito Puente was appearing at one of his clubs he persuaded the artist to switch from Tico to RCA Victor, a move that enraged Goldner. Confronting an apparently contrite Levy, Goldner made a deal wherein Levy would promote Goldner's records for a piece of the company and the publishing rights. "Gee" was assigned to Levy's Patricia Music, but despite Levy's supposed influence the record moved very slowly, finally reaching the hit charts in Los Angeles in December. In March 1954, it appeared on the pop charts and a month later made its debut on the much shorter R&B list. Sales were strong, but the Crows were unable to repeat.

Artie Ripp, who became Goldner's factotum, recalled to Joe Smith, "The incredible thing was, the majors at that time—Columbia, RCA, Decca—were not in the business of selling kid music by kids to kids. The independent guys, like George, discovered that kids actually had creative value. And what's more, you could put that value on record. It was a brand new industry and it didn't require a thirty-seven piece orchestra to make the music happen."

Even Goldner was not yet in the business of selling records by kids to kids. In April 1954, hot on the heels of his one big hit, he had started another label, Gee, but was unable to find any hits from its mixture of jazzy pop, R&B, and mambo artists. Rama continued with a string of releases that drew from all fields of music but met with indifference from the record-buying public. Goldner, reportedly a chronic gambler, was increasingly dependent on transfusions of capital from his partner Levy in order to keep operating.

Singer-songwriter Richard Barrett moved from Philadelphia into New York City's riotous record scene in late 1954 and took over the leadership of a quartet called the Valentines. After one record on Hy Weiss's Old Town label, the group moved to Rama where their first release, "Lily Maebelle," was a regional hit in the fall of 1955. Barrett started working with Goldner as his connection to the Harlem music scene. According to writer Ralph Newman, "Richard hung around the office constantly, and came to perform a variety of functions. He would act as a chauffeur, sweep out the office, help with promotional activities, and he would make creative suggestions…[he] was permitted to bring in his own discoveries and to assist George Goldner in the production of their records."

Translating a cappella street-corner-group songs such as "Lily Maebelle" into finished recordings was done with incredible informality, as Barrett related to writers Marcia Vance and Walter DeVenne in 1972. "Instead of writing arrangements, the arranger would get the musicians together in the studio and hum the song. The band would have the arranger hum the song until they got it. Then the recording would start and as the band members heard different things happening with the music, they'd stop the take and say 'put this in here,' and so forth. They'd start again and when it sounded good, they'd do a take, figuring there was nothing more they could do to enhance it."

227

The ease of making the records was offset by the difficulty in getting them played on the air—an absolute necessity in making a hit. Fortunately for Goldner, his partner Levy had become close friends with Alan Freed. In February 1956, *Billboard* magazine gave Freed full credit for translating record-spinning into blockbuster stage shows: "Freed didn't pioneer the presentation of R&B stageshows by jocks— Tommy (Dr. Jive) Smalls, WWRL, New York, for one was active before. But shrewd station promotion and the fact that the timing of his shows coincided with the peak of the rock 'n' roll craze among teenagers brought him into national prominence. His first show last spring at the Brooklyn Paramount grossed the all-time house record of $125,000, while his second show at the same theater later that year piled up another record-breaking gross of $155,000, and his Christmas weekend bill at the Academy Theater, New York, pulled in another $125,000."

With Freed on board, airplay was assured for Rama and Gee artists, and, in turn, Goldner supplied talent for Freed's enormously successful and profitable stage shows at a minimal cost to the disc jockey. By the end of 1955, the trade papers were noting that it was becoming more difficult to "break" a record in the marketplace because of the plethora of good new releases swamping the radio stations. One solution to gaining exposure was payola—paying the disc jockey for play—a practice then rampant in the industry, and not illegal. Still, the record had to be good to sell.

It was in this atmosphere of quick and easy fame that dozens, perhaps hundreds, of vocal groups were formed in large cities all across the nation. Throngs of eager youngsters, well practiced in the intricacies of group harmony, besieged the small record companies. Artie Ripp recalled, "Manhattan was like a nuclear test site. Everybody was coming into the record business. Every kid had a group. And it didn't cost you anything. All you had to be able to do was hit a chord and sing. You didn't have to have a piano, or a guitar, or anything. You just needed to be able to sing. It was an amazing, energetic time. People hustling, bustling. Hearts being broken. With so many people getting into it, it got to a point where you had to think like a piranha and act like a snake, just to survive. Suddenly, being artistic and creative wasn't enough."

According to Little Anthony Gourdine, who made several hits with George Goldner, money was sometimes the furthest thing from an artist's mind. He told Joe Smith, "A hit record to me was always when your friends heard you in your neighborhood, or heard your record on Doctor Jive. If Doctor Jive played your record for more than a week, you were in. That's all that interested me, that the guys in my little world in Brooklyn heard it. Never saw any money, but you're talking about a new entity, something no one really understood. If you played jazz or were a big-band dude, you were respected, you had this sort of air about you. But rock 'n' roll was like noise. 'They can't sing. That's not music.' Really good lawyers didn't want to handle that sort of thing. We had lawyers from the garment district, and they didn't know anything about the music business. They were just as ignorant as we were. So here I am running with girls and traveling. I was way better off than I'd ever been. It didn't take much to please me."

While youthful buoyancy and passable voices could get a group on school or local club stages, record companies were not interested in clever imitations of current hit songs. Original material was the key that opened the doors to the recording studios. The lucrative publishing royalties that would be collected by the lucky company with a hit song was another important reason for insisting on new material to record.

Most small companies had a house publishing arm to which new songs were assigned. The growing pop acceptance of their songs made publishing a profitable endeavor.

This sometimes caused a conflict of interest that hurt the original artists as pop cover versions garnered the bigger sales figures. One illustration of this is the song "Tweedle Dee," written by Robie "Winfield Scott" Kirk and assigned to Atlantic's Progressive Music Company. As the original version by LaVern Baker began selling heavily, Progressive licensed the song to Mercury Records, which rushed a version by Georgia Gibbs onto the pop market. Baker lost sales as Gibbs's disc swept up the charts, but Progressive and, ultimately, Atlantic enjoyed greater financial returns from having a pop hit. In the same way, Chess Records benefited from the McGuire Sisters' cover of "Sincerely," and Duke Records combined royalties from both the Johnny Ace original and the Teresa Brewer cover of "Pledging My Love." Other cover versions enriched rather than infuriated the independent record companies. A lot of debate about the ethics of pop cover versions stealing record sales from R&B artists filled the trade papers, but the smaller companies with publishing rights safely in hand were in a no-lose situation.

The unschooled composers and singers who actually wrote the songs were usually unaware of the value of a copyright or the money to be derived from publishing royalties. It was alarmingly easy to get papers signed that transferred all song rights to the record company owner or one of the owner's employees. Chuck Berry in his autobiography recalled the contract signing that took place after his first session at Chess Records—the session that produced "Maybellene."

"The recording contract he [Leonard Chess] handed me seemed to be a standard form, having no company name heading at the top. The other paper he gave me was a publishing contract, a segment of the business I was totally ignorant of. It was printed on a double sheet, but I didn't understand most of the terms and arrangements of publishing either. I did see the word 'copyright' several times as I read it through and thus figured if it was connected with the United States government it was legitimate and I was likely protected."

Some of the terms that confused Berry and many other singer-songwriters were "residuals from mechanical rights," "writer and producer's percentages," and "performance royalties and publisher

229

fees," but happy at last to be connected with a record company, Berry signed everything, took his copies of the contracts and went home. As time was to prove, this scene was repeated hundreds of times in the mid-1950s by hundreds of starry-eyed singers and musicians.

While the Premiers were sharpening their Latin-rhythm version of the Valentines' "Lily Maebelle," they were also working on material of their own. Most of their songs were collaborative efforts—the usual procedure within vocal groups. Herman Santiago worked out a catchy rhythm number about "going downtown" (high on the list of favorite teenage activities in the '50s) called "I Want You to Be My Girl." Jimmy Merchant told Wayne Jones in 1982, "Every time we attacked a new tune—inasmuch as I was the one who handled a lot of the music, vocals and making up the harmony—I always tried to do something different. But at the same time we made sure we were letting everyone know that it was us and that we did have our own style."

One tune came from a neighbor in Sherman Garnes's building. His lovestruck girlfriend had been sending him love poems and he offered a stack of them to the group of hallway kids harmonizing outside of his door. One of the poems, entitled "Why Do Birds Sing So Gay," was immediately taken up and given the full collaborative treatment. According to music historian Phil Groia, the song's transformation was accomplished quickly.

230

"Right there, they decided to change the standard type of group bass intro usually employed on an R&B tune. They wanted to improve on the usual natural 'doom-doom-doom, doom-doom-doom.' Sherman tried it in the usual way, but Jimmy suggested he try it this way: 'doom-wop, doom-wop, doom-wop-ah-doe-doe.' Frankie made up a melody line to the lyrics. Joe, Jimmy, and Herman started inventing background sounds to the lyrics using 'why do fools fall in love' as a response to the lead singer's call. The Premiers now had their own song to do in the hallways."

The Stitt Junior High School building was kept open at night as a recreation and social center for teenagers, who paid $2 a year for the pleasure of having a place to congregate away from the streets, and it was used by many novice vocal groups and singers who monopolized the old piano in the music room. Richard Barrett's own Valentines, hit record notwithstanding, found this arrangement attractive as it was much cheaper than renting a rehearsal hall. Barrett, whose position at Goldner's record company included talent scouting besides songwriting and preparing groups for recording, heard the Premiers doing their original material at Stitt and was sufficiently impressed to offer them an audition.

Barrett was intrigued by Santiago's Spanish accent and thought an R&B song with an authentic Latin lead singer would be a selling gimmick. He took the Premiers and another one of his discoveries, the Millionaires, to audition for Goldner. According to show business legend, Herman Santiago had a cold and could not do the lead singing on "Why Do Birds Sing So Gay" at that audition, so Frankie Lymon took over his spot. However, Jimmy Merchant pointed out to Wayne Jones, "I don't think we would have gotten past the audition if Herman was singing the lead. Once you see a group and you know there's a strong voice within the group that's not up front, then you try to get the strongest voice up front. And this is what happened. While we were auditioning they discovered there was not only someone with that strong voice but a rather charismatic individual who owned that voice. So they encouraged us to try Frankie on lead. We tried it, they liked it, and so did we." Lymon took his place as lead in the group from that point on.

Goldner saw the star quality in Lymon's showmanship and vitality. Barrett agreed ("I have never seen a kid with so much dynamite—naturally. This kid was a born entertainer") but recognized that the group's featured song needed some work. He changed the ungrammatical title to "Why Do Fools Fall in Love" and sent the boys home to work on the vocal arrangement with Lymon as lead.

The success of "Lily Maebelle" in the fall of 1955 had revitalized Goldner's standing in the record community and he resumed issuing an odd mix of artists on his Rama label: the Wrens, an R&B vocal group, pop groups like the Five Encores and Bachelors, pop singer Carole Bennett, and even boxer Rocky Graziano stumbling through "Grander than an Old Grand Piano." In November 1955, he resurrected his Gee label with a bright new label design, and his first release, "You Baby You," by the Cleftones, sold very well. Sometime in late November or early December, the Premiers, Duvals, and Valtones trooped into the studio for a recording session to be shared with saxophone virtuoso Jimmy Wright. The Duvals were the Millionaires who had previously recorded for Gee as the Five Crowns (and later became famous as the Ben E. King version of the Drifters). Wright was music director for Goldner's labels and his big-toned honking tenor was the equal of sax

231

stars Sam "The Man" Taylor, Freddie Mitchell, Big Jay McNeely, and Red Prysock.

Split sessions such as this were common practice with small labels, done in order to get the maximum number of usable masters in the shortest possible time. Hy Weiss of Old Town Records sometimes managed to record ten vocal groups in one all-night session. The groups were expected to have their vocals well rehearsed on their own time, and the backing musicians learned the songs in the studio—lead sheets and written arrangements were a luxury only the major labels could afford. The simple chord progressions of R&B songs were easy enough to pick up for the moonlighting jazz musicians who earned a living doing several R&B sessions a day. On-the-spot changes would be made as the company owner nervously watched the studio clock—jump tunes were turned into ballads and vice versa at the suggestion of the band leader, and lyric changes were common. The Premiers came into the studio without written music and left a few hours later with two completed masters and a new name for their group. Jimmy Wright had suggested an obvious name change and they became the Teenagers.

To illustrate the extent to which Goldner "owed" Morris Levy, "Why Do Fools Fall in Love" was assigned to Patricia Music, a publishing company owned by Levy and named after his first wife. The flip side of the record was assigned to Kahl Music, Phil Kahl being Levy's publishing partner. Kahl, supposedly without Levy, was also in the management and booking business with Levy's friend, Gaetano Vastola, whose name appears as a writer on several records by the Cleftones. Kahl's brother, Joe Kolsky, was Goldner's partner and became manager of the Teenagers. The tangled and seamy web of Levy's and Goldner's business arrangements has been well document-ed in the book *Hit Men* by Fredric Dannen. The initial release of "Why Do Fools Fall in Love" credited Lymon, Santiago, and Goldner as writers but Santiago's name was quickly dropped on repressings.

"Why Do Fools Fall In Love" was released in the last days of 1955 and quickly attracted the attention of the trade papers. *Billboard* awarded the record a Review Spotlight on February 4, 1956, declaring, "Here's a hot new disk which has already sparked a couple of covers in the Pop market. The appealing ditty has a frantic arrangement, a solid beat, and a sock lead vocal by 13-year-old Frankie Lymon. Jockeys and jukes should hand it plenty of spins and it could easily break pop." The record was already No. 4 on the best-seller charts in New York City.

232

Pushing sales along was another of Levy's business associates, Alan Freed, who was busily promoting the term *rock 'n' roll* as a replacement for the racially specific *rhythm and blues*. Goldner's and Levy's artists frequently comprised up to half of the acts on Freed's spectacularly popular stage shows. Lymon and the Teenagers were to make many appearances on those stage shows in the next year.

The effect of "Why Do Fools Fall in Love" on teenagers cannot be overemphasized. At the time of its release the top-selling R&B record in the country was "The Great Pretender" by the Platters, a group which, if not exactly from an older generation, was composed of post–high school singers. Little Richard was selling big numbers of his "Tutti Frutti." In the top 15 R&B records, the Cadillacs' churning rocker, "Speedoo" represented the new wave of youth groups in competition with old timers like the Clovers, the Spiders and the Clyde McPhatter-less Drifters. Bluesy hits by Little Willie John ("Need Your Love So Bad"), Bubber Johnson ("Come Home"), and B. B. King ("Crying Won't Help You") were reminders of the roots of R&B.

The later Queen of the Phil Spector sound, Ronnie Spector, remembered, "I was twelve years old when I first heard Frankie and the Teenagers singing 'Why Do Fools Fall in Love' on my grandmother's radio. Frankie had the greatest voice I'd ever heard, and I fell in love the minute that record came on. I couldn't tell if he was black, or white, or what. I just knew that I loved the boy who was singing that song. I would sit by my grandmother's old Philco every night waiting to hear him sing 'Why do birds sing so gay'. And when he finally came on— with his innocent little voice and perfect diction—my hands got all sweaty, my toes curled up, and I climbed right under that old box radio, trying to get as close to that sound as I could. I pressed my head into the speaker until I got Frankie going right through my brain."

The clarity of Lymon's vocal had a lot to do with the universal appeal of "Why Do Fools Fall in Love." It was the same reason the Platters attracted sales all across color and demographic lines. Spector said, "I was amazed when I found out that Frankie was black. 'Where did he learn that perfect diction?' I wondered. Not at home. I went to a black church, and I couldn't understand a word they said." Tim Hauser, founder of Manhattan Transfer, said "Frankie Lymon and the Teenagers are why I'm in the business. They performed in the first rock 'n' roll show I went to when I was a kid. I went backstage and met them, and when they sang a cappella in the dressing room, I was just blown away. I knew that's what I wanted to do." In far-away Detroit, young Smokey Robinson found something he was looking for, too. He told author Gerri Hirshey, "The blues is torment or some degrading type of thing. Kids weren't ready for that. I liked Frankie Lymon, Sam Cooke, or Jackie Wilson—the plush, pop kind of singers whose music wasn't hard-core blues." Mary Wilson of the Supremes forgot her teenage dreams of becoming an actress and tried to get into a vocal group fronted by Aretha Franklin's sister, Carolyn, after seeing the Teenagers. "When I saw Frankie Lymon and the Teenagers—a very clean-cut young black quintet—singing on Ed Sullivan's television show one Sunday night, the die was cast. I wanted to sing, and I decided that getting into Carolyn's group would be the best way to start."

Local New Yorkers could see the Teenagers on television a bit before the rest of the country got a glimpse of the hit group. The late Ralph Cooper, longtime emcee of the Apollo Theater's Amateur Night contests, had a WATV-13 variety show called *Spotlight on Harlem*. In his autobiography, Cooper gave this version of events:

"One day I was walking down the street and there was a group of kids on the corner doing the doo-wop. The leader of the group was a mere child. But this little boy had a fantastic voice. I walked past dozens of street singers every week in those days, but this group stopped me dead in my tracks. I thought, 'Man, this is too good to be true.' I talked to the leader, the young kid, and he surprised me by calling me Mr. Cooper. It turned out he knew me because he had performed on Amateur Night as a drummer for a group called the Esquires. So I invited him and his group to audition for *Spotlight on Harlem*. They were great singers, and I made a spot for them on the next show. The show was done live on Saturday night and right after it aired I got calls from four or five different record companies wanting to sign Frankie Lymon and the Teenagers." Although he got the chronology of events a bit wrong, there is no doubt that Cooper was among the first to feature the hot new group on television and his version of the story was repeated in several national magazines.

"Why Do Fools Fall in Love" appeared nationally on the Top 100 pop chart on February 11, 1956, in the No. 86 position. The most auspicious debut record that week was Les Baxter's slick instrumental "Poor People of Paris," which slid in at No. 46. *Billboard* declared, "The inroads that this disk has made in both the Pop and R&B fields in the past week prove it to be a two-front threat on the order of 'The Great

Pretender.' The Teenagers are now showing on both Pop and R&B territorial charts and are moving up toward both national charts. Unusually good volume was reported in Cleveland, Cincinnati, Detroit, St. Louis, Nashville, Baltimore, Philadelphia, New York, and Boston."

The record appeared on the shorter national R&B chart one week later and shot to No. 1 in just one month. It remained the top R&B song in the nation for a total of five weeks. More significant in terms of sales numbers, "Why Do Fools Fall in Love" reached No. 6 on the pop "Best Sellers" chart on April 14, and remained a strong seller for a total of 21 weeks. This meteoric rise brought with it an astonishing number of personal appearance engagements.

Goldner had laid down only two masters by the Teenagers at their first session. The group was whisked into the studio on February 4, and again on February 16, to obtain a follow-up to "Why Do Fools Fall in Love." The top side was selected from many takes of Herman Santiago's "I Want You to Be My Girl" (now credited to Goldner and Richard Barrett) and the flip was "I'm Not a Know-It-All," written by Tin Pan Alley veteran Buddy Kaye in an awkward teenage voice.

The Teenagers' debut on stage was at the State Theater in Hartford, Connecticut, as part of a bill that included the Cadillacs, Valentines, and Fats Domino. Like other youthful acts, they were included in the uproar and hysteria that followed the so-called rock 'n' roll stage shows from city to city. The blame for the violence and civil disobedience (that resulted more from overcrowding and wild enthusiasm than anarchic threats) was laid squarely at the feet of the music, and many cities and towns banned stage performances by rock 'n' rollers.

On March 16, the Teenagers worked in New Brunswick, New Jersey, and no doubt tried out the new dance steps shown to them in Hartford by the Cadillacs, considered by many aficionados to be the best choreographed group. During the ten-day run of Freed's "Easter Jubilee" at the Brooklyn Paramount, the Teenagers shared top billing with the Platters, and the show grossed $240,000, with many fans turned away at the door. Meanwhile, up in Harlem, rival disc jockey Dr. Jive had filled the Apollo Theater with a roster that included the Schoolboys, a group reportedly made up of nine-year-olds. Clearly, the piping of prepubescent boys was becoming more popular.

The typical Alan Freed show had the acts performing three to six songs, depending on the reaction of the audience. Freed also insisted

235

Frankie Lymon and the Teenagers

on having a new record by the artist to introduce on the show—the Teenagers debuted "I Want You to Be My Girl," which had just been released. Following this spectacular arrival in the big city, the group made an appearance on the "Chrysler Shower of Stars" TV show and then hurriedly prepared to leave town on an extended tour of one-nighters with Bill Haley. The Teenagers closed the first half of the shows, and Haley closed the second half. Called The Biggest Rock 'n' Roll Show of 1956, it also featured LaVern Baker, Joe Turner, the Drifters, the Teen Queens, Bo Diddley, the Colts, the Flamingos, and Red Prysock's big band.

The promoter, Irvin Feld, was one of the unsung innovators in rock 'n' roll. He was the first packager of big touring rock shows. According to *Variety* in 1984, "The Feld brothers, Irvin and Israel, started by selling snake oil at a circus, and were doing well at it. Although snake oil is not a standard ingredient in a pharmacy, it helped the Felds accumulate enough to buy a drugstore, which boasted a record counter as well. He listened to the music which inspired him to do the rock shows, and became the foremost promoter in the field." After promoting a few dates for the Ringling Brothers circus, he became an owner and with his son, Kenneth, eventually moved into the Ice Follies and Holiday on Ice (which were combined into Disney's World on Ice) and several other national shows.

"I Want You to Be My Girl" appeared on the pop charts at the end of April, and entered the slower-reacting R&B chart in the first week of May 1956. "Why Do Fools Fall in Love" was still selling very strongly against stiff competition from Gale Storm, the Diamonds, and Gloria Mann, and "I Want You to Be My Girl" did not do as well, reaching only No. 13 pop and No. 3 R&B. Still, it was their second national hit.

Following the February session that produced "I Want You to Be My Girl," Lymon was recorded separately from the group and backing band. This arrangement solved several problems that had been vexing Goldner. His young superstar was not the most pliable and agreeable singer to work with, and precious studio time (and money) was being wasted getting Lymon's vocal right. Rather than have musicians standing around through multiple aborted takes, Goldner could record the backing tracks at his convenience and work Lymon through the songs alone. It also served the purpose of accentuating Lymon's light voice above the backing (multiple tracks were not available at the time).

237

The results were pleasing to the ear and undetectable to the listener.

Lymon's exploits offstage while on tour were becoming whispered common knowledge in the music business. He certainly didn't act like the usual 13-year-old when it came to booze and girls. Ronnie Spector recalled her surprise when he was a guest at her house in 1956 and she smelled whiskey on his breath. According to his own account in *Ebony* magazine, his childhood had never existed. "I never was a child although I was billed in every theater and auditorium where I appeared as a child star. I was a man when I was 11 years old, doing everything that most men do. In the neighborhood where I lived, there was no time to be a child."

The rest of the group had mixed feelings about their star leader. He was, after all, a newcomer to an already established group. Yet, their very first records emphasized "Frankie Lymon" over the group. On the other hand, they were sharing in phenomenal success and public attention as long as Lymon was out front. The group simply wasn't important anymore. They needed him, but he didn't need them. This fact was not lost on the management of Roulette; they began devising a scheme to promote Lymon as a solo artist. From Goldner's point of view it made good business sense. The salaries of a group could be eliminated, traveling expenses reduced, and promotion concentrated on one man (or, in this case, boy).

The third single, "I Promise to Remember," presented an unusual case of the Teenagers imitating one of their imitators. Written and first recorded by Jimmy Castor, a "twelve-year-old prodigy who plays clarinet, sax, drums, and piano, and also composes," according to a press release, it was released by Castor as "I Promise" on Mercury's Wing subsidiary two days after the Teenagers recorded their version. This quick turnaround was typical of the record business at the time. The tune was originally published by Buchanan & Goodman (later of "Flying Saucer" fame) and was undoubtedly shopped around to other record companies. Goldner snatched it up in a deal that gave Levy's Patricia Music a share in the rights while Buchanan & Goodman profited by having their song recorded by a superstar act. Castor was a classmate of Lymon's and had performed with him in his pre-Teenagers days.

On August 6, filming began for the Teenagers' first motion picture appearance, a rock-exploitation film that exemplified the term *quickie*. "Completed in less than two weeks," said Alan Freed's biographer John

Jackson, "*Rock, Rock, Rock* had all the markings of the rush job it was." The plot was nonsensical, the acting was worse, and audiences laughed at the poor overdubbing (Connie Francis's voice for Tuesday Weld) and sloppy editing (Teddy Randazzo's sports jacket kept buttoning and unbuttoning itself). Musically, it was more satisfactory. The musical sequences were filmed in New York with just two cameras, but there were memorable performances by Chuck Berry, the Moonglows, Flamingos, and LaVern Baker. The Teenagers, spiffy in their white sweaters, rocked through "Baby Baby" and "I'm Not a Juvenile Delinquent," written by Bobby Spencer of the Cadillacs and sold to the decidedly unjuvenile Morris Levy. "Baby Baby" and several other songs in the film were credited to one of the producers, Milton Subotsky, and all of the performers had ties to Freed and his friends in one way or another. Freed initially received publishing rights to 15 of the 24 songs in the film, with the rest held by Phil Kahl and Morris Levy. Just before the film's release, Freed sold his rights to Kahl and Levy. *Rock, Rock, Rock* was rushed into the theaters in December 1956.

Following the filming of their segment of Freed's movie, the group left for shows in Ohio and Pennsylvania and spent the remainder of the summer on the road. In late August, they returned to the studio where they recorded their next single release, "The ABC's of Love" and "Share." Rave personal appearances notwithstanding, the group's records were not selling all that well. "The ABC's of Love" charted for only three weeks in the R&B lists, peaking at No. 14 and enjoyed only two quick weeks in the bottom rungs of the pop chart.

Although the Teenagers cannot be called "one-hit wonders," their slide from the top reaches of the sales charts was swift and unexpected. In late 1956, Goldner took the bold step of issuing a lavishly packaged LP by the group, but sales of this album (and, indeed, other early rock 'n' roll albums, except for those by Elvis Presley) were slight. All was not well within the group, either. Lymon was becoming increasingly difficult to handle. On one occasion, the star singer failed to make the bus departing for a major tour and Jimmy Castor had to be plucked from school as a hurried replacement. Eventually, Lymon caught up with the tour and Castor was sent home. Richard Barrett, even less believable as a "Frankie Lymon," had to substitute for the elusive singer in Detroit.

Amid all of this behind-the-scenes anguish, the group did their shows and spent weeks away from home traveling the length and

239

breadth of North America. As 1956, the year of the Teenagers and the year of teenagers, drew to a close, plans were being made for a tour of the United Kingdom, France, and Australia. At the same time, Goldner, Levy, Kahl, Kolsky, and Alan Freed were planning a new record label, Roulette.

For one week starting February 22, 1957, the Teenagers were headlining Alan Freed's first big stage show at the New York Paramount along with the Platters, Ruth Brown, Nappy Brown, the Cadillacs, the Cleftones, and the first two hit-makers on the new Roulette label, Buddy Knox and Jimmy Bowen. The group then left for two appearances in Colon and Panama City, Panama (where the press mobbed Lymon and ignored the rest of the group), before returning to New York and preparing for their European excursion.

At the end of March, Goldner sold his part of Roulette, Rama, Gee, and Tico for $250,000 to Morris Levy. Hugo Peretti and Luigi Creatore, former producers at Mercury Records, became partners in the new combination, with Peretti as president of all four labels, and Creatore as executive vice-president. Joe Kolsky stayed on as sales manager and was also an executive vice-president. Roulette was to concentrate on pop music, Rama and Gee would feature jazz and R&B, and Tico would stay with Latin music. Goldner's sudden departure from the companies he had labored so hard to build was not too surprising. He was a compulsive gambler, forever selling his old labels to Morris Levy for desperately needed cash. Goldner would build them up with Levy's financial help, then have to sell them to pay off his debts. Levy said, "He liked horses. He always needed money. Any degenerate gambler needs money all the time. It's like being a junkie, isn't it?" A week later, Goldner launched his Gone and End record labels.

Frankie Lymon and the Teenagers opened at the London Palladium on April 1 amid a blizzard of publicity and promotion that included the premiere of *Rock, Rock, Rock* in the United Kingdom. The Teenagers fulfilled all expectations, negative and positive, during their stay in Great Britain. Their London Palladium shows were sellouts, and they performed for Princess Margaret. The press and various hotel managers found their offstage conduct objectionable. Particular attention was focused on the group's tutor, a lovely young lady named Lulu Carter, who unfortunately let slip that she found Lymon "very precocious." The *Manchester Guardian* reported, "Frankie Lymon, 14-year-old singing star and members of his rock 'n' roll quartet, the

Teenagers, were severely rebuked by officials of two hotels in England where the youngsters were on tour." Lymon was banned from a London hotel following a party in his room. The chief receptionist at the Park West Hotel said, "We can't go into details, you can draw your own conclusions."

The partying was perhaps partly to blame for an initial breakdown in the group's usually tight stage routine. *Melody Maker* reported, "The Teenagers don't have an act. The group did little more than provide harmonies for Frankie's lead and join him in a couple of dance routines which will require a lot more polish before they are any help to the presentation." Then Lymon made the mistake of saying in an interview, quite truthfully, that he preferred modern jazz such as Stan Kenton, Dave Brubeck, and Ted Heath to rock 'n' roll, a statement that was widely repeated in the press.

The LP project also turned out to be less than satisfactory for the group. Levy had sent Rudy Traylor with the group to arrange their London sessions. Traylor, who was born in Rhode Island in 1918, had been a drummer and arranger with Earl Hines (including the session that produced Billy Eckstine's hit "Skylark" in 1942) and had worked with Jimmie Lunceford and Noble Sissle after the war. Prior to his signing with Roulette as leader and arranger for their house band, he had spent three years as a studio musician for the Columbia Broadcasting System. Traylor only recorded Lymon while in England, although the rest of the group expected that this time they would be overdubbed later. Then the group received some bad news from home.

"We received a letter from the States telling us that our latest release, 'Out in the Cold Again,' was another smash but the flip side of the record, 'Miracle in the Rain,' was just Frankie singing by himself," Jimmy Merchant told Wayne Jones. "So people asked what in the hell happened. Of course, we had no idea the record company had planned on releasing it and doing it in a shady way. We consulted each other on it and decided to write a letter to the record company. Despite the fact that we were only 16 years old we had some sort of sense as to what was going down. We really didn't know what happened until it came time for everyone to sign the letter, and Frankie said he wasn't going to sign the letter because he was aware of the group being split, with him going solo. So he didn't sign it and that was the beginning of a nightmare."

There was more at stake here than just the survival of the group. The songs Lymon was doing in the Abbey Road studios were not rock

241

'n' roll; they were hip pop arrangements of old standards—"Yours" (1932), "Glow Worm" (1907), "Begin the Beguine" (1935), "Love Is the Thing" (1933). Merchant had an idea of where this sudden shift in style originated. "I didn't have a grudge with Frankie; I just felt that Frankie was too young to make that decision on his own and that it probably came from either his parents or the record company. Through their manipulation, I believe they felt this was the thing to do, and that they foresaw something that never really happened, which was Frankie becoming another superstar like Sinatra or Sammy Davis, Jr."

At that time, albums were selling mainly to adults and it is probable that Goldner and Levy had hopes of marketing Lymon in the pop mainstream while still maintaining his popularity with rock 'n' rollers. Certainly, the picture of a diminutive 14-year-old belting out "Fools Rush In" on a Las Vegas stage is not too far-fetched. At any rate, the brief heyday of the black vocal groups on the pop charts was over—only the Coasters and Platters were consistently scoring big national hits, and the Teenagers without Lymon had nothing to distinguish them from hundreds of other quartets and quintets.

"Out in the Cold Again" was the last R&B hit for Frankie Lymon and the Teenagers, and it spent only one week on that chart. "Goody Goody," a 1936 vintage Johnny Mercer tune, was recorded (according to group members) with the Teenagers, but the released version had Lymon backed by a large choral group, possibly the Ray Charles Singers. It debuted on the Top 100 on July 22, shortly after the group had returned from their overseas tour. After peaking at No. 22 on September 16, 1957, it slid off the chart eight weeks later. It was the last chart hit carrying the name "Teenagers." Their moment in the spotlight had lasted eighteen months.

On July 19, Lymon and the group appeared on Alan Freed's *Big Beat* ABC-TV program, which aired on Friday nights. Jack Hooke, Freed's partner, said of that show, "Alan's show closed with the kids in the audience coming out and dancing. Frankie Lymon grabbed a little white girl and started to dance with her." Dozens of protests flooded in from southern viewers and Freed was reportedly given the choice of using only all-white acts on future programs or dropping the show. He chose to give up the program after only four telecasts. Five days later, ABC inaugurated daily national broadcasts of *American Bandstand* with Dick Clark.

Freed's favorite acts, including the Teenagers, Chuck Berry, Little Richard, Clyde McPhatter, the Moonglows, and LaVern Baker were featured in his fourth movie, *Mister Rock 'n' Roll*, released in July 1957. Lymon and the Teenagers, in their last appearance together, sang two songs, neither of which had been released at the time. Lymon's split from the group was made official in August as was his switch from the Gee label to Roulette. That same month the group was in the studio again, this time with white vocalist Billy Lobrano. According to historian Phil Groia, the group didn't think Lymon was serious about going out alone until more solos by him began appearing.

Lymon still had a lot of drawing power and Levy spared no expense in recording and promoting him. In October, an LP entitled *Frankie Lymon at the London Palladium* was released along with Lymon's first Roulette single, "My Girl." The album included some tracks recorded in London and others made in the United States—all pop standards but for one track. At a time when rock 'n' roll itself was still the subject of intense debate, and rock 'n' roll singers were looked upon with some derision, it is mystifying to reflect that Roulette apparently intended to sell Lymon as a "serious" artist to a wide pop audience. The arrangers responsible for the album used every gimmick in their well-worn bag of tricks—alternately presenting the singer in a sentimental, uncomfortable adult setting or running the old pop songs through a quick rock 'n' roll rinse to give them a modern driving backbeat. Who were they expecting would buy this record? The thin, rangeless piping of the singer, which had been arresting in the framework of a vocal group, was glaringly exposed in front of a dizzy array of strings, blaring brass, Latin percussion, and convoluted arrangements. Energy and enthusiasm were there in abundance, and Lymon's much-vaunted showmanship shines through some of the most unfortunate choices of material in record history. Jumpy "teenage" tunes were issued as singles in early 1958—all of them failed. There were simply much better records on the market.

Reflecting the confusion or bad judgement at Roulette, Lymon's next album was composed of cover versions of hit rock 'n' roll songs by other artists—just the sort of thing a pop star would be expected to do. This production completely ignored the trend away from cover versions in favor of originals. It was a pretty safe bet that people who wanted to hear "Jailhouse Rock" would want to hear Elvis Presley do it, and fans of "Wake Up Little Susie" didn't need any version other than the original by the Everly Brothers. The most satisfying cover was "Silhouettes"; Lymon was at ease with this simple rhythm ballad

243

and vocal group backing, but the Rays had done it so much better.

Lymon's efforts to find a new audience while maintaining his old fans continued throughout 1958. Few of the tracks he cut during the year were released at the time. There was nothing wrong with them, but there was nothing special about them, either. Roulette, investing considerable money in the recording sessions, wisely decided not to spend even more money issuing records with almost no chance of selling them. As the music changed with the times, time was also eroding Lymon's one hold on fame. His little-boy voice was changing. The natural deepening of his voice was gradual and, according to his brother Louie, it never bothered Frankie. His ambition to become an all-around singer, as evidenced by his Palladium set, would be helped by a more mature voice.

Lymon's struggles to find an identity in the pop music world were mirrored by those of his former group. The Teenagers, with Billy Lobrano in the lead spot, took a short tour with Roy Hamilton, whose flagging career had been rejuvenated with the smash hit "Don't Let Go." The Teenagers discovered that they could no longer share top billing with the headliners on these shows. Although the drawing power of their name was still strong, they had difficulty getting bookings without Frankie Lymon. The group left Roulette and followed Goldner to his End label a year later. All of the labels formed by Goldner eventually ended up in Morris Levy's stable, usually after a phenomenal period of success after which Goldner would spend more money than he had made. Hy Weiss said, "Guys like us were destined to go broke. We were living for today. Yesterday's gone, today is here, tomorrow's an illusion. If I got a hot record, I took off for a year. Goldner would do the same in his way. Other guys like Ahmet Ertegun were smarter. They built for tomorrow."

Author Tony Scherman summed up Goldner's downfall. "To understand Goldner's business—cleaning up 15-year-old Harlem kids and launching them into brief orbit while picking their pockets; traveling the country with a briefcase of 45s; learning every angle and playing it for all it was worth—is to understand the rock 'n' roll business of a vanished day. But beyond this value as a prototype, what attracts one to Goldner are his flaws, the almost systematic way he managed to undercut his victories."

Of course, the artists had to suffer along with Goldner's rise and fall, unless they were smart enough to change labels and managers, and adjust to changing musical tastes. The Teenagers failed on all counts. Two singles on End failed in 1960. A potentially lucrative contract with Columbia Records in 1961 dissolved into a single release. By this time the revival was beginning—a growing nostalgia for records and sounds only four or five years old—so quickly had the heyday of the vocal group passed. The Teenagers (the original four always intact) with several female lead voices replacing the little-boy pipes of Frankie Lymon found work in the revival circuit. Of course, the crowds only wanted to hear the old songs and even today the pathetic sight of four or five aged and gray Teenagers weaving and doo-wopping through 40-year-old jump tunes can be seen in concerts, locked in some sort of Dr. Who-esque time trap.

Lymon escaped the revival trap mainly because he didn't live long enough to descend to that level. For a time his popularity kept his bookings frequent and lucrative but the lack of a new hit record eventually brought him down. Contradicting the general view that record companies dropped their hapless artists as soon as they hit a cold spell, Roulette kept recording Lymon all the way into the fall of 1961. By that time he reportedly had a drug problem and his unreliability caused Roulette to drop him from their roster. Single record releases for TCF in 1963 and Columbia in 1964 went unsold. In 1967, he recorded for the last time, for manager Sam Bray's Big Apple label.

245

In a 1967 interview in *Ebony* magazine, the singer candidly told of his addiction to heroin, which he claimed started at a party in New York in 1959. He attempted to stop using the drug in 1960, but was convicted of narcotics charges in 1964. After two years in the Army he tried to resume his career without success. Although he declared in his interview that "I have kicked the habit for good," he was dead of an overdose a few months later. He had apparently celebrated a recording session with an injection of heroin, and died in his grandmother's apartment on February 28, 1968.

Jimmy Merchant, reflecting on the sad end to Lymon's life, told Wayne Jones, "What killed Frankie was the same thing that killed a lot of other teenagers from drugs. A lot of it was the environment they were in. Frankie was a very talented artist and there are a lot of talented artists that do not know how to cope—like Michelangelo and Picasso—although Picasso was somewhat luckier in fulfilling his dreams. But there were many like Frankie who passed away early that were also quite talented. They were confronted with many emotional and sensitive things they simply had no governing over their lives. In Frankie's case, his mom had died early on and his management couldn't keep up with him 24 hours a day. So he just got involved with the wrong people in his own neighborhood. He took to the drugs because it appeased him and helped him escape the rigors of show business."

Merchant and Santiago are the only surviving members of the Teenagers at this time. The genial bass-voiced giant Sherman Garnes died on February 26, 1977. According to Merchant, "Sherman's contribution to the group was phenomenal. He was a guy I met in the ninth grade on my first day of school. He was probably the truest baritone-bass singer that was born. He had a real, true resonant bass voice. He lived long enough to show the world what he was. He had a heart condition and had open heart surgery. He died as a result of that."

Joe Negroni died on September 5, 1978. Merchant said, "Joe Negroni we'll always respect because he was the great dreamer and wanted to realize his dreams. He had always dreamed of being involved with a vocal singing group. He was the one who said he was going to find a group, and he realized his dream. At the point when he died he was a hell of a writer and was writing a book that had just been accepted. He died rather suddenly from a brain tumor." A book coauthored by Negroni on the subject of the pornography industry, *The Price of Heaven*, was published in 1984. He was also reportedly working on a screenplay about the Teenagers' rise to fame at the time of his death.

George Goldner died at the age of 52 of a sudden heart attack on April 15, 1970. His last years had been spent building and losing a spectacular label, Red Bird, which had produced smash hits by the Dixie Cups, Jelly Beans, Shangri-Las, and the Ad Libs. This time, an abortive attempt to take over Atlantic Records had alienated his partners, songwriters Jerry Leiber and Mike Stoller. They left the label, and it quickly died. According to his friend Clay Cole, "George had given up. When business starts failing, your mind does things with you. You start thinking, 'Shit, I never deserved any of what I got anyway. They've caught up with me and taken it all away.'"

The other key player in the story of the Teenagers, Morris Levy, died of liver cancer in 1990 in the midst of a comical and protracted legal battle over the rights to the copyright for "Why Do Fools Fall in Love" that had no less than three women claiming to be the widow of Frankie Lymon (including Zola Taylor of the Platters). Levy, in failing health and under indictment for extortion in an unrelated incident, sold his music business holdings for $55,000,000 shortly before his death. In November 1992, a Federal jury decided that "Why Do Fools Fall in Love" was actually written by Jimmy Merchant and Herman Santiago, a decision that should have brought financial security to the singers. A British television documentary caught them celebrating their victory, but their elation was short-lived. Levy's music publishing holdings had been taken over by Windswept Pacific Music, which appealed the ruling and got it reversed.

Despite the Teenagers' relatively short sojourn as hit-makers, their influence was far-ranging and pervasive. Besides the obvious off-shoots of similar kiddie groups (with ever younger members), they also had a profound effect on the direction rock 'n' roll was to take in the ensuing years. Today, 40 years later, it is accepted and expected that rock 'n' roll will be teenage music, and it was the Teenagers who first showed that this was necessary and possible.

Revivals of their songs, particularly "Why Do Fools Fall in Love," are frequent and include hit versions by the Happenings, Diana Ross, and Joni Mitchell. Their two film appearances are available on video, they are always included in documentaries about the rise of rock 'n' roll, and their music is used in films based on the period, including *American Graffiti* and *Hollywood Knights*. The film *American Hot Wax* features the Chesterfields playing roles loosely based on the meteoric rise of the group. Santiago and Merchant now sing with a group called Frankie Lymon's Teen-Agers, with Lewis Lymon in place of his famous brother. By the time this book goes to print, a movie about Frankie Lymon and the Teenagers, *Why Do Fools Fall in Love*, will have gone into general release.

Some small part of the magic of the cheerful and grinning 13-year-old Frankie Lymon and his teenaged friends can be found in records and films, but the enchantment and joy of the times will still be missing. There is a part of the past populated by sights, sounds, and thoughts where no casual traveler can go. Only our memories can carry us there, and the glimpse of those happier times is fleeting and, somehow, truly sad.

These notes accompanied a 5-CD box, Frankie Lymon: Complete Recordings *(BCD 15782).*

Contributors

Rick Coleman

Rick Coleman is a native Louisianan (although he was actually born in the Republic of Haiti, where his parents were missionaries). He has a Bachelor of Arts degree in Anthropology from Louisiana State University. Coleman has done freelance work on New Orleans R&B for over a dozen years, conducting some 200 interviews. He has produced radio programs for New Orleans radio stations WWOZ and WYLD. He has written extensively for the New Orleans music magazines *Wavelength* and *Offbeat*, as well as for the *New Orleans Times Picayune, DISCoveries, Billboard*, and *Rolling Stone*. He has written historical notes for many records, including multi-CD sets on Little Richard, the New Orleans Mercury sessions, Joe Banashak's New Orleans labels, the Spiders, and Fats Domino. His Fats Domino biography, *Blue Monday*, is nearing completion.

Hank Davis

Hank Davis has worked as a producer/annotator for Bear Family Records since 1983. His most recent projects for the label include the *Charlie Rich Sun Box* (BCD 16152) and *The Complete Sun Singles*, a series of six boxed sets. Hank's music credentials go back to the 1950s, when he recorded a number of rockabilly singles on obscure labels. These tracks have been collected along with some unissued material on a CD called *Blue Highway*. Hank's music reviews and feature articles appear frequently in *Goldmine* magazine.

Colin Escott

Colin Escott is the author of *Good Rockin' Tonight: Sun Records & The Birth of Rock 'n' Roll, Hank Williams: The Biography*, and an anthology, *Tattooed on Their Tongues*, the latter published by Schirmer Books.

Rob Finnis

Rob Finnis is a London-based consultant to Ace Records, and the author of *The Phil Spector Story*.

Peter Grendysa

Peter Grendysa of Milwaukee, Wisconsin, has been a record collector since 1955 and a freelance writer since 1971. Over 400 of his articles, reviews, and columns have appeared in specialist music magazines, and he has contributed booklet essays for more than 100 albums and CDs. He was the principal researcher for the books *Top R&B Singles 1942-1986* and *Top Country Singles 1944-1986*, and a contributor to *Blackwell's Guide to Soul Recordings*. Mr. Grendysa was voted Best Music Journalist in Rhythm & Blues by *Goldmine* magazine in 1985 and was awarded a Grammy Certificate for the album set *Atlantic Rhythm & Blues* in 1986. In 1993 he received the Award for Excellence in Jazz History from the Association of Recorded Sound Collections. He earned a Grammy Nomination for his work on *The R&B Box* from Rhino Records in 1996.

Jeff Hannusch

Jeff Hannusch is a graduate of the University of Western Ontario who has lived in New Orleans since 1978. He has written liner notes for more than 100 albums, as well as articles and reviews for *Billboard, Rolling Stone, Offbeat, Elle, Living Blues, Blues Access,* and *Juke Blues*. His book, *I Hear You Knockin': The Sound of New Orleans Rhythm & Blues* won an American Book Award in 1986.

Bill Millar

The author of books on the Drifters and the Coasters, Bill Millar was also consultant editor of Panther's *Encyclopedia of Rock* and Orbis's *History of Rock*. His "Echoes" column was a feature of *Record Mirror, Let It Rock,* and *Melody Maker*. His liner notes have appeared on numerous albums including most of the major label rockabilly anthologies. In 1996, he was awarded the MBE (Member of the British Empire) for services to a government department.

Wayne Russell

Canadian Wayne Russell was born and raised in Winnipeg, Manitoba, before moving to Brandon, Manitoba, where he managed the Country Music Center for 22 years. In addition to issuing two slender volumes of his *Footsoldiers and Kings* in the '80s, he has written liner notes and contributed articles to magazines like *Now Dig This, Goldmine,* and *New Kommotion*. He is currently at work on a comprehensive '50s *Rock 'n' Roll Discopedia*, a combination bio-discographical work.

Billy Vera

As a singer/songwriter/actor himself, Billy Vera's writing about popular music provides a very different perspective: he's been there. His vocal hits began in 1967 with "Storybook Children," a duet with Judy Clay, and include 1987's No.1 hit "At This Moment." Billy's songs have been recorded by artists ranging from Ricky Nelson, Fats Domino, and the Shirelles to Bonnie Raitt, George Benson, Robert Plant, and Dolly Parton, who reached No.1 with Billy's "I Really Got the Feeling." He coproduced three Top 5 albums for Lou Rawls, including the No.1 jazz album, *At Last*. He has produced over 200 reissue albums. Awards include a star on the Hollywood Walk of Fame and the George Peabody Award for Excellence in Radio Broadcasting.

Ian Wallis

Born in Essex, England, Ian Wallis is a lifelong rock 'n' roll fan. Since 1983, he has been the rockabilly columnist for Britain's leading country music magazine, *Country Music People*. His first book, *The Hawk*, a biography of Ronnie Hawkins, was published in 1997. He organizes European tours for several American rockers, and jointly promotes the Rockers' Reunion in London every January.

Index

251

781.66
ALL   All roots lead to
        rock

$ 24.95

DUE DATE